CM0106446O

THE MANDOLIN MANUAL

The Art, Craft and Science of
the Mandolin and Mandola

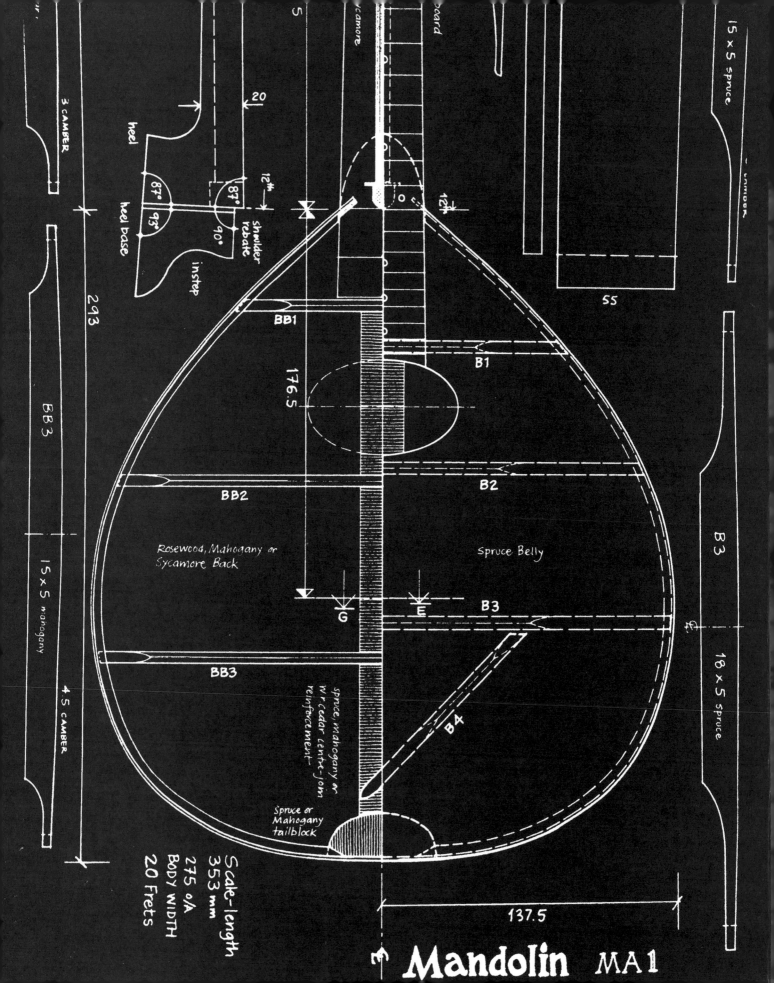

Mandolin MA1

Scale-length 353 mm
275 o/A BODY WIDTH
20 Frets

The Mandolin Manual

The Art, Craft and Science of the Mandolin and Mandola

John Troughton

The Crowood Press

First published in 2002 by
The Crowood Press Ltd
Ramsbury, Marlborough
Wiltshire SN8 2HR

© John Troughton 2002

All rights reserved. No part of this publication may be reproduced
or transmitted in any form or by any means, electronic or mechanical,
including photocopy, recording, or any information storage and retrieval
system, without permission in writing from the publishers.

British Library Cataloguing-in-Publication Data
A catalogue record for this book is available from the British Library.

ISBN 1 86126 496 8

Dedication
This book is dedicated to Manny and Rose Emanuel, two lovely people
and fine musicians, who not only indulged my turbulent occupation of
their first floor but suffered my practice of the violin with truly remarkable stoicism, hoping that one day I might choose to play a mandolin.

Acknowledgements
I am extremely grateful to the following individuals and organizations for
their encouragement, assistance and invaluable contributions towards
the preparation and compilation of the typescript, illustrations and
photos; without their help this book would not have been possible: The
British Library Document Supply Centre; Viv Dyson, for her infectious
optimism, food parcels and pub lunches; Chris Lavender, for her
patience and expertise in opening *Windows '95* to me; Bev Lawton, for
his IT skills in rescuing and re-formatting my original typescript; his
computer, monitor, keyboard and floppy disks; his string-lifter and
enthusiasm; Suffolk County Library service at Halesworth and Bungay;
Susan Reilly, for her guitar and photos; and James Yorke, Furniture and
Woodwork Collections, The Victoria & Albert Museum.

Photograph previous page: Blueprint of a mandolin.

Line illustrations by the author.

Typefaces used: M Plantin (main text) and Helvetica (labels).

Typeset and designed by D & N Publishing, Baydon, Marlborough,
Wiltshire.

Printed and bound in Singapore by Craft Print International

CONTENTS

INTRODUCTION

The mandolin in its present form, despite looking like a soprano lute – which suggests it may originally be an early Renaissance instrument – is of mid-eighteenth century origin. Whether bowl-backed or flat-backed, if it has four pairs of steel strings, each pair tuned in unison, in fifths: G, D, A and E as the violin, it is a *Neapolitan* mandolin. The flat-back varieties – which are the subject of this book – are sometimes referred to as 'Portuguese' mandolins; others, such as the Gibson archtop, have carved bellies and backs but these are all essentially Neapolitan mandolins. It is probably correct to describe the eighteenth-century Neapolitan mandolin as 'traditional': having a bowl-back made of narrow, thin ribs and a raked belly, with a pressure bridge and strings running on to hitch pins in the tail. The 'traditional' Neapolitan instrument is more difficult to construct than a flat-back and is beyond the scope of this book. If building a 'traditional' bowl-backed instrument is your particular passion, then this book will prove useful together with a manual on lute-making for the detail and construction of the bowl, but the belly template, rake, bowl depth and profile will have to be worked out.

Fig 1 The mandolin's nomenclature.

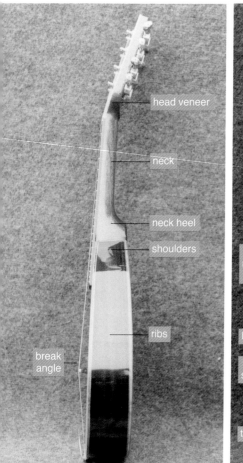
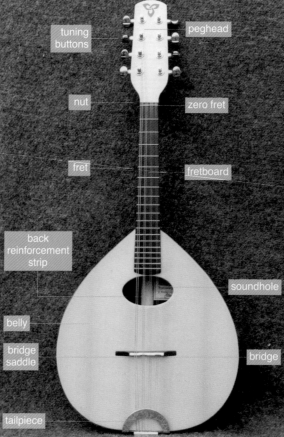
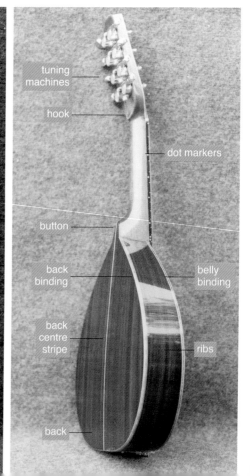

The mandolin is descended from the ancient stringed instruments originating in central Asia, from which other double-strung instruments have evolved, such as the Arabic oud, European lute and cittern, Greek bouzouki and Spanish bandurria.

The most famous violin-maker of them all, Antonio Stradivari, made mandolins, but these were not an early form of the Neapolitan as they were gut-strung soprano 'lutes' and had a flat belly with a fixed tension bridge and gut frets. The body was small and very almond-shaped, similar to the Renaissance mandore, with an elaborately carved soundhole rose and sickle shaped pegbox, but the tuning was different, as was timbre, and five or six courses of strings were used. The Milanese mandolin, being a Baroque adaptation of the mandore, was in use up to the end of the nineteenth century, when the Neapolitan type proved to be more popular as it was easier to tune, keep in tune (the advantage of wire strings) and not such a challenge to play (*see* Fig 1).

There is no evidence of a transitional model between the Baroque and Neapolitan instruments. Rather like a flash of inspiration or as the result of an expressed need for a mandolin tuned as a violin – perhaps dictated by fashion or musical taste – the Neapolitan instrument jumps on to the stage around 1760, the finest examples of which were made by the Vinaccia family in Naples. The technology already existed for this type, as the earlier cittern, known in Europe from the late-fifteenth century, had a 'floating' pressure bridge and wire stringing in double courses with metal frets. A larger, older brother to the Neapolitan mandolin is referred to as the 'pandura' in Naples in 1722 and existing examples show a mandola-sized instrument, being a scaled-up version of the Neapolitan mandolin. It would be incorrect to state that the Neapolitan mandolin has always been recognized by its metal strings: the earlier types were

strung with a combination of gut, silk and steel. Chapter 15 is devoted to greater detail of types, tuning and stringing.

The early part of the 1900s saw a craze for the Neapolitan mandolin, that became popular enough for Italian and German factories to mass-produce instruments far more decorative than tuneful. In the late nineteenth century, tuning machines – instead of friction pegs – had been introduced and the

Fig 2 Mandolin in spruce/rosewood.

ABOVE: Fig 3
Left-handed mandolin
in spruce/sycamore.
ABOVE RIGHT: Fig 4
Octave mandola in
spruce/rosewood.

frets were now the familiar 'T' or 'mushroom' sections of nickel-silver or brass. These innovations greatly improved tuning up and playability and whole mandolin orchestras came into being (*see* Figs 2 and 3).

Mandolins currently being produced in Italy, Spain, Japan, Korea, China, Romania, Eire, USA and the UK are usually the flatback, flat-top Portuguese style, with perpendicular ribs (sides) and the soundholes being either round or oval. The carved archtop and arch-back mandolins made by the Gibson Co. (USA) are much copied by other makers and these have either 'f' holes or oval soundholes; some copies are not necessarily carved but made from plywood formed into an arch and veneered – this is a factory process and does compromise quality and tone.

The Portuguese style does not involve any difficult carving or the need for specialist carving tools and can be made – without too much fuss – with general woodworking tools, producing a very playable instrument with excellent projection, a bright well-balanced tone and robust enough to pass on to your great-grandchildren; I am that confident in the adhesives, materials and construction used. The design of the neck to body joint is simpler and more reliable than the standard dovetail arrangement. This method is taken from the best luthiers' 'slipper-heel' through-connection, that permits a small margin for error, should the alignment of the neck need slight adjustment. All the techniques and methods of construction are identical for all the instruments mentioned herein, the only real differences being: scale-length; fret spacings; body size and depth; whether the neck joins the body at the 12th or 14th fret position; bracing sizes (bars); spacing of strings and gauges of strings (*see* Figs 4, 5 and 6).

I am not saying that to follow the instructions is the simple route to a successful instrument – a person who never made a mistake never made anything – however, there are pitfalls to be avoided and where these can lie in wait for an out-of-sequence cut, impatient moment or a blunt chisel, I shall emphasize the potential snags at the appropriate sequence of construction. If the text reads '*don't*' then don't! The tools you will need are usually to hand if you are a woodworker. Various items, specialist tools and equipment are needed, but you can fabricate all these yourself – I did – and there is nothing you need to use that was not available to a seventeenth-century luthier, except

Figs 5 & 6
Tenor mandola in spruce/sycamore.

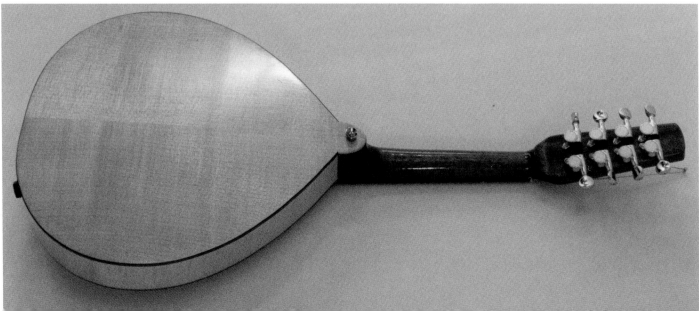

that electric light is quite an advantage and today's adhesives are superb. You will need a clean, dry and naturally ventilated work space and a clean, flat worktop bench with a woodwork vice. If you are fortunate enough to have a spare room, commandeer it if it will not cause a revolt in your family. You will also need good-quality sharp tools; the right equipment; the correct materials; patience and complete detachment from the modern 'hurry up' world – at least some of the time. *See* Chapter 1 for a list of tools and equipment you cannot do without.

The constructional plans (*see* pages 147–9) will need the outlines for neck, belly and ribs to be transferred to a grid of 25mm squares to bring the scale up to full size. A large sheet of cartridge paper is fine, but white or ivory-coloured mountboard is preferable and can be obtained from picture framers and suppliers of artists' materials. You will not need a drawing board to create a full size 'blueprint' from the plans and details given, but you will need an accurately calibrated, long steel or alloy ruler and a table or worktop. All dimensions and sizes quoted are in metric using millimetres (mm) which are now being universally adopted by luthiers. Those of you used to Imperial (or USA) inches can be assured that there is less chance of an error occurring when using millimetres, and fret spacing calculations and marking out are easier too. Figures and diagrams appearing in the text will provide the outlines, details and dimensions of components not able to be shown or fully described on the constructional plans. Photos are included of parts, workpieces and assembly sequences.

The importance of a working area that is clean and can be heated in cold weather and maintained with a low air humidity cannot be overemphasized. Those of you living in the higher latitudes might like to occupy yourselves during the long dark winters in instrument-making and it is necessary from the very start to be aware that the weather does not aid the instrument-maker who uses real woods that expand and contract with every rise or fall in the relative air humidity; instrument-makers in New Mexico, South Australia and Mongolia will have the edge over the rest of us. If Stradivari had worked in the north-west of the UK, I have good reason to suspect that not many of his instruments would be playable today. The climate of Cremona had much to do with the success and longevity of the instruments made there.

Do not give up at this stage if the only work space available is in the back of the garage or the garden shed; you can overcome any cold or damp and make a 'warm cupboard' to keep the tonewoods in, for gluing up the workpiece, and for drying finishes. An old blanket-box stood on end, with a 40-watt tungsten lamp fixed inside at low level is ideal.

Do not feel daunted by the procedures or methods described in this book; firstly, I had no real joinery experience except for a brief and disastrous encounter with a project to make a tie rack at school and sometime later with more successful plywood furniture at college. Secondly, I built my first instrument whilst handicapped by a fracture at the base of my right thumb: as I couldn't draw for a living, I had plenty of time to visit the library to research and abuse off-cuts of wood. What information was available on mandolins seemed rather scant and I came to the conclusion that luthiers must be shy, secretive creatures who do not give much away. However, I managed somehow and made the mistakes the uninitiated would, but the mandolin turned out fine, plays well and has a great tone, but above all it is unique and improving with age.

The aim may be perfection, but it will be a target difficult to reach; it is quite in order to start off badly and get better. Try things out on old off-cuts of similar woods before attempting the real thing. I hope this book will help to save you wasted time and butchered material. My advice is:

don't take shortcuts; don't attempt any sequence unless you've got enough time and everything you need; don't allow yourself to be interrupted whilst gluing and clamping up; keep the cutting edges of your tools razor-sharp and keep sharp edges away from you – trying to get a bloodstain out of a piece of pure white spruce is not easy. Antonio Stradivari lived to be over 90 years old, so he had plenty of time to make mistakes and correct them. Above all, enjoy what you do; it will be reflected in your craftwork and do take heed of the Carpenters' Commandments:

◆ Measure twice; cut once.
◆ Leave the workpiece as long as you can.
◆ Don't rush and don't force – let the tools' cutting edges do the work.
◆ Blunt tools are only useful to lend to your neighbour.
◆ Keep the bench top and floor clear from off-cuts, shavings and tools.

And please note: I use the word 'clamp' rather than 'cramp' throughout the text. This indicates that gluing up is always done with moderate pressure applied, rather than a torque-wrench setting. The woods are thin and easily distorted or split by over-zealous clamping. The rule to adopt is: stop tightening up when the glue line is fully closed – that is,,no extra turns of the screw 'for good measure'.

THE MANDOLIN FAMILY

The mandolin has a bigger brother in the tenor mandola that is tuned a fifth lower in C, G, D and A; the scale-length, from zero-fret (or nut) to bridge, is usually about 420mm. The next relative is the octave mandola (called the octave mandolin in the USA) that is tuned an octave below the mandolin in G, D, A and E. The scale-length is about 530mm. (Some luthiers argue that there is no such instrument and this should be labelled a bouzouki;

however, the bouzouki is long-necked, has a scale-length of about 670mm, is tuned C, F, A and D and its two bottom pairs of strings are not equal gauges but are tuned an octave apart.) Next and even bigger is the mando-cello which is tuned an octave below the tenor mandola in C, G, D and A and has a scale-length of about 640mm. At the very top of the range there is a beast called a mando-bass and this is tuned E, A, D and G and has a scale-length of about 1070mm. However, it is not within the scope of this book to describe or detail the working patterns to construct a mando-cello or mando-bass. The figures on pages 147–9 contain the grid outline plans for mandolin, tenor mandola and octave mandola, respectively.

All the above-mentioned instruments have identical construction techniques and dynamics – it is just a question of size and tonal range. The mandolas are no more difficult to build than the mandolin; in fact, you may find the larger instruments less fiddly to make. The larger scale of the mandolas may appeal to those whose taste is for a more guitar-sized instrument with a similar tonal compass and a more conveniently sized fretboard that may better suit their hand size and finger stretch. It is interesting to note that one does not need small hands to play a mandolin, the fret spacing just seems very cramped when compared to the more usual guitar fretboard.

With the loose bridge employed on these instruments, that is, one that is held down on the belly by string pressure alone, accurate intonation, regardless of string gauges chosen, can always be achieved as the bridge can be moved towards the neck or tail depending on whether you need to lengthen or shorten the scale-length in true relationship to the frets. This position is critical because the bridge does not lie exactly on the theoretical scale, but a few millimetres beyond. This is called 'compensation' and will be dealt with in greater detail later. Because a loose bridge can wander about when strings are changed and can tilt forward when the strings are tensioned, it is important to ensure that the bridge is always perpendicular to the face of the belly and aligned with the marks on the belly for accurate positioning.

THE DESIGN BRIEF

The principle applied to these instruments is no different from that for a guitar, banjo or lute. A string is tensioned at a given pitch (frequency) anchored between two points: the bridge and the fret at which the string is held down (stopped) to give the chosen note; the string is plucked to vibrate freely until its energy expires. Now a vibrating string does not move much air, so the volume (projection) of the sound is barely audible. The belly, coupled to the ribs (sides) and back provides a soundbox to amplify the vibrating string. This soundbox (or body) must be capable of some remarkable and seemingly paradoxical qualities: flexibility to vibrate freely; rigidity to be stable and withstand the tensions and compressions; light in weight for dynamic response and sweetness of tone; dense and solid for warmth and sustain and specially shaped to enhance and balance all the frequencies within its range, avoiding unwanted harmonic horrors caused by over-sympathetic resonance of the soundbox. All these elements are not easy to tie together, but an understanding of what matters will get you closer to building a very good instrument.

Even the volume of air inside the soundbox and the size of the soundhole(s) can make all the difference. Hi-Fi loudspeaker manufacturers get very scientific on this particular subject and I know a guitar maker who insists that the woods used are not as important as the ratio of the soundhole open area to the volume of air inside. It is certainly true that 'jumbo' soundboxes are responsive to the bass frequencies and have a warmer tone, whilst shallow sound-

boxes produce better projection and a more brittle tone: a flamenco guitar can certainly be described as one of the latter. There is no doubt in my mind that the volume of air and related soundhole size can improve the instrument's response to the lower notes; this is called 'air resonance'. I would claim from my own experiences that an oval soundhole does give a more balanced sound to the lower notes and the longer axis of the ellipse does permit more of the belly to vibrate in front of the bridge. Circular soundholes are more common as they can be cut out simply and decorative inlays (roses) to surround them are available 'off the shelf'. The advantage of an oval soundhole is that you can look inside the instrument more easily and gain access to insert contact microphones and jack sockets for sound reinforcement or recording applications.

Whatever you decide, the soundhole should be a beautiful shape with silky smooth, well-finished edges to show the full thickness and grain and that the belly is obviously not made of veneered plywood. The soundhole sizes outlined and dimensioned are correct for the soundbox volumes and should not be increased unless you wish to make an instrument with deeper ribs than suggested. It is the open area that matters rather than the shape, and any shape you choose should be equal in area to that specified. It must be said here that larger soundholes (or deeper soundboxes, for that matter) do not give greater loudness: this is due to the effective air-moving surface area of the belly being diminished as the soundhole size increases!

The belly of the mandolin has to act in the same manner as the cone or diaphragm of a loudspeaker: free to vibrate, light for transient response but rigid enough to avoid physical distortion or collapse. The belly construction must be able to cope with the pressure imposed on it from the string tension transmitted via the bridge and the compressive force acting between the neck and tailpiece; the wood used must possess the tonal qualities required for a sweet, bright sound. The belly construction should not be so robust that it prevents the vibrations of the strings being freely amplified. The designed dome that is maintained by the internal bars and ribs' profile will enable lightness, strength and adequate flexibility. Without consideration of these points an instrument can still be built that will never fly apart or cave in when strung up to concert pitch, but it will be a poor performer with a thin sound. *Do not* be tempted to omit the dome to the belly and back; it is not difficult to plane a low convex curve on the bars and ribs. If you don't plane a camber on the bars, when they flex under string pressure the belly will dish (go 'hollow'). The term 'flat-top' *is* a little misleading!

The ribs (sides) and back are made of thin, solid pieces of hardwood selected for their suitability as a stable, rigid and dense timber that does not distort or 'move' too much. Some luthiers use fibreglass bowl-backs as this material has the preferred qualities, however, I advise using wood as the solvent vapours from the fibreglass resins can be most unpleasant and unhealthy.

The neck of the instrument deserves much attention – it is probably the most difficult component to craft well, but a badly crafted neck can ruin an otherwise good instrument. It must be slim, light and strong with just a hint of springiness and be reliably connected to the body. The insertion of a truss rod will counter the tendency of string tension to bend the neck beyond playability and this rod should be full length and adjustable. Neck material should be selected for straightness and direction of grain; do not skimp on this.

The bars used for internal bracing of the belly have got to be best quality, straight-grained spruce, absolutely knot- and blemish-free, with the grain running with the depth of the bar as shown on the plans and detailed illustrations. The illustrations do show the grain directions correctly for each function and component: no 'artist's licence' has been permitted; if the grain is shown parallel to the sides then it must be so. If the grain runs 90 degrees in the wrong direction by mistake, it can lead to disaster.

You will not regret buying the best belly, neck and bracings and save money by omitting the inlays and decoration, as these do nothing for the tone and actually promote weak areas. If you can afford attractive woods for the ribs and back, and plain hardwood bindings, you won't go wrong. Avoid using synthetic (plastic) bindings as these man-made bindings and inlays may not prove compatible with the chemical make-up of the adhesives, oils, varnishes or polishes used. Wood, steel, brass, tin, bone and mother-of-pearl are fine – plastic: much less so. I have deliberately not mentioned tortoiseshell, which was once a very popular adornment on instruments, but whose use is now discouraged. There is, however, nothing wrong with being resourceful and should you come across two suitably sized book-matched pieces of quarter-sawn Bahia rosewood lying on top of a skip (or a piece of ivory for that matter), make full use of them.

The bridge of the mandolin is one component that has not always received the attention it deserves. It is not just a stopping point; its role must be fully appreciated. The majority of flat-top instruments have bridges that are too low and do not have a hard saddle such as bone. Some are just badly fitted, leading to strings having an unnecessarily high action or are too low because the neck angle is inadequate. This results in the bridge not transmitting the string vibrations fully to the belly, so rogue rattles and poor projection are the outcome. It is most important with a 'floating' pressure bridge to get it right and achieve the correct 'break' angle to the tailpiece.

The height of the bridge above the belly will determine the dynamics of the sound: a bridge too low means sloppy string tension and less energy transmitted to work the belly; the low bridge can also move sideways during vigorous playing because there is not enough pressure to hold it in place. A bridge too high means over-tight strings with too much pressure on the belly (which stifles flexing) and attenuates the projection. A bridge too far away or too close to the nut or zero-fret means that intonation will be completely wrong at all fret positions, except on the open strings!

A bridge height of around 16 to 17mm is the optimum, with a minimum of 14mm for mandolins and 19mm about the upper limit for mandola. Even if low bridge heights gave good performance, you will find the plectrum scratches the belly and will pick out the softer earlywood not protected by a pickguard. A hard saddle is necessary on the bridge to prevent the strings from 'cheese-wiring' themselves into the wood, thus lowering the action as time passes, resulting in strings rattling on the frets. Strings that have chewed their way into a plain wooden bridge do not sound so bright, as the surrounding wood effectively dampens the energy like a violin mute. A hard saddle of materials such as ivory – look out for old cutlery handles and piano keys – bone, mother-of-pearl, brass or nickel-silver should be inserted or bonded onto the bridge. The strings should sit in just enough of a groove on the saddle to prevent them from moving or squeaking about. A common problem can be the point at which the string 'stops' on the bridge saddle. This must literally be like the edge of a precipitous cliff, with no uncertain or sloping facets. The saddle should also be 'compensated' for the strings' gauges: the theoretical scale-length has to be slightly adjusted for each pair of strings, so the saddle has stepped indents progressing to the thinner strings. Sometimes a single slanted saddle is adequate to ensure correct compensation and intonation on the octave mandola.

The mandolin's dynamics are very different from those of a guitar; this may be the

reason why it has remained an underrated and somewhat misunderstood instrument. The classical and steel-strung guitar employs a fixed bridge with the belly in compression forward of the bridge and in tension behind the bridge, whereas the mandolin belly is wholly in compression, therefore different principles apply to the structural bracing. The guitar belly is being *pulled*: the mandolin belly is being *pushed*. This dynamic produces the brighter, more brittle, ringing nasal tones of the mandolin family. The mandolin *can* be just as versatile as a violin: in the hands of a virtuoso, it can emit the most evocative and delightful sounds. It also has the capacity to be biting and exciting: from J.S. Bach, Castello, Handel and Vivaldi to American Bluegrass and Celtic reels and jigs. If you have yet to hear the sublime collection of mandolin albums by Simon Mayor or the recordings of American players such as Bill Monroe, Bobby Osborne, Ronnie Reno, David Grisman, Andy Statman, Dan Biemborn and Roger Landes then you are in for a treat; and if you are interested in the sound and timbre of the Baroque (Milanese) mandolin, then check out the recording *Baroque Music for Mandolin* by Duetto Giocondo with Caterina Lichtenberg on mandolin. You may also hear a mandolin built by Antonio Vinaccia (1765) and played by Kevin Coates on the album *L'Art de la Mandoline Baroque*.

You can never be absolutely certain how *your* instrument will sound – you will have a good idea of what to expect and this can be the most exciting of all anticipations. You will not be disappointed with its tone and very pleasantly surprised when you hear someone else play it: that is the ultimate test. Reflect for a while on the fact that time can only improve it and then contemplate that your next instrument will be even better. I may be being fanciful, but the passion, care and attention you give to your work is always well rewarded and I have yet to meet someone who made *just* one instrument.

1 TOOLS AND EQUIPMENT

TOOLS THAT YOU WILL DEFINITELY NEED

Tenon saw; bow saw; razor saw (available from craft or model makers' shops); scalpel and No.10A blades; chisels: 6, 9 and 25mm; steel straight-edge marked in millimetres at least 600mm long; steel rule in mm; try-square; sliding bevel; block plane; smoothing plane; spokeshave; marking knife; files: flat and half-round; set of needle files; hand-drill and bits: 1, 1.5 and 3mm diameter and 'clean-cut' bits 4, 5, 6, 8 and 10mm diameter and 18mm diameter flat bit; steel scraper or cabinet scraper; 4oz

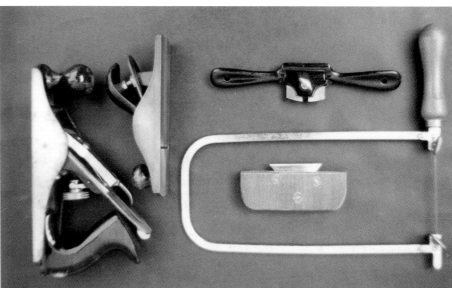

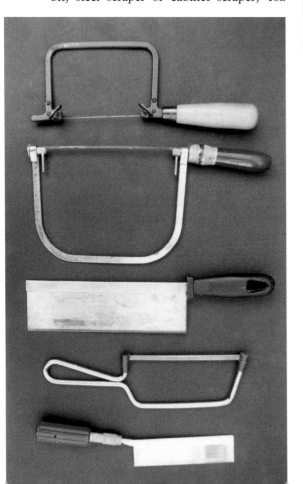

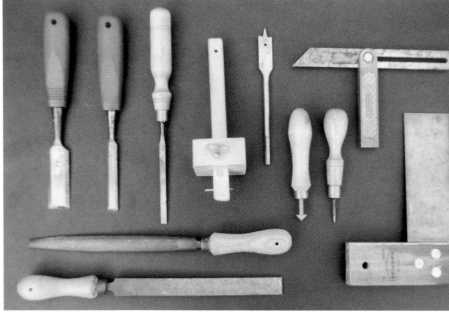

LEFT: Fig 7 Saws: piercing, coping, dovetail, junior hacksaw and razor.
TOP: Fig 8 Smoothing and block planes, spokeshave, scraper and fret saw.
ABOVE: Fig 9 Chisels, files, marking gauge, squares, bradawl and countersink.

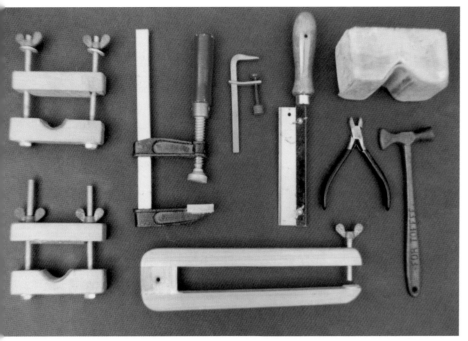

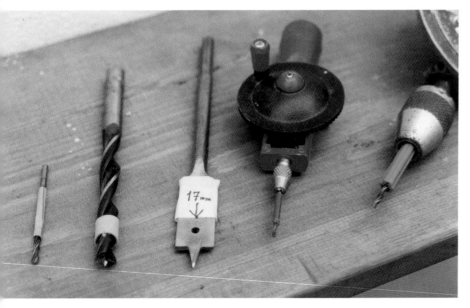

TOOLS THAT MAKE LIFE EASIER

Electric jig or scroll saw with fine-cut blade; electric drill with variable speed and reverse; band saw; electric router with 6 and 9mm diameter straight-cut bits; electric hobby drill and accessories; purfling cutter (adjustable) and soundhole cutter (optional).

EQUIPMENT
(*See* Figs 10, 11 and 12)

Where an item is marked with an asterisk (★) you can save money by making these yourself. Sturdy flat-top workbench at least 1200 × 600mm and 900mm high, with a top of 25mm plywood, blockboard or MDF★ (chipboard is unsuitable); a 200mm carpenter's vice with wooden jaws; bench-hook★; shooting-board★; winding sticks★; bending-iron★; cello clamps★; neck/fret-board clamps★; forty wooden (spring type) clothes-pegs; cowhide sheet 3 to 4mm thick by 600 × 600mm (available from a saddle and harness-maker or craft shop); plywood about 1.5 to 2mm thick (available from model-makers' shops) to make the templates; piece of thick-pile carpet or foam mat about 900 × 600 mm; as many 'G'

TOP: *Fig 10 Fretboard clamps, 'G' clamps, thickness gauge and fret tools.*
ABOVE: *Fig 11 Various drill bits with 'collars' as depth gauges.*
ABOVE RIGHT: *Fig 12 'Clean-cut' drill bits for wood, sizes 5, 8 and 10mm diameter.*

(100g) hammer with convex ground and polished face; marking gauge; protractor; small set-square; large set-square; junior hacksaw; side-cut wire cutters with face ground to cut 'flush'; coping saw; fret saw; fretting saw with interchangeable blades; cork sanding block; grade 2B pencil and white pencil crayon; small flat-head and cross-head screwdrivers; bradawl; counter-sink bit; home-made scratch-stocks and a small 'hobby' vice.

clamps as you can lay your hands on; cork floor tiles to glue to the vice jaws to make them 'soft'; a thicknessing gauge★; and large sheet of white cartridge paper or mount-board to create your full-size 'blueprints'.

OTHER ITEMS

Medium grit, 'free-cut' aluminium oxide abrasive paper; fine grit 800 and 1200 grade 'wet or dry' paper; Cascamite powdered resin glue; waterproof C3 PVA wood adhesive or Titebond wood adhesive; Araldite epoxy resin adhesive; artist's flat bristle paintbrush about 6mm wide (cheap one); 25mm wide masking tape; red button thread; thin parcel paper; filler wax, dark brown and black; white spirit; oil-based varnish; Danish, tung oil or teak oil; mounting paper or thin card to make 'masks'; hardwood 'V' block with suede-lined faces; old credit cards; dust mask; eye protection; clean rags; a good quality sharpening stone (the diamond grit ones are *superb*); honing guide for plane irons and chisels; clean water; first-aid kit and, of course, the kitchen sink.

SAFETY

As a general precaution, it is wise to wear protective goggles for power drilling, sawing and routing. Timber dust can be very irritating to the eyes, nose and throat and some species contain extractives which may set up allergic reactions, inflame the mucous membranes and cause breathing problems; wear a breathing mask when sanding. Blunt tools are more dangerous to use than razor-sharp ones. Chisels are excellent and incredibly versatile for luthiers' work, but make sure both hands are always behind the cutting edges. Craft knives are razor sharp and can cause hideous wounds; always use these with great care with a 'safety' straight-edge to avoid slicing the ends off fingers and thumbs. Keep tools well clear of the bench and workpiece unless they are actually in use. Don't mount a shelf over the workbench to place tools on as they can roll off and damage you or your workpiece.

Keep oils, stains and varnishes well away from the workbench. Make sure any gas-fuelled bending-iron is burning correctly and that volatile liquids and inflammable materials are contained and stored out of harm's way. Keep an eye on the bending-iron burner flame even when it is warming up. And lastly – the greatest irritant – don't be a Pavlov's dog when the phone rings just when glue has been applied on the belly to ribs' join; at this stage *nothing* can be more important.

THE TEMPLATES
(*See* Figs 13, 14, 15 and 16)

To make the templates from the outlines and profiles shown on the grid-scale plans, you will need to buy the thin birch ply that is sold in craft or model-makers' shops. This is about 1.5 to 2mm thick and is sold in sheets about 900 × 450 mm. Mark on the shapes for belly half, ribs, neck profile and peghead using a sharp pencil; then cut out the shape with a fret saw or electric scroll saw about 1mm outside the line. Finish the edges off to smooth curves using the file until you are exactly on the line; then rub the edges with the medium grit abrasive paper until smooth and splinter-free. Mark on them the bars' register lines taken from the plans in thin, black felt-tip pen and give the templates one coat of Danish oil or tung oil. It is a good idea to drill a 6mm diameter hole through the templates so you can hang them up – and let them dry. The back and belly outlines must use the same template that is deliberately half the shape to ensure mirror-image symmetry both sides of the centreline (the long axis of the instrument).

The template for the ribs (sides) must include the gently curved edges at the neck ends to allow correct neck heel and fret-board alignment and to ensure the bridge height is that recommended. It is best to

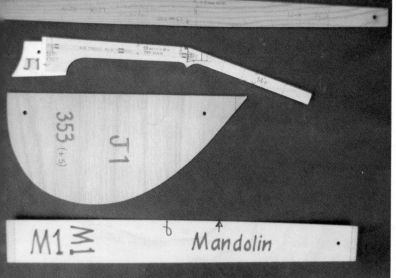

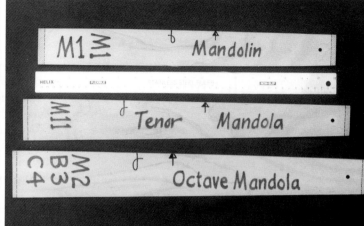

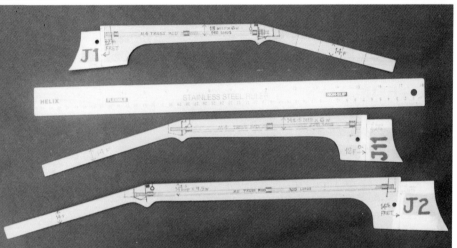

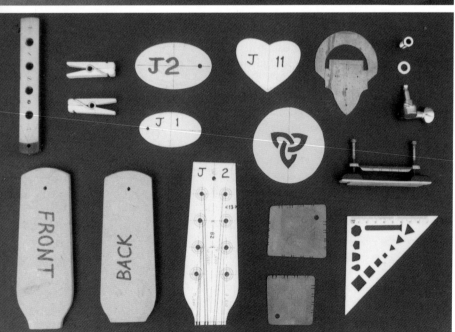

ABOVE LEFT: *Fig 13 Templates: camber, neck, belly and rib.*
ABOVE: *Fig 14 Templates: ribs for MA1, MA2 and MA3.*
LEFT: *Fig 15 Templates: necks for MA1, MA2 and MA3.*
BELOW LEFT: *Fig 16 Templates: peghead, soundholes, tuners and strings.*

make the camber template from an actual strip of thin wood 3mm thick, as this can be planed better than plywood to a low convex curve, rising at the centreline about 3mm one edge and 4.5mm on the opposite edge. These two profiles will give you the camber for the bars B2, B3, BB2 and BB3. The bars B1 and BB1 which are fitted to the neck end of the soundbox have no camber.

I strongly recommend a template for the peghead to ensure it is quite symmetrical and that the hole centres for the tuning machines are correctly spaced. It is all too easy to fashion an awful peghead – keep it simple and tapered towards the end to avoid the usual problem of strings being deflected when passing across string posts and other strings, which leads to tuning difficulties. Some popular peghead designs flare out towards the top end, which makes a mess of the stringing geometry. I have shown a peghead that will accommodate back mounting (posterior) tuning machines as these are far superior to the side-mounted, four-on-a-plate types and can make restringing almost a pleasure.

Bearing in mind that 10 per cent of the population are left-handed, the plans and details shown will be of use to a person who wishes to build a left-handed instrument. However, you will have to work from the plans as viewed in a mirror to ensure the nut, the fretboard, fretboard edge marker dots, bridge height, saddle compensation, treble bar, tailpiece and stringing are correct for left-hand use. You will note from the details that the fretboard is not a flat section but is thicker on the treble side; why this is so will be explained in Chapter 10.

THE MOULDS

The moulds for the body (soundbox) shape are made from 19mm plywood or blockboard (MDF or chipboard is not suitable). It always pays to have a snoop around your timberyard, builders' merchant or DIY store for off-cuts from larger boards; take the belly template with you to try for adequate size, so that the board will be at least 50mm wider than the full belly width and about 100mm longer than the belly length. You will also need to buy a length of 19 × 19mm 'quadrant' moulding – larger section if available – usually sold in 2.4m lengths. This needs to be sliced up like a loaf of bread into 15mm wide segments with your tenon saw or band saw, so you end up with a lot of 'little cheeses' as a visitor to my workshop once described them.

Sandpaper the feathery edges off all these segments and put them in a box out of the way. Take the blockboard or plywood mould base and mark the centreline down the length and score this line with the marking knife so it remains obvious; place the belly template with its straight edge on the centreline and clamp it down. Now drill two 3mm diameter holes through the template about 150mm apart and 5mm deep and screw fix through these to hold the template tight down to the mould base. Now take out the quadrant

segments and apply C3 PVA wood adhesive to one flat face of the segment and stick these down onto the board so that the clean perpendicular faces are touching the curved edges of the belly template leaving about a 16mm gap between each. When they are all in place from tail to neck, leave for about two hours for the glue to set hard.

Next unscrew the template, flip it over so that the straight edge lies on the centreline

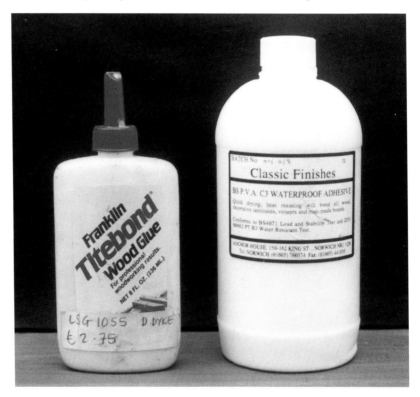

Fig 17 Adhesives: only the best for lutherie.

again to mirror-image what has been done, screw fix it to the mould base in its new position and repeat gluing on the quadrant segments around the curved side of the template from tail to neck again, with 16mm gaps between them, and allow two hours for the glue to set hard. With a 'clean-cut' 8mm diameter drill bit, drill through the mould's baseboard completely between every second quadrant segment (see Fig 18). Once all these holes are drilled, drill a hole about 10mm diameter on the centreline about

Fig 18 The body mould for a mandolin.

40mm in from the neck end; this is so that you can hang the mould on a nail in the wall! Give the mould and glued-on segments two coats of gloss-finish oil varnish.

You will need to find a 25mm diameter broomstick and cut off about 1 metre. This will be sliced up into pieces about 25mm thick with the tenon saw or band saw to make the twenty turn-buttons. When sliced up, rub them smooth on both faces on the medium grit abrasive paper (glued onto a piece of flat board). With a bradawl point, prick on the eccentric hole centres so the buttons become 'cams'. Drill through each button on the eccentric centres with a 4mm diameter 'clean-cut' bit. Countersink one side of the hole and rub the other side with candlewax. You now have rolling about your bench twenty little wooden wheels with their axle-holes off-centre. Fix these turn-buttons to the mould base at about every third segment, using 40mm × 8 gauge CSK woodscrews so that the 'locked' position just touches the perpendicular faces of the quadrant segments as shown. Screw these down so that the turn-buttons are a secure fit, but can be easily rotated by hand (*see* Fig 19).

The mould for the body (soundbox) is now complete, so the ribs of the instrument, as you will find out in Chapter 7, will be heated, bent and fitted into the mould,

then clamped up tight with the turn-buttons, allowed to cool down and dry out, when they will retain their curved shape. The design of this mould has the added advantage of securing the ribs in the exact template profile, so the tailblock and linings can be glued on. When it comes to gluing the back to the ribs, the ribs are left in the mould, clamped up tight with the turn-buttons while the back is clamped evenly down onto the ribs with long-bolts passing through the holes in the mould's baseboard, utilizing cello clamp spindles and 6mm wing-nuts, as described in Chapter 7. This method works well and avoids distorting the body shape from the template outline. Once the glue has set, the long-bolts are released and withdrawn, it is then possible to ease the ribs/back assembly out of the mould by inserting the 9mm chisel between the quadrant segments and prising between the baseboard and the ribs, levering upwards as it is not possible to gain access to the turn-buttons at this stage. I have never experienced any problems, but if a blob of rogue glue has stuck a rib to the baseboard (it shouldn't if the gloss oil

Fig 19 Detail of the mould's turn-buttons.

varnish was applied), use gentle persuasion, working systematically around to tease up the ribs, like you would if levering off a bicycle tyre. *Never* pull the ribs/back assembly out of the mould by hanging on to the overhanging waste edge of the back: you could fracture the glue joint or split the very thin hardwood of the back.

Of course, you could adopt a different mould from that shown, although the one I use is easy to make if you do not have access to band saws and piles of MDF board. The recommendation that you seal the mould and quadrant segments with gloss oil varnish is to protect the mould from water damage, staining and degradation of the glue. It is not advantageous to oil the turn-buttons; these will swell slightly when the hot damp ribs are locked in them, then shrink on cooling and drying to ease removal of the ribs/back assembly from the mould. The ancient Egyptians used timber wedges driven into mortices cut into rock and soaked with water to swell and split stone for quarrying; we are using shrinkage, in this case, to our advantage.

THE SHOOTING-BOARD

This piece of equipment is essential for planing a true, straight edge to the two halves of the belly and the two halves of the back, where they are to be glued together on the centreline. It is also very useful for planing a straight line on anything else. This device guides the sole of the plane along the fence, which has to be dead straight, thus cutting the workpiece edge dead straight as well. If both belly and back halves have their meeting edges planed simultaneously on the shooting-board, they should join perfectly, at least in theory! A thin glue line for the centre-join is not only cosmetically satisfactory; the simple truth is that glue joins are stronger the thinner the film of glue is.

The shooting-board can be made according to the pattern (*see* Fig 20). Mahogany is

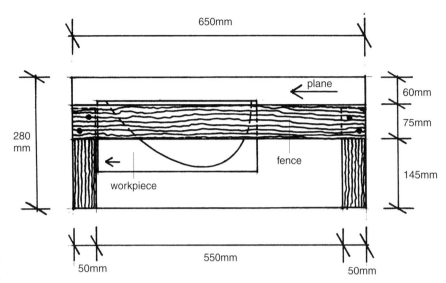

Fig 20 Detail for a shooting-board.

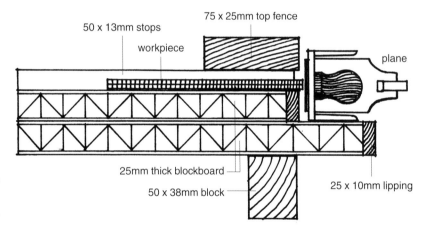

Fig 21 Section for shooting-board showing top fence.

the best for the fences as it is dimensionally stable; utile or red lauan can also be used. The top and bottom fences will become planed away by the plane during shooting, which leaves the untouched extreme edges guiding the sole of the plane always on a true, straight course. The shooting-board is greatly improved by the addition of the top fence and you should take the trouble to make and fit this (*see* Fig 21). Gluing and

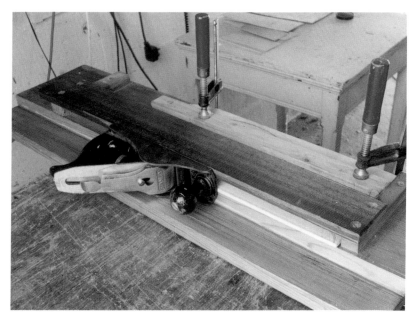

Fig 22 The shooting-board in use.

screwing on the 38 × 50 × 300mm block to the underside of the board will allow you to clamp the shooting-board secure in the vice during use (*see* Fig 22).

CELLO CLAMPS

You can purchase these from luthiers' suppliers and you will need about twenty-four of them. You can make your own from the remains of the 25mm diameter broom handle sliced up squarely into 20mm pieces, with 7mm diameter holes drilled through the middle (*see* Figs 23 and 24). The laborious bit is cutting out the forty-

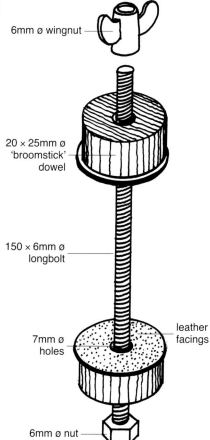

6mm ø wingnut

20 × 25mm ø 'broomstick' dowel

150 × 6mm ø longbolt

7mm ø holes

leather facings

6mm ø nut

ABOVE: Fig 23 Cello clamps in use to glue on the belly.
RIGHT: Fig 24 Cello clamp detail.

eight pieces of leather washer to glue onto the face of each wooden spindle. The sort of leather used for handbags is fine; glue them on with the C3 PVA glue, suede face uppermost. Buy 150mm × 6mm diameter long-bolts if you can, or the 1m lengths of mild steel studding found in DIY stores, and hacksaw it into 150mm lengths. Araldite adhesive will hold fast the hexagonal nuts you screw on to one end, pass them through the wooden spindles, add a steel washer and 6mm diameter wing-nut and your cello clamps are complete.

If you have made the mould, the shooting-board and twenty-four cello clamps then you have proved to yourself you can now make an instrument, so carry on and make the four neck/fretboard clamps.

NECK/FRETBOARD CLAMPS

These are worth the trouble as the art of simultaneously holding packing pieces, off-cuts of cowhide and 'G' clamps is beyond the abilities of two-handed humans. Pine is fine for these. Use pieces about 100 × 25 × 35mm. The 6mm diameter long-bolts and wing-nuts will come in useful again. Cut one 'jaw' of the clamp either in a semi-circle or a 'V' shape and glue on a piece of leather, suede side uppermost. The other 'jaw' of the clamp needs to be flat and also lined with a piece of leather. Use the two long-bolts and a couple of wing-nuts to screw the jaws together (see Fig 25).

CLOTHES-PEG CLAMPS

These have to be the wooden type with a coil spring. You will need about forty of these and the jaw is to be sawn off at the point where the semi-circular clothes-line recess begins, so the shorter jaws have flat meeting faces. To shorten the jaws of the pegs in this way means that they clamp better with more pressure. These clamps are used to hold on the linings whilst being

glued to the ribs. When you have sawn off the part of the jaws not required, dip the pegs in Danish oil or tung oil and hang them up to dry so that any glue that may get squeezed out onto the peg jaws does not adhere to them. If you really want to do a good job, take a flat file and chamfer the ragged sawn edges off the new jaw ends; they look much less like vandalized clothes-pegs if you do this. The discerning clothes-peg enthusiast will note from her or his browsing in hardware stores that some wooden clothes-pegs are rather slim matchwood hopeless cases. Seek out the white willow robust-looking ones with heavy coil springs and don't settle for anything less.

Fig 25 The fretboard/neck clamp.

HARDWOOD 'V' BLOCK

This is useful for supporting the neck (after it is fitted to the body of the instrument) to provide a solid backing when tapping in the frets. Sycamore, beech or oak are fine for the block, about 100 × 50 × 75mm. Line the 'V' with leather from a discarded shoe or bag, glued on with C3 PVA, the suede side uppermost. You will find this device useful to support the mandolin lying on its back when fitting the nut, machine

Fig 26 The 'V' block to support the neck.

heads, truss rod cover plate, tailpiece, bridge and strings.

THICKNESSING GAUGE

This device can be made from pieces of pine half-housed and glued and a 6mm diameter bolt. It is a necessary device to ensure the belly and back material is thicknessed fairly evenly over its whole area before the transverse bars are glued on (*see* Figs 27 and 28 for a suitable home-made design).

Fig 27 Detail for a thicknessing gauge.

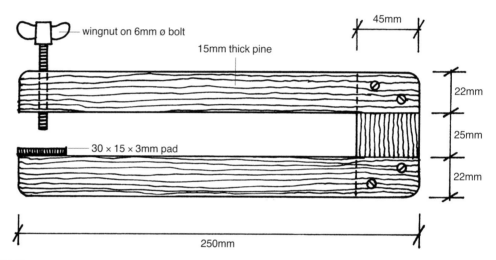

wingnut on 6mm ø bolt

15mm thick pine

30 × 15 × 3mm pad

45mm

22mm

25mm

22mm

250mm

Fig 28 The thicknessing gauge in use.

2 TREES AND THE NATURE OF WOOD

This chapter is written particularly for those who are not too familiar with woodworking.

Trees are definitely the most beautiful and useful of plants; while they live they give shelter in winter and shade in summer. Forests balance the atmosphere and the climate, so that all other life can exist, even in the rivers and oceans. When trees are felled for timber or fuel, this is thought to be the best gift of Nature to man – the most creative and destructive animal of all. Wood is certainly the finest of natural unprocessed materials with its many uses and qualities. It is light in weight, strong in section, easy to work, warm to the touch, a natural thermal insulator, and the variety of species, properties, grain pattern and colour make every wooden artefact unique. Working and fashioning wood is without doubt as old as knapping flint.

The procedure for obtaining timber today is a contentious issue. There is a good deal of propaganda from both the timber trade and the environmentalists. What is plain is that massive deforestation of virgin woodlands has happened on an unprecedented scale without any consideration paid to the long-term effects or attempts to replant. This commercial vandalism occurs not just for marketing supplies of timber for carpentry, joinery and construction, but for fuel, to clear land for stock grazing, cropping, new roads, car parks, airports, tourist developments and the suburban sprawl needed for the rising tide of population growth. Over half the timber felled is burnt for fuel and a lot more burns in the forests in situ from bush fires and deliberate 'torching'. What

actually gets to be sawn, planed and fashioned into something useful and beautiful is about 7 per cent of felled timber and burned forest. Our weather patterns are changing as our woodlands diminish: the UK has now only about 8 per cent of its land covered by forest (Belgium has about 34 per cent and France over 45 per cent).

Some countries operate good forest management; others are beginning to operate programmes for selective harvesting rather than the 'bulldozer' technique of the last century and plans to conserve and replant are being adopted, with local timber producers taking more control than the predatory big multinational companies who were only interested in getting as many logs shipped as possible. It is edifying to note that some timber merchants are consciously giving their patronage to the more ethical and enlightened timber producers where milling and conversion is undertaken by the country of origin to increase local employment and secure their economies.

With this trend towards less exploitative methods of timber acquisition, we have our part to play in the selection of the woods we wish to use; if a material is demanded, there will be a market for the supplier. Some of the most perfect woods for instrument-making have become endangered species because of over-harvesting and inappropriate use. Stocks of these 'tonewoods' are therefore currently low and becoming expensive. Future imports of the 'exotic tropicals' will become rarer and cost will eventually prohibit their use. American and Cuban mahogany, for example, proved to be a timber suitable for everything –

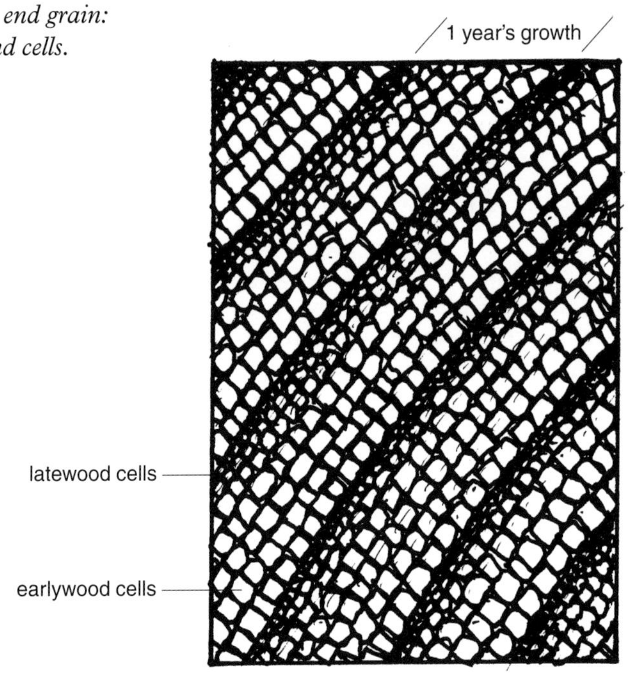

Fig 29 Wood's end grain: annual rings and cells.

1 year's growth

latewood cells

earlywood cells

and the narrower, darker, denser band being latewood. The earlywood is the part of the annual growth ring that conducts the sap and other nutrients through the larger, thin-walled cells during the spring rapid-growth season; the latewood is the outer part of the annual ring that is more dense because of the slower rate of growth resulting in the smaller, thick-walled cell structure of the darker band. The width of the annual growth ring will vary depending on climatic conditions during the growing season. A wide band indicates moist, favourable conditions; a narrow band, drought and hostile conditions. Fast-growing softwoods, used for pulping, have broad annual growth rings, while slow-growing trees in mountainous or arid regions have very narrow ones. The nature of the wood you will work with has the earlywood that cuts easily, then adjacent, the harder latewood, that does not (*see* Fig 29).

It is this annual ring that we refer to commonly as the 'grain' – although the actual grain is something quite different. For determining the appearance of the face of a piece of timber, the direction of the growth rings is important when the green log is converted by the sawmill into planks, boards or scantlings for seasoning. A particular lengthwise slice down the log will produce a particular 'grain' that may be desired. The two common methods of converting logs are shown (*see* Fig 30). Note the direction of the 'end grain' (annual growth rings) and the 'grain' (figure) on the face of the boards. For our purpose, we are interested in 'quarter-sawn' boards and scantlings, which just happens to be the most expensive way of converting a log. Most timber sold for general carpentry and construction use is 'plain-sawn' and quite unsuitable for instrument making. Note how the conversion of timber from the log will affect the shrinkage of a given section when seasoning takes place (*see* Fig 31). You will note that shrinkage on the quarter-sawn sections distorts less.

for example, for boat-building, furniture and instrument-making it is manna from heaven, but unnecessarily wasted on doors and windows. Of course, you should not give up on a suitable species from sustainable forestry operations and it is pointless to argue that you should not use mahogany or rosewood when there may be a pile of the stuff that has been stored for years. I have used 'second-hand' mahogany for neck, backs and ribs which is always worth seeking out. We tend to forget that trees have a natural lifespan and felling one before the whole structure becomes ripe for rot, decay and termites is very resourceful. Norwegians are enlightened: for every tree felled, they plant two.

When a tree is felled, the cut end of the trunk shows the annual growth rings. Some species do not have very conspicuous growth rings, but those that are obvious, like pine and spruce, display the variation in cell structure between 'earlywood' (spring-wood) and 'latewood' (summerwood), the paler, softer, broader band being earlywood

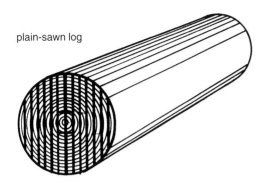

plain-sawn log

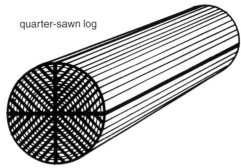

quarter-sawn log

Fig 30 Conversion of logs into boards.

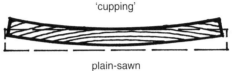

'cupping'

plain-sawn

Fig 31 Shrinkage of various wood sections.

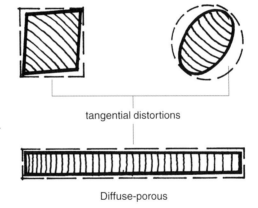

tangential distortions

Diffuse-porous

Shrinkage is much less between the annual rings (radially) than around them (tangentially). The shrinkage that occurs during seasoning along the length of a board or scantling (longitudinally) is so small, it is negligible and is due to the actual cellular structure of timber being composed of long, cylindrical vessels, looking (on cross-section under a microscope) like a bundle of reeds tied tightly together.

The cellular structure of wood is really what defines its density and texture; the individual cells of cellulose fibre are round, rectangular or polygonal in cross-section, tapering to closed ends. The direction of the length of the cells is the same and in line with the length of the trunk. The light-weight softwoods have thin-walled cells; the denser hardwoods have thick-walled cells. The texture of wood is determined by the size and arrangement of the cells. Ash and oak are coarse-textured woods because they are 'ring-porous', that is, the earlywood cells are very large compared to the latewood cells. Other coarse-grained woods are 'diffuse-porous' where the larger and smaller cells tend to mix in groups so the annual growth ring is less obvious, as in woods like meranti, utile and mahogany. Most of the tropical woods are 'diffuse-porous' which accounts for their dimensional stability and open grain (*see* Fig 32). Horizontal groups of cells run radially from the centre of the trunk and these are called 'medullary rays' that show

Fig 32 Diffuse-porous and ring-porous grain.

diffuse-porous

ring-porous

as the transverse flecks or 'silver figure' on the quarter-sawn faces of oak, for example. Medullary rays also conduct nutrients; they are smaller and not so obvious in softwoods.

There are other ingredients in timber apart from cellulose and lignin: toxins are found in rosewood, teak and greenheart that protect the living tree from woodborers and fungal attack. A splinter of greenheart may cause septic wounds and the oil in rosewood can irritate skin, eyes and mucous membranes. The fine dust from sanding down can induce allergies, be very bad news for asthmatics and can be carcinogenic. The presence of silica in tropical woods causes problems when trying to keep those much-desired razor edges on your cutting tools and is the reason why such 'exotic' tropical woods as teak are so hard to work. Softwoods contain negligible amounts of silica.

The tree trunk has another feature that will affect the choice of timber cut: the very centre of the trunk is the oldest wood and tends to be pithy and prone to fungal decay, but radiating outwards from the centre is the 'heartwood' that forms the strong structural core of dead cells that no longer conduct sap or nutrients up the tree. The heartwood is therefore the mature timber and is darker, denser, more resistant to fungal attack and woodborers. Outside of the heartwood is the living 'sapwood' which is lighter in colour, has thinner walled cells and is more prone to shrinkage and warping when seasoned. The sapwood is more likely to attract woodborers and fungal attack as it has juicy nutrients within the living cells. Sapwood is the timber that will contain the most moisture, knots and intrusion of cambium and bark, but is – take note – not inherently inferior in strength to the heartwood.

Because tree trunks taper as height increases, true straight grain will not figure on a long board unless the longitudinal saw cut is parallel to the outside of the trunk, not the centre axis.

SEASONING TIMBER

Newly felled timber when converted into boards or scantlings still contains a lot of water in the cell cavities and cell walls. (Trees should be felled in winter when the 'sap is down', but this is not always done these days.) Most of the weight of the timber while 'green' is water, in a ratio of up to 12 parts water to 10 parts wood tissue. For wood to be useful, it must have its moisture content reduced to a level approximately equal to the humidity of the environment in which it will be used. As the cells of wood are closed, the water contained in them can only dry out by evaporation through the cell walls, that are themselves saturated with about 25 per cent of the moisture in the wood. The drying process or 'seasoning' must be gradual and carefully monitored since once the moisture content drops to below 30 per cent the cell cavities are dry but the cell walls remain at fibre saturation point and further moisture loss from the cell walls will result in shrinkage taking place. Rapid drying out will therefore damage the timber, as sudden stresses caused by the fast-shrinking cells promote warping or splitting that is usually evident at the end of the boards. Once the wood has reached a moisture content in equilibrium with the ambient atmospheric humidity, shrinkage will cease.

The purpose of seasoning timber is to reduce, gradually, the moisture content so that warping, splitting and distortion do not occur, with the result that the timber is dimensionally stable and its 'movement' in a given environment will be (almost) predictable. The period needed to season timber varies with the species: 22mm thick pine boards may be seasoned in six months, but 22mm thick oak planks may take twelve months or more. Natural seasoning by the traditional air-drying process will reduce the moisture content to perhaps 16 per cent, which is fine for external use or use in an unheated building, but the timber will need to be dried further if it is to be used in a heated building. The best method to acclimatize timber is to leave it stacked in the building where it will be fixed or used for ten to fourteen days before cutting and jointing. This is not always possible since tight schedules and deadlines mean timber with too high a moisture content is fixed in heated buildings, where shrinkage will inevitably occur; you have only to look at the tawdry joinery of contemporary estate house-building. Fixing joinery with a moisture content of 18 per cent inside a new centrally heated house is asking for trouble that the hapless new owner inherits.

As a rough guide, the moisture content of timber can be as high as 22 per cent for external use in damp climates, but for internal use needs to be reduced to below 16 per cent for unheated buildings and below 11 per cent for use in heated buildings. In an arid climate the timber may need the moisture content reduced down to 5 per cent. For musical instruments, we need woods with a moisture content of about 9 per cent.

There is an alternative to seasoning by natural evaporation and this is 'kiln-drying'. This sounds somewhat alarming since we know timber must be dried out gradually. However, it is necessary to reduce moisture in timber to be used internally as we have seen and kiln-drying provides a relatively fast option for having timber delivered directly from the merchant with a specified moisture content. Needless to say, once you have taken delivery, the timber cannot be left out in an unheated shed, otherwise it will take up water vapour readily from the air. The ability of timber – and velum drum and banjo skins – to sponge up airborne moisture is truly remarkable.

Some woodworkers turn up their noses at the idea of kiln-drying, although the wood technologists confirm this method in no way reduces the quality or nature of the timber and does, in fact, lessen the chances

of the timber being prone to attack by fungal spores, which can and does occur during air-drying. Simply, the kiln-drying process is a controlled operation whereby the drying rate is speeded up, in accordance with the specified times for each species and size of timber section.

Even well-seasoned timber will move with fluctuations of humidity in the atmosphere. Here in the UK we can experience rapid changes due to weather fronts appearing suddenly, and it is possible to enjoy four seasons in one week. Humidity and temperature changes can cause havoc as far as

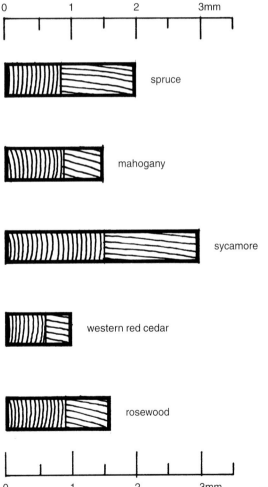

Radial and tangential moisture movement for a 10 per cent relative humidity change on a 300mm wide board

Fig 33 Comparison of movements in the tonewoods used.

wood is concerned, especially where more than one species is coupled together in a workpiece. Some woods have more capacity for swelling or shrinking (movement) than others and since we cannot control the weather we have to accommodate the movement in timber that can take place. Note the amount of movement due to relative humidity for the species of woods used (*see* Fig 33).

Attempting to prevent movement in timber is futile; even varnishes, paints and oils do not provide an impervious film to water vapour, whichever way it is heading. Protective coatings on timber can cause the entrapment of moisture, raising the content so that it becomes ripe for fungal attack. 'Wet' rots cannot infect timber with a moisture content below about 17 per cent, although the fungal spores can lie dormant within the cells, waiting for conditions to improve! Dry Rot, the terror of every timber house owner, is something very sneaky: it can infect healthy dry timber by feeding moisture into it via the strands of mycelia it sends out from the fruiting body of fungus. Science fiction would find it hard to come up with anything creepier. If the vulnerable timber is well-ventilated and the source of moisture removed, dry rot can be eradicated.

The moisture content (MC) of timber can be checked with a 'moisture meter' that either works on the principle of a small electric current passing between two electrodes that penetrate the wood to measure the resistance across the gap, or by magnetic resonance. Low moisture content means high resistance and high moisture content means low resistance; this degree of resistance is then converted to a digital or analogue read-out of 'percentage MC'. As the electrode devices will leave two small holes in your unblemished tonewoods, choose an off-cut or waste area to test. Take several spot readings – but be warned – if the wood section is thick the electrode-type moisture meter won't have a

clue what the MC at the heart of the timber will be and if you test the end grain, this is no indicator either as moisture evaporates quickly from the cut ends.

It is always far better to buy in your tonewoods and set them aside in a warm place for at least two months before you intend to use them. This will ensure that moisture content will be low and that further shrinkage after fashioning and gluing up will be unlikely.

Any piece of wood with a marked movement due to moisture cannot be restrained without meeting trouble. A workpiece prevented from shrinking (for example: glued between a rigid frame or box) will have to split along the grain, usually between the interface of latewood to earlywood. A workpiece prevented from swelling will either burst or fracture the rigid frame that restrains it, or will 'belly out' or 'dish' if the restraint does not yield. Considerable compression and tension can build up in timber that wants to move but can't and these forces are not welcome in the components of a musical instrument, especially as the tonewoods are costly and one may have spent many hours labouring away on them. There are people who believe that an oil leak in an engine will eventually clog up and seal itself; they are like the woodworkers who believe that wood, once well-seasoned, glued up with indestructible adhesive and given a glass-thick coat of catalyst laquer will never move; they will be disappointed.

The woods we will select for instrument-making are those species that have proved stable, reliable, acoustically beneficial and have very small movement radially. Spruce and sycamore have moderate movement compared to mahogany, western red cedar and rosewood, but spruce for lightness, strength and unsurpassed tonal qualities has to be used for soundboards. Sycamore seems to like to move rather more than spruce, but 'flamed' figure sycamore is so beautiful for ribs and backs, we must tolerate the tendency of some timbers to expand and contract. We must accommodate the foibles and qualities of the tonewoods and couple them together so that they react with and enhance their neighbours' properties. To conceive that any element of a stringed musical instrument is somehow 'inert' is quite incorrect: the whole assembly 'works' and 'lives' from tuning post to tailpiece; there is no 'deadwood' packed in anywhere.

BENDING WOOD

It will be necessary to bend wood during the construction process and whilst wood like ash, well soaked in water, will bend a fair amount before fracturing, the hardwoods used, alas, are not as compliant as ash. Steaming the thin workpieces for the ribs (sides) is possible: you can heat wood in a steam-box up to 140°C, but this method is not the preferred one, as it makes the surface fibres woolly. The wooden ribs of violins, guitars and all the mandolin family of instruments are best bent to the shape required by the hot iron method. Heat is the primary agent to soften the wood cells and fibres to make them plastic, but not too much heat, nor for too long. The wood needs to be kept moist otherwise rapid shrinkage will take place and splitting along the grain can occur. The workpiece needs to be soaked well beforehand and then continuously (when held against the bending-iron) with a broad paintbrush dipped in water, as the wood is gently persuaded to take on a bend around the profile of the hot iron. The wet wood will spit and steam wildly when pressed on to the hot iron and further dousing with water on both faces must be done when the wood stops steaming. Never try to bend timber by just heating it; you need the steam to rapidly penetrate the fibres and the bending-iron must not be too hot: the right temperature is gauged when a droplet of cold water dropped onto the bending-iron cap sizzles

and evaporates quickly – if the droplet explodes like a bomb, the iron is too hot. When the curve of the rib is about right – still warm and damp – it is locked into the mould where it cools down and excess moisture will evaporate, leaving the rib to retain the curve you gave it.

Bending the ribs' shape can be disastrous for a novice; I suggest practising on some waste material of similar species and thickness, where you will get a 'feel' for the amount of pressure you need to apply as the wood 'gives' just that slight amount. It is better to have several soft approaches to this than one or two attempts to wrap the rib around the iron. The golden rule here is: plenty of water, the right heat and plenty of time. Be mindful that ribs come in bookmatched pairs, so to break one by over-zealous bending means you will have the other on which to practise getting it right. However, this is an expensive way to learn.

Wood has one other property that we must consider: the cellular structure will gradually distort under stress from forces imposed by string tension and the wood will take on a 'set'. A straight piece of wood will, if under a constant load, assume a curve that will partially remain even when the load is removed. Humidity and high temperatures can accelerate this 'setting' which is why medieval longbows were unbraced (the bowstring slackened) when not in use; violin bows are slackened off when not in use for the same reason and it is unwise to leave a vintage instrument permanently tuned to concert pitch as the neck will pull up into a set and make the action too high. The set on a neck can be corrected by the use of a heated neck clamp that will pull the neck back down – however, this remedy is only temporary. The insertion of a 'truss rod' to counteract the pull of the strings is now common practice although the rod *must* be from peghead to heel, as shorter rods will permit local setting where the truss restraint cannot act. I have seen many fairly new guitars with an adjustable truss rod that stops short of the peghead and sadly a set has occurred between the nut and the 3rd fret which raises the action and wrecks the playability of an otherwise good guitar. This kind of attention to detail separates good from bad and the convenience of factory-fitted truss rods can compromise the quality of a neck. The contentious subject of truss rods will be dealt with in Chapter 8.

SELECTING TIMBER

When choosing your woods for instrument-making, examine the pieces carefully for defects. Often on sawn material it is not always easy to see the run of the grain, nor the end grain direction to tell you if the piece has been quarter-sawn. Take a knife and scrape a patch to view the surface; this will give you an idea of what it will look like when planed; wet the patch to see what it will look like when varnished or oiled. Do this to the end grain to make the annual growth rings obvious. Sight your eye down the length of the board or scantling to check there is no twisting or bowing and that the grain is fairly straight and the growth rings are not too wide. It is usual for the growth rings to increase in width across a board, but avoid material with sudden wide rings as this can lead to a line of weakness. Disregard material with much wavy and wild grain but do not confuse any 'flamed' figure on sycamore or maple as wild grain; this is much sought after and fetches a high price.

Avoid material with knots, pinholes, pith, shakes, splits, checking, ingrown bark, fungal staining and woodborer flight holes. However, you can't be too fussy as I've yet to turn up the perfect piece of wood. Merchants who offer material for luthiers' use often dip the end grain of boards into paint or wax, which prevents rapid drying and splitting at the sawn ends; this can be cut off as waste or planed off when you prepare the sawn board for thicknessing. Beware of being offered material that has not been

properly seasoned or has been stored in open sheds. You will pay a high price for this selected material so you are entitled to have it well-seasoned and supplied with a low moisture content. Any boards that have a twist suggests bad seasoning or 'reaction' wood that has grown stresses in it; this twisting may not be remedied when you plane to thickness, so it is wise to pass by and select the next best. Really interesting grain on boards is attractive, but can be risky.

Once you have bought what you need, lay it in store in the warmest room in your house for a week or two; you will soon discover if it was correctly seasoned. If it warps or splits then take it back. Always look for woods at the sawmill that have a good layer of dust on them. If a merchant doesn't give you licence to rummage around the stock to select your material, then give your patronage to a dealer who appreciates why you're being picky. Take the instrument's templates with you when you visit the timberyard; this will help you quickly establish suitable sized woods without measuring up. You may also find you may be comparing worthwhile notes with other luthiers. I have spent half a day selecting enough suitable material for just two instruments; it does pay to be selective. Once you have secured your prized tonewoods, store them carefully so they don't get damaged, bent, bruised, stained by paint or other solvents or spirited away to put under the foot of the fridge to stop it rocking. I say this because the rough sawn panels of spruce look like old bits of packing crate!

THE GRAIN IN TIMBER

The hardwoods you will use will have cell structures that wave about, curl and some pieces or areas may display 'wild grain' or 'interlocked grain', where the long tubular cells change direction alternately from one growing season to the next. This spiral of growth: clockwise one year, anti-clockwise the next, gives the 'ribbon' figure on some quarter-sawn tropical hardwoods, such as mahogany, utile and meranti. These coarse-grained hardwoods tend to have wild and interlocked grain in them to a greater or lesser degree and whilst it may be our aim to select woods with grain like Regency wallpaper, it is inevitable that somewhere the grain will provide us with an unwelcome challenge.

Any divergent grain will matter when we start to plane a workpiece. Planing with the grain must be done to avoid the plane iron snagging and chopping out chunks from the face of the work (*see* Fig 34). You may need to turn the workpiece 180 degrees in the vice to get the plane to shave cleanly. Where the grain is so wild and interlocked that no direction of planing will produce a good longways cut, then try planing diagonally, or even at right-angles to the grain (*see* Fig 35).

All softwoods that are true quarter-sawn boards tend to behave a little more predictably, where a clean shave is possible in one and the same direction, but when you turn the board over to plane the other face, face 'B' may be in the opposite direction.

Fig 34 Plane with the grain to avoid tearing.

plane with the grain

planing against the grain

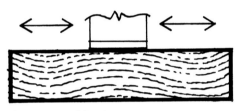

plane across wild grain

Fig 35 Plane across the grain for interlocked or wild grain.

Fig 36 Plane with the grain to thickness the belly.

You will need to imprint this indelibly on your memory when preparing to thickness the spruce boards for the belly and most probably the back and ribs as well. I always mark the 'plane with the grain' direction on a corner of the board (which becomes waste material) by stabbing in an arrow mark with the 6mm chisel. Pencil marking this feature is no good as it will get planed off instantly (*see* Fig 36).

Because all timber has a lighter, wider, open-pored area directly adjacent to the darker, thinner, close-pored latewood line, the surface nature will be of an alternating harder and softer material. Where these growth rings are tightly spaced this property will not be so important, but where the growth rings are wider, as they probably will be the farther they get from the centreline, any abrasive paper will tend to remove more of the softer fibres of the earlywood leaving the harder latewood proud, giving a corrugated effect. Spruce is especially prone to this problem when rubbed

down, so the solution, in complete contrast to everything you may have been told before, is to rub down across the grain using the medium grit, 'free-cut' aluminium oxide abrasive paper on a flat cork block. I strongly recommend this particular abrasive paper as it is hard-wearing, does not clog and does not leave scratches on the surface like sandpapers.

When the oiling and polishing to finish the belly of the instrument is complete, the final surface will show the very slight corrugations once the timber has taken up moisture to balance it with the atmosphere's relative humidity. Too thick a finish will obliterate the grain's slight corrugations and change its acoustic value, however, you do not want the surface to resemble a 'washboard' by removing too much of the earlywood. It is not desirable with spruce – or any softwood for that matter – to dampen it to 'raise the grain' prior to sanding; this will only result in the 'washboard' effect being increased.

3 DYNAMICS, ACOUSTICS AND EARS

A string, whether gut, nylon, brass or steel will behave in a certain way when it is tensioned between two fixed points and plucked, it will spring back and forth from the energy given to it by the plectrum until all the energy is used up in vibration and the string returns to its 'rest' position. The distance to which the string moves away from the resting position is called the 'amplitude' and the more vigorously it is plucked, the greater the amplitude. In practice a string does not vibrate back and forth exactly on the same plane as the direction of force from the plectrum, but during its vibration period will oscillate in all directions (*see* Fig 37). For a given string length and thickness (gauge) the amount of tension on a string will determine how many vibrations per second (pitch) it will make. 'Pitch' in musical terms means 'frequency' in cycles per second or Hertz (Hz) in physical science. Slacker tension produces slower vibrations of the string and therefore lower pitch; tighter tension produces faster vibrations and therefore higher pitch. A tensioned string is, in effect, a spring. There is just one difficulty with this simple arrangement for varying pitches of a string and that is that slack tension for the low pitches lowers the potential energy of the string: the string will not vibrate with any springiness and will lose its energy fast, it will be floppy, have little sustain and sound dull. Tightening the string will improve performance as the greater tension will cause the string to oscillate with more energy, increasing its amplitude and sustain, and it will sound brighter.

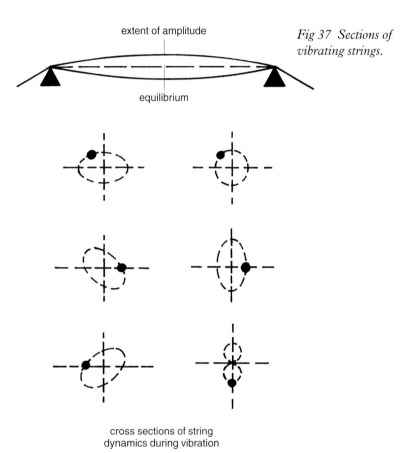

Fig 37 Sections of vibrating strings.

extent of amplitude

equilibrium

cross sections of string dynamics during vibration

To achieve a fairly even balance in dynamics across the range of pitches an instrument can produce, the strings used can be the same gauge but of graduated decreasing lengths as on a zither, harp and hammered dulcimer. With a mandolin, where all the string lengths are virtually identical to a preferred scale-length, these strings must have varying gauges and weights to achieve optimum tension and balanced performance for the pitch range needed. The basic principles for all strings are that pitch will rise with:

◆ shortening the string
◆ increasing the tension
◆ reducing the gauge (thickness).

Of course, to lower the pitch, you do exactly the opposite of the above three.

If we look at the mandolin or mandola it is now obvious why strings of different thicknesses are used, with the thicker wound strings for the bass pitches and the thinner plain strings for the treble pitches. Logically this seems fine and mathematical formulae should provide the perfect gauge

required for a given length and a given pitch. However, it is not so elementary as the perceived performance is subject to many considerations, just as personal preference for a 'good tone' may not be appreciated by others and will be difficult to define.

The way in which the human ear hears and how the sound impulses are transmitted to the auditory nerves and brain are part of the reason why pitch would appear to perform inconsistently. The graph (Fig 38) shows how the perception of loudness by the human ear varies with pitch. Higher frequencies (with a peak at 3,500 Hz) are heard more easily (the ear has a natural resonance of about 3,000 Hz) and appear to be of greater volume. The lowest note on a piano at about 32 Hz needs to be much louder to be perceived as the same volume of 3,200 Hz: about 60 decibels louder, in fact. There are other agents at work that will make the issue of perceived loudness even more complex and these include age, gender, health of the ear and auditory nerves, air temperature and relative humidity, acoustic environment, extraneous and ambient noise levels and whether the people around you are wearing thick woolly sweaters! Whilst we have little control on the above it would seem there is more to achieving a balanced range of pitches from the construction of something as seemingly basic as a hollow wooden box.

It is not within the scope of this book to enter into environmental physics or human biology in detail. Suffice to say that high frequency pitch is very directional and more easily absorbed by the sort of general furnishings and finishes around us and that the low bass frequencies are less easily absorbed, are more penetrating and reflected more readily. Compare this with the very low pitch of a broad dispersal ship's foghorn and the high-pitched directional squeak of a dolphin's 'sonar'. For whatever reason, women *are* more sensitive to the very low frequency sounds and can

Fig 38 Our perception of loudness varies with pitch.

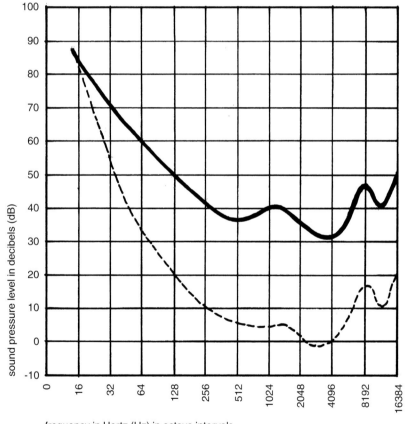

perceived equal loudness

threshold of hearing

detect them even at very long distances and low volume levels. It has been found that noise pollution generated at very low frequencies from factory machinery, turbines and ships' engines can sometimes *only* be perceived by women. Women, perhaps, have developed this ability as an evolutionary asset: the advantage of knowing well in advance of the approach of a storm, a seismic event or even a large herd of buffalo would allow her time to repair to safety with her brood. Animals and birds seem to know of an impending earthquake.

The strings that interest us for the mandolin and mandola are made from steel. Steel strings are manufactured from: (a) plain high-carbon steel wire, plated with silver or tin to protect the steel from corrosion; or (b) a steel core wound with a spiral covering of brass, bronze, nickel, copper or even stainless steel. Type (a) are the thin gauges used for the higher-pitched trebles, whilst type (b) are for the heavier gauges needed for the lower bass pitches. The wrap-around cover on type (b) will affect the projection, brightness and longevity of the string but the gauge of the core wire is what counts for optimum tension and hence, vibrant performance. The gauge and alloy of the wound covering wire will enhance the string's acoustics and, as a rule, bronze alloys are best as they impart a warmer, richer tone needed for the bass pitches. For attack and bite the stainless steel wound coverings are preferred and give the long-scaled octave mandola, which has rather low-tensioned strings, a bit more 'buzz'. The strings you will prefer on a specific instrument can only be found by trial but I would say that phosphor bronze wound are best suited on a responsive handmade instrument and work well on the instruments featured in this book.

As string technology deserves a publication of its own, I shall confine myself to mentioning the other properties that affect the vibrating string and are those of which instrument-makers should be aware. A string being of relatively small diameter, even when vibrating vigorously, does not have much surface area to move much air and therefore cannot project much sound. The type of alloy cover will, as we have seen, make a bit of difference to the tone, but the actual size of the winding and its cross-section can increase the response to overtones and brilliance. Large-gauge windings will improve the brightness; small-gauge or flat windings will produce less harmonics and a mellower sound. The rougher covering of 'roundwound' strings actually energize small additional air fluctuations, enriching the sound. String-makers are at great pains to manufacture improved wound strings: the winding alloy can loosen from the core wire and wreck the string, but hexagonal or fluted section core wire can be used for the best quality strings as this grips the wrapped around covering more securely. Good strings are more expensive because of this specially extruded core wire, but they do have a longer playing life. Steel strings are subject to initial stretching and metal fatigue: new strings have an elasticity and spring to them that is lost after many hours playing, so never try to assess the tone of an instrument unless the strings are fresh; a good, responsive instrument with tired old strings does not make for a fair audition.

When a string is plucked, the sudden release of energy will spring the steel wire into life, oscillating to a pitch dependent on the degree of tension, length and weight of the string. Initially the string will vibrate slightly sharp for a tenth of a second or so, settle to the exact pitch for a longer period of perhaps four to twelve seconds and then decay to a flatter pitch before coming to rest. It is the nature of this response that will give the instrument its particular 'timbre' and is so characteristic that even the electronics wizards can't quite replicate this with synthesized sound; electronic keyboards can produce a sound *like* a piano or harpsichord, but it is too compressed and contrived, missing out those subtle overtones that come into play on the real assemblage of strings, iron, brass, wood, air spaces and resonances. Where a string is plucked matters as well: the vibrations wander in all directions and the string will find its harmonic overtones and segment the fundamental note into octave, third, fifth and seventh divisions to a greater or lesser degree depending on where it was plucked. Pluck it near the 12th fret (half the scale-length) and the fundamental harmonic will respond giving a pure, flute-like tone; pluck it near to the bridge to excite the other overtones into life and the tone is brighter, richer and with more bite.

Because the amplitude will increase with the stronger flick of the plectrum and the peaks and troughs along the string's length change with the stopping at a chosen fret, the height of the strings above the fretboard (action) is critical; too low an action will cause the strings at full amplitude to rattle or buzz against the frets in front of the stopped string: too high an action results in difficulty in stopping the string on the chosen fret, excess tension and tendon strain in the wrist and arm and poor intonation as all the stopped notes become progressively sharpened; all this is enough to discourage you from playing. How many would-be guitarists have given up because their first instrument had too high an action?

As if there were not enough to think about already, steel strings will go dull very quickly if the player has sweaty hands (some people's perspiration is more acidic than others), or if left out of the instrument's case will collect dust. Grime will clog up the wound coverings to wreck their brilliance and wear from the frets will eventually distort the strings causing the loss of their response to the overtones. There are patent solutions on the market that claim to rejuvenate your strings and improve their playability. They may well clean off some of the grime and lubricate them but there is no miracle cure for distortion or

metal fatigue; strings need to be replaced regularly. As a string becomes old and worn it loses any elasticity it possessed; to try to tune an old string to pitch will become increasingly difficult as it will never sound right: it will have become brittle and is now just ripe to snap at the first opportunity. To have old strings on an instrument tensioned up to concert pitch is not recommended as the lack of any 'give' in the string will cause greater stresses on the neck especially, and on vintage instruments without truss rods, this can be permanently damaging and create a bad 'set'.

You will learn to hear old strings: they sound more like the reinforcement rods in concrete – and feel like them. I have seen so many mandolins in junk shops and antique dealers that haven't got many strings on them usually, but the remaining ones are so old and rusty the neck of the instrument has taken on the form of a banana. These old, neglected bowl-backed mandolins are, sadly, destined to hang up as decoration.

The stringing of the mandolin is done in double courses, that is, in unison pairs with the gauge of the pair of strings being identical. To discover why anyone would want to create this complication by doubling the strings and giving the player twice as many to keep in tune can be demonstrated when a string snaps: pluck the one remaining and you will notice this sounds dull with no sustain or 'zing'. You will also notice (when you have replaced the broken string) that if you tune them and then just pluck one of the pair, the other one will vibrate in sympathy. If you now tune up the second string of the pair *just* slightly sharp and pluck both of them, they sound brighter than exactly tuned unison pairs. This is no trick of the ear (for once) as two strings side by side at exactly the same pitch tend to cancel out each other's dynamics. This doubling up to reinforce the projection is a paradox as organ builders discovered when they placed pipes of the same pitch adjacent to each other: one pipe would mute the sound of the other because of 'out-of-phase' pressure waves meeting each other and neutralizing the fluctuations in air; in practice, organ pipes of equal pitch are placed well away from each other. If the pitch of one string is sharpened slightly, then this does give the note more reinforcement, aids sustain and increases projection. Because the mandolin is a short-scaled instrument with tight stringing, pairing of the strings is done to improve the sustain. Triple-strung courses on 'Sicilian' mandolins get over this problem of double-strung projection, but it does mean you have twelve strings to worry about. (Of interest, whilst on the subject, check out the inside of the next piano you see; the mid- to bass ranges are 'trichord' strung: triple-stringing of these heavy brass wound strings increases their sustain and projection.)

The mandolin, although being tuned the same as a violin, does not project as well simply because the bow of a violin constantly sustains the strings at a great amplitude. A plucked violin string is a very different sounding short-lived 'plink' with no bite whatsoever.

The longer scale-length mandolas, citterns and even longer-scaled bouzoukis have paired strings as well to give that distinctive ringing tone. The tremolo technique of picking is much aided by pairs of strings – whether unison or octave tuned.

THE BELLY AND SOUNDBOX

The selection of tonewood such as spruce for the soundboard is critical as the belly of an acoustic instrument should efficiently project the sound to the audience. The properties of the belly material, the type and arrangement of internal bracing and the flexing of the soundboard will determine the performance and tone of the instrument. One must understand the dynamics of how the bridge transmits the vibrant energy of the plucked string to be amplified by the belly and this action is best described as a combination of tiny rocking and pumping motions made by the bridge feet directly exerting its influence on the belly, that must be able to vibrate correspondingly. This principle is similar to the voice-coil of a loudspeaker pushing or pulling the attached cone to set up oscillating pressure waves in the air to create sound; however, there the similarity ends as the belly does not share the same definite linear motion as the loudspeaker but 'rocks' with the bridge. The face of the belly rocking downwards partially cancels out the pressure wave of air being generated by the face of the belly rocking upwards, causing considerable loss of projected sound to the listener. This effect can be well illustrated by two loudspeakers placed so that they face each other, with one of them wired up to the amplifier 'out-of-phase', connected by reversed polarity. When one cone moves out the other facing it moves in, neutralizing the sound pressure wave, so the projection to the listener is diminished greatly. (Incidentally, new loudspeakers are 'run in' by this technique to get them to optimum compliancy and efficiency quickly.) To prevent such an unwanted neutralizing effect occurring on the belly of an instrument, the bracing underneath the soundboard is designed to stiffen the treble side, so the bass side will vibrate with greater vigour. A violin uses a 'soundpost' near the treble foot of the bridge to stiffen the belly, but with a mandolin or mandola a diagonal bar is used, strategically placed to tighten up the dynamics of the treble foot of the bridge. The choice of restraining the treble side is quite deliberate as the bass side of the belly can use the more uninhibited surface area to flex more freely and project the lower-pitched, longer wavelengths whilst the stiffened treble side is aptly suited to the higher-pitched, shorter wavelengths, thus achieving balance and brightness across the whole tonal range. Again we can compare these actions to the loudspeaker's large surface area 'woofer' for the low pitches and the small 'tweeter' for the highs.

To appreciate fully the need to have a belly that does not respond symmetrically, imagine (but please *do not* try this) the instrument standing on its tail and the soundbox filled with water right up to the edge of the soundhole. If you pressed one half of the belly in whilst the other half sympathetically came outwards, no water would be displaced from the soundhole and, for that matter, no air either, so the projected sound is nil. Restrain the belly on the treble half and press the bass half inwards and you will force water out; water or air, you have improved projection! It is a common criticism that many mandolins fail to perform well within the bass ranges: the G and D strings can sound dull and slack even if they are fresh and of a heavier gauge than standard. This is a problem caused by the bracing dynamics being woolly and can be avoided by careful design, application and crafting of the bars.

Having established that the belly must be able to flex in a controlled way, the structural bars must support the belly across its width from going hollow or collapsing under the pressure from the string tension across the bridge. This presents us with a fly in the ointment: the bars must have adequate stiffness but must also be compliant enough to allow the belly to vibrate in all manner of ways and directions. Ideally, one bar would be fine, but for practical purposes more have to be incorporated to prevent local weaknesses at soundholes and to maintain the gentle doming so acoustically and structurally necessary to the soundboard. The bars should be the same species as the belly tonewood, although I have experimented with spruce belly and pine bars that prove quite compatible and give the tonal quality a more nasal timbre with improved sustain, working well on the larger-bodied mandolas and bouzoukis.

The size and shaping of the bars will be critical for excellent performance; the camber must be planed on the top edge of the bars B2 and B3 that will maintain the gentle outward curvature of the belly top. (The bars BB2 and BB3 to the back should reflect the doming of the belly too.) There are two good reasons for the doming: firstly, without a dome the string tension would pressure the belly inwards and become 'hollow': this is not a desirable feature. If the belly is dished then an increase in moisture content and subsequent swelling of the wood will cause compressive forces to dish the belly even further, straining and stressing the bars making them less compliant and therefore less effective. Furthermore, if the belly dishes, the 'action' is reduced and string-rattles on the frets will be the outcome. Secondly, the doming will induce the belly to bow outwards when swelling occurs, as the same compressive forces are directed upwards against the pressure of the bridge. This tendency is advantageous as it has a compensatory effect: as relative humidity rises this produces greater tension on the strings (with an increase in pitch) just as the strings under such conditions tend to go flat. The effect of climate fluctuation is, therefore, somewhat mitigated.

The doming also has an aesthetically pleasing appearance, of which the ancient Greeks had been most conscious: the inclusion of the 'entasis' to a vertical column, whereby the sides had a slight bulge to make them appear visually straight. (The Parthenon in Athens even has a slight rise at the centre of the pediment's entablature to effect a perceived straight horizontal.) It is worthy to note that there is not one straight plane on a mandolin, except for the edges of the fretboard. But here there is a theoretical complication – strings are *only* straight when they are not being played! It would not be too obsessive in one's quest for perfect playability to have an 'entasis' to the edges of the fretboard to follow the curve of the vibrating or stopped string to allow for the lateral force sometimes applied by the fingers to 'pitch-bend' a note.

The amount of camber designed on the bars B2 and B3 of 3mm and 4.5mm, respectively, can be increased slightly, but don't overdo it for the mandolin which, having a narrower body width than the other instruments, will not need a higher curvature than recommended. The need for the doming to the back of the instrument to reflect the belly is not just cosmetic to prevent it going 'hollow'; sound waves are reflected in the same way as a snooker ball rebounding off the cushion. The angle of incidence equals the angle of reflection, so the opposing internal surfaces of the soundbox do not want to be absolutely flat or parallel. Unwelcome resonances will occur in any enclosure with parallel faces, especially if they are rigid and smooth-faced. This particular acoustic foible can be demonstrated in a subway by clapping your hands once, then listening for the series of rapid interval echoes as they bounce back and forth between the parallel tunnel walls; the closer the wall surfaces, the quicker the flutter. As parallel surfaces will encourage the formation of standing waves such as 'wolf notes', the irregularity of shape of an enclosure (or soundbox) will diffuse any tendency towards the generation of flutter echoes or booming resonances.

The back of the instrument vibrates as well, which is why holding the instrument tight to your chest when playing is not recommended: your body will mute the sound.

Regarding unwanted resonances within musical instruments, we can only suppose that the manufacturers of loudspeaker enclosures utilize rectangular shapes for economic reasons as the most irregular shapes conceivable would be ideal. The latest fashions tend to diverge from this habit and strange space-age shapes are appearing in the Hi-Fi stores. One

designer I knew built cabinets for his loudspeakers in the proportion of a perfect 600mm cube. It did not seem strange that he never invited anyone to visit his studio to listen to his fabulous handmade Hi-Fi. The irregular shape of an enclosure (or soundbox) will produce a broader response without favouring any particular frequencies, which is just what we desire. In fact, the only straight line is the long axis or theoretical centreline. The doming that proves so useful to the integrity of the belly also proves fortunate when considered as a feature improving the internal acoustic properties of the soundbox. This is why the doming to the back should be included as a complementary element.

You will have noticed the arched belly and back and the figure-of-eight shape of the violin, viola, cello and double bass. These details are not a mere whim of Baroque styling, otherwise this fashion would have been superseded. The shape *is* beautiful and eminently purposeful – no one has been able to improve upon the shape and inherent dynamics of a violin, and the moulds of N. Amati and A. Stradivari still reign supreme.

There is one other subtle curve that needs to be mentioned: you will see on the plans that the ribs taper slightly from the tail to the neck in a long, low convex curve. This tapered feature to the ribs' profile prevents the belly and back from being parallel to each other, but it also serves another function – it promotes a very slight longitudinal dome to the belly (and an even slighter one to the back) ensuring that the belly does not go 'hollow' lengthwise from the compression exerted on it from the tailpiece being pulled towards the neck by string tension. *Do not* omit this feature by planing the edges of the ribs perfectly straight. Make sure the templates for the ribs follow the plan's outline religiously. You could, if you wish, make the ribs' depth lesser or greater, but *do not* omit these gentle curves

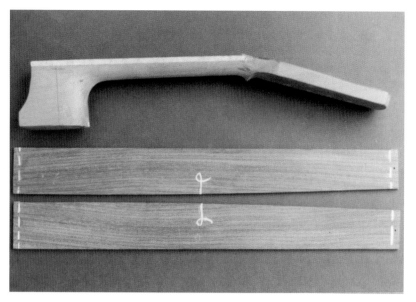

ABOVE: Fig 39 The ribs' cambered edges.

BELOW: Fig 40 The recurved ribs' profile at the shoulders.

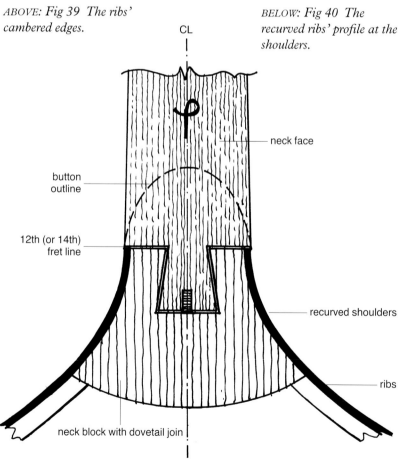

unless you want a belly with a self-lowering action! (*see* Fig 39).

It would not be out of place here to mention the design of the ribs-to-neck join. Choose the method of fitting the rib into shoulder slots in the neck. This simplifies the bent curve and anchors the rib securely into the neck. The alternative 'recurved' rib design of the 'tear-drop' body shape, that is commonly used for flat-back mandolins, has a separate neck block carved to accommodate the ends of the ribs, that are rebated and glued in so they lie flush with the sides of the neck (*see* Fig 40). This arrangement incorporates a dovetail join between the neck block and neck: a detail that is not so easy to fashion and scribe to the angles required, and does not allow much flexibility when having to make a final adjustment when checking the angle of the neck. The pull of the strings creates a turning moment at the shoulders as the tail wants to move forwards to the neck and the neck wants to move upwards towards the tail! The neck/neck block join becomes a reluctant 'pivot' that can stress the thin ribs where they are glued to the neck block. The solid 'through-neck' heel design as recommended is superior, more reliable and less stressful to the ribs (*see* Fig 41).

The internal bars of the belly are fashioned in such a way that they are slim and light in weight. The direction of the grain increases the bars' stiffness, so provided the grain is aligned as shown, the light wooden bars can be very strong for their cross-sectional area. Spruce is, of course, famous for its strength-to-weight ratio. The bars are not straight rectangular sections like a structural beam; although they must support like a beam, they must be able to flex just the right amount. They are scalloped to increase their bending moment towards the edges of the belly, thus making the whole structure more compliant to literally 'pump' out the sound to the audience. This gradual tapering prevents any local point of weakness on the span of the bars, so the thinnest section is at the end bearing on the rib linings (*see* Fig 42). Attention to detail when fashioning the bars cannot be skimped; a bar is rarely seen by anyone but the luthier, but you should work at this as though it is to be fitted on to the outside – this will ensure you make a proper job of it. If too much material is left on, the bar will be too stiff and too heavy; if you shave too much off, the bar can distort under load from the bridge's pressure and at worst, pull away from the rib linings or shear where it is thinnest. Such distortion or failure of a bar will wreck the instrument, since effecting a repair is terribly difficult; a new belly would be the best restorative solution.

One unavoidable truth is that the bars lengthwise will not shrink or swell as much as the radial aspect of the belly grain. This is because the bars run at right-angles to the belly grain and longitudinal shrinkage is negligible compared to radial as mentioned in Chapter 2. This does mean that the bars, once glued on, will have a definite restraining effect on the belly's movement due to relative humidity, but the tensions and compressions in the belly material will still be there, depending on the whims of climatic conditions. It is absolutely necessary, therefore, to ensure that the belly will not shrink appreciably after the bars have been glued on. If the moisture content of the belly is higher than recommended, then subsequent drying and contraction may promote a split down the weakest line of grain. This miserable occurrence does not herald the end of the world or of the instrument, but do take every effort to reduce the belly material to its 9 per cent MC. For the same reason, avoid applying a reinforcing strip to the belly centre-join internally. The more structurally minded may desire to add something, but it is not needed on instruments with such lengths of body as these: the bars B2 and B3 do a good enough job.

The belly will have, as a result of the designed cambers to bars B2 and B3, its

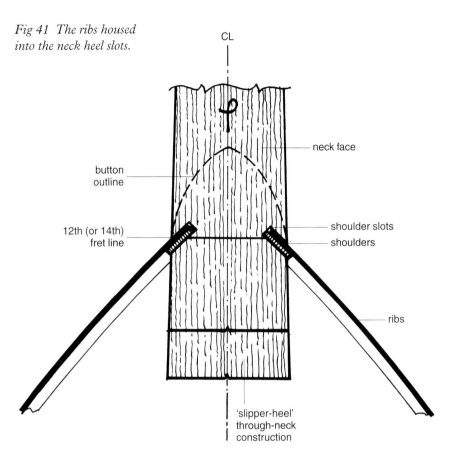

Fig 41 The ribs housed into the neck heel slots.

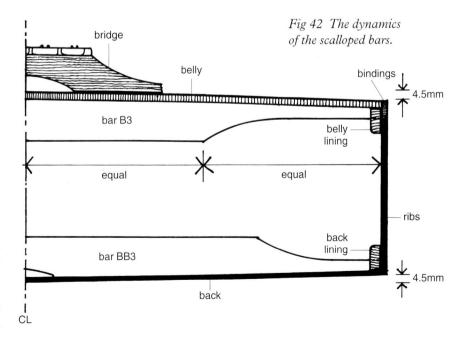

Fig 42 The dynamics of the scalloped bars.

greatest curvature at the bridge position, diminishing gradually towards the sound-hole and then quite level across its width at bar B1 that is flat on its upper edge. The belly does not want any curvature neckside of the soundhole as this area must be flat for the fretboard shim to fit neatly between fretboard and belly, and the belly's neck end sits level and squarely into the shoulder rebate in the top face of the neck (*see* Fig 43).

Whilst the belly is constructed to work as hard as it can to amplify the energy of the

100mm or 200mm diameter will reproduce all the pitches from 50 to 10,000 Hz, but the smaller cone will favour the higher notes, whilst the larger will favour the lower, and the discerning listener will detect this tendency. Because the vibrating diaphragm of a loudspeaker is a cone, the diameter will decrease with depth and the various pitches will be emphasized somewhere on the cone. The elliptical cones, now rarely used, were designed to give an overall response within the variable radii available. It is no surprise

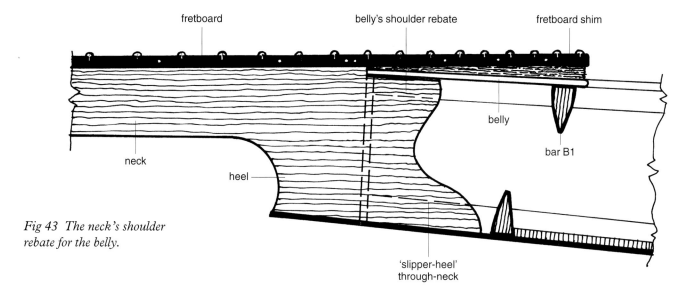

Fig 43 The neck's shoulder rebate for the belly.

vibrating string(s), it is not the case that a particular half of the belly will act especially or be dedicated to a given pitch. The bridge transmits vibration via two feet to enhance the rocking motions, yet there is no simple division between bass and treble ranges to their respective halves of the belly. The lowest string will act primarily on the 'bass' foot, but will impart energy to the 'treble' foot as well – hence the rocking moment. The whole belly reacts to a greater or lesser degree depending on the pitch and all we can hope to achieve is a good broad balance in vibrancy, projection and sustain. If we return to the ubiquitous analogy of the loudspeaker again, the cone, whether

then, to look at the shape of the mandolin body and conclude from its almond shape – 'mandola' stems from Italian *mandorla*, meaning 'almond' – that it is a distorted ellipse for a good reason. This ovoid area will, therefore, have at least some part of it that responds to a given pitch and if the belly has this ability to respond equally to each pitch within the instrument's compass then you have a *very good instrument*.

There are other agencies at work on the belly that need consideration and one is the finish applied to it. This finish, whilst protecting the soft spruce from abrasion, bruising and making some attempt to stabilize the movement due to humidity, must not be too hard, too thick or too thin. The best finish, but not the most durable (you are not varnishing a floor) is oil. Such products as Danish oil, tung oil, teak oil or Tru-oil (USA) are superb as they are 'soft' enough to allow the belly to do what it likes and are transparent enough not to attenuate the tone. The fact that oils are so much easier to apply than varnishes or sprayed lacquers makes finishing an instrument an absolute doddle. I often wonder, looking back to when I first started making mandolins, why I did not use oil finishes. There were all those layers of oil varnish that were applied to be cut down again and again, plus those suicidal insects, dust and loose varnish-brush hairs that always seemed to put two fingers up at me on the final coat. Oil: the luthiers' saviour! The thick glass-like synthetic lacquers used commercially are not suitable for handmade solid wood instruments; they can contain unhealthy substances and spraying them around your workshop, kitchen or spare bedroom is not desirable. Excellent results can be had from oiled finishes and a good final polish. Applications of oil finish, hand polished will be discussed in Chapter 12: suffice it to say here that a good protective finish, cut down and buffed to a French polish-like sheen needs to be about seven or eight coats. This may sound excessive, but the process of cutting down between each coat reduces the overall thickness to produce a silky-smooth surface that never feels tacky and does not 'drag' on the hand as a high-gloss lacquer does on the neck of the instrument.

Another element that has a bearing on the belly's performance is the type of adhesive used for gluing the bars to the belly. The belly wood will expand and contract far more than the bars, so the adhesive must not be flint hard, otherwise it will shear. The softer, generally available PVA woodworkers' adhesives are too elastic and will permit creeping. One adhesive that outperforms the rest is the high-grade C3 PVA, which has all the right properties for belly, bar and linings and is waterproof, heat-proof, bomb-proof, and so on. Franklin's Titebond (USA) is also suitable for the high-stress belly components. One does not want to risk using an adhesive that will fail: re-gluing a loose bar is an impossibly fiddly and uncertain affair.

The edges of the belly sit on top of the ribs of the soundbox. The ribs are only about 2mm thick so the area for gluing is increased by the use of linings, which adds some substance to the join between belly and ribs. These linings must also allow some movement as well, and light, soft and strong wood is used here and the section of material should not be too large as it would constrain the belly from flexing. If you look at Fig 42 again it will be apparent that as the belly flexes, the strain on the join between belly and ribs is quite high and therefore the joint is potentially weak. The linings 'spread the load' at this junction but allow a reasonable degree of flexing as they are not a rigid material. The linings should not be regarded as the dead internal framing of the soundbox: they are as complementary to the instrument as the bars and should be selected, fashioned and glued on with care. Any 'dry' areas of the lining/rib/belly glued joint will cause rogue rattles, so be liberal with the adhesive and wipe off or chisel off excess glue, as necessary, later on.

Mandolins, loudspeakers and wooden clinker boats seem to share similarities and they are all dependent on their measure of success by an understanding of the nature and compatibility of the components and materials used and by having a good idea of how they will behave when assembled together. The mandolin is quite an astonishing device – there is a great deal going on when one plays it and it is only the bringing together of art, craft and physics that will get the best out of it. At last we arrive at the point where theory ends and handling wood begins.

4 MATERIALS AND TONEWOODS

GLUES AND ADHESIVES

One component that is definitely the most remarkable is the adhesive that not only sticks the various woods together but must withstand the tensions and shear forces imposed on it by shrinkage and swelling as we saw in Chapter 2 and must also, on a mandolin for example, cope with a pull of 38kg at concert pitch or about the full draw weight of the lighter English medieval long-bow. (I was a first-class archer, but even so, I would find it difficult to draw a long-bow with a 'weight' of just 28kg.) These comparisons show the lightness of con-struction of such a thing as a mandolin and the cunning diversion and dissipation of forces and dynamics it contains, yet it plays so sweetly and doesn't fly into pieces when tensioned up to concert pitch. Addition-ally, when a note is plucked the tension of that pair of strings momentarily increases.

I have never ceased to be amazed that nothing more than a viscous liquid turned solid by dehydration or chemical reaction is the only thing that keeps the instrument intact; not one mechanical fastening at all is used in the traditional luthier's methods: good gluing is 99 per cent efficient. It is not surprising that wood is so strong: its struc-tural fabric once supported a tree and kept it there during 120kph winds; but glue – well, the mind simply boggles at its ability to hold on.

The mandolin family of instruments, unlike the violin, are not constructed to be opened up later on in life. Violin-makers use traditional hide glue and this hot-melt product enables the violin to be dismantled by application of a hot knife inserted under the fingerboard or between joined surfaces to replace split, damaged or worn-out components. The problem with animal glue is that it:

◆ does not allow much time for assembly and clamping;
◆ softens in warm, humid conditions that allows it to 'creep';
◆ decomposes and is attacked by fungi.

For these reasons I don't recommend its use. Mandolins are not designed to be pulled apart as they have bindings let into the side of the belly and perhaps the back join with the ribs. Adhesives used must not degrade, attract fungal spores, soften with moisture or creep over a length of time. One adhesive I have used that is excellent is Clas-sic Finishes C3 PVA, available from their store in Norwich, UK. Franklin's liquid ali-phatic resin 'Titebond' (USA) is also very good and used by many luthiers. Good old Cascamite, the powdered resin glue, is still on the shelves of most hardware stores and is an excellent non-staining adhesive that is very good for centre-joins, linings, inlays, bindings, head veneers, back to ribs' join, belly to ribs' join and fretboard to neck.

Whichever adhesives you can obtain must be tenacious. Never glue up in cold, damp conditions and never glue up wood with a moisture content above 10 per cent. Some adhesives will not cure or set if the tempera-ture is below 5°C and this is one way of making sure you do not stand around in a miserable, draughty shed getting frozen.

Always make certain the surfaces you are about to glue together are free from grease and dust. Planed or scraped surfaces tend to glue better than ones sanded down, as abrasive papers tear up the fibres making the joint face soft. A good gluing face is one slightly dampened to open the pores, but only when using water-soluble adhesives. Araldite, the stick 'anything to anything' adhesive, is to be used where suggested to areas that bear incredible stresses and must not fail. The adhesives I recommend in the text are proven to work well – stick to them! Make sure you buy adhesives that are factory fresh, thus avoiding dusty or rusty containers!

THE TONEWOODS

The woods you will need should be supplied 'quarter-sawn'. A timber merchant who prepares stock for musical instrument makers will supply quarter-sawn material and you will pay a premium for this selected stock. The end grain will show how suitable the section or board is (*see* Fig 44). The importance of quarter-sawn material will become apparent when the two halves of the belly or back are joined 'book-matched' so the grain is a mirror image either side of the centreline. The second reason for quarter-sawn wood is that its 'movement' is more predictable and less marked than the usual 'plain-sawn' timber available generally. The third reason for choosing quarter-sawn material is for its strength: aligning the run of the grain so its growth rings are parallel with the direction of stress results in a stronger section and is the same principle behind the technology of laminated timber beams; you will notice on a garden fork or spade that the ash handle is fitted with the grain running at 90 degrees to the flat of the blade.

All wood should be free from knots, pith, shakes, pinholes and fungal staining. Use only close-grained and straight-grained material – curly, wavy or fan-shaped grain

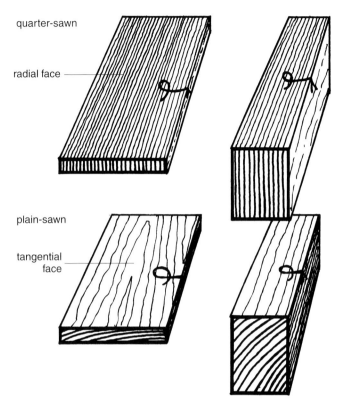

may look lovely and it is excellent for veneers but this kind of figure can cause problems because of the differential movement at shrinkage or swelling: fan-shaped grain can result in warping and splitting as the varying degrees of tension across the face of the timber will seek out the weakest line of grain and the unthinkable can happen.

The wood must be well-seasoned and there is no reason to avoid kiln-dried woods, that are quite suitable (*see* Chapter 2) despite what many woodworkers think of kiln seasoning. Store the wood somewhere warm and dry for as long as possible before you start construction – this will reduce the moisture content. Greenhouses and conservatories are no good for reducing moisture content, even if they do get very hot. Stack the timber so air can circulate freely to all faces. A thin board of spruce, for example, laid on a table or bench will only lose moisture from the exposed surface and it can

Fig 44 Sections of quarter-sawn timber.

'cup' as a result. Don't use hairdryers, hot-air paint strippers or any direct sources of heat to reduce moisture content and never store wood in plastic bags.

SUITABLE WOODS FOR ALL FRETTED STRINGED INSTRUMENTS

The Belly

Coniferous (evergreen) softwoods are used as they are strong, very light in weight and have the tonal qualities required. The grain as seen on the radial faces should be close, quarter-sawn, straight with about seven growth rings per 1cm, tighter at the centre of the belly (*see* Fig 45). Very close grain gives brittle tone that is needed for the mandolin; wider grain imparts a more mellow tone and is suited to the larger bodied mandolas, bouzoukis, citterns and guitars. Slow-grown high altitude softwoods are best as the annual growth rings are fairly regular and tight. Fast-grown softwoods are quite unsuitable, except for fence posts and paper. European (Alpine) spruce, *Picea abies* is the belly material par excellence, the best coming from the mountain areas of central and south-eastern Europe. This used to be known as 'Swiss Pine' by violin-makers. Sitka spruce, *Picea sitchensis* from western USA and Canada is a good optional belly material and you may find more of this spruce available on the market than *Picea abies*. Western red cedar, *Thuja plicata* also from north-western America can be used as a belly material, but because of its very light weight is more suited to classical guitars and fretted instruments with tension bridges and nylon or gut strings. I have never used cedar for a belly, but if you do, allow it a fairly generous finished thickness of 3 to 3.25mm. Brazilian mahogany, *Swietenia macrophylla* can also be used for bellies.

The sawn boards of quarter-sawn belly material need to be supplied 5 to 6mm

thick as you will plane these down to a fair face both sides, aiming for a 3mm maximum planed finished thickness. The longer the timber has been stored the better, as spruce (especially) is more stable if it has had plenty of time to season; maturity also enhances the acoustic qualities

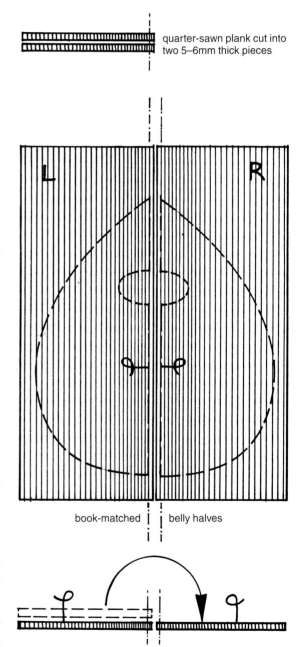

quarter-sawn plank cut into two 5–6mm thick pieces

book-matched belly halves

Fig 45 Grain pattern for the belly halves.

and the finished instrument will attain a good tone much sooner than freshly seasoned stock; look for wood that is dusty and has been lying around for some time and has 'yellowed' (the discolouration soon planes off). I should mention here that spruce with wider annual growth rings than recommended is neither weaker nor inferior to the closer-grained material, at least radially. The closer-grained timber is certainly stiffer lengthwise, which is an advantage for a material that is required to be so thin and so light and will have to bear a pressure bridge to energize it.

The Back and Ribs
Hardwoods are used for the back and ribs (sides) and these must be selected quarter-sawn on the radial faces, close straight-grained pieces, preferably from the same log. Hardwoods that have proved eminently suitable are: Brazilian mahogany, *Swietenia macrophylla*; Brazilian rosewood, *Dalbergia nigra*; Indian rosewood, *Dalbergia latifolia*; American cherry, *Prunus serotina*; American walnut, *Juglans nigra*; and European sycamore, *Acer pseudoplatanus*. Other hardwoods that can be used are European beech and Spanish cypress, although beech does have large 'movement' and is not the most attractive of hardwoods, despite its excellent bending properties. Spanish cypress is also an option, if you can obtain some, and is the traditional back and ribs' material for the shallower-bodied flamenco guitars.

The three tropical hardwoods mentioned are tending to become difficult to obtain because of over-harvesting and the conscious refusal of merchants and woodworkers to give patronage to unethical exporters; both rosewoods are endangered species and the import of the American mahoganys pricks too many consciences. If you do use any variety of rosewood, then be aware it is a very oily wood, the dust can cause allergic reactions, it is difficult to glue unless you de-oil it with petroleum spirit and has a

tendency to split along the grain if sudden heat is applied, so care must be taken when bending on a hot iron. However, it is a most attractive wood: superb material for the back and ribs. (The old Hindu proverb: 'the most beautiful snakes are the most deadly' certainly applies to rosewood.) European sycamore with 'fiddleback' figure is excellent, provided it is thoroughly seasoned; its moisture movement is more than any other tonewood used. The beautiful 'flaming' makes it hard to work: you need to plane in the direction of the 'flaming', not the grain. The back and ribs material should be supplied sawn about 4 to 5mm thick to be planed to a fair face both sides to about 3mm for the back's finished thickness and about 2mm for the ribs' finished thickness.

The Neck
This billet should be quarter-sawn, close and straight-grained and running in the direction as shown (*see* Fig 46). The most suitable woods for the neck are: Brazilian

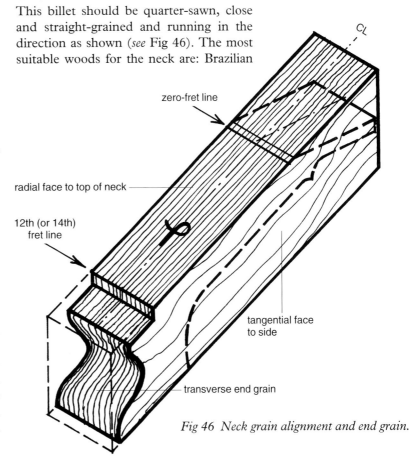

Fig 46 Neck grain alignment and end grain.

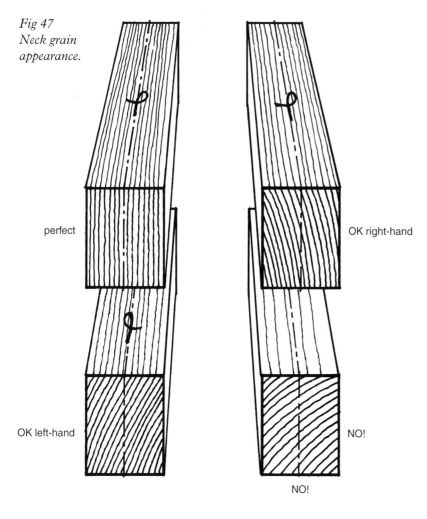

Fig 47
Neck grain
appearance.

perfect

OK right-hand

OK left-hand

NO!

NO!

mahogany; European sycamore; and light red lauan (meranti), *Shorea pauciflora*. You can utilize smaller sections and glue on the extra material required to heel and peghead or laminate a neck from, for example, a mahogany–sycamore–mahogany 'sandwich'. I always prefer to use a one-piece neck and use the off-cuts for shims, end blocks, wedges, tool stocks and truss rod slot fillets. The neck billet must be planed square and true with no 'winding' and the top face absolutely level to a steel straight-edge. Inspect it carefully for grain appearance and any flaws and blemishes, selecting the best way round to mark it out for head and heel direction (*see* Fig 47). Timber showing shakes from the end grain or cracks, however hair's-breadth, should be discarded. Make certain any originally sawn end grain becomes a good portion of waste – this will have colour, paint or wax on it, or perhaps just stencilled or stamped-on letters or numbers. The truss rod cover fillet should be quarter-sawn Brazilian mahogany or Indian rosewood – no other woods have the compressive strength required to react against the tension of the truss rod as much as these two. In this application the 'grain' *must* be perpendicular to the plane of the fretboard.

Bars and Linings

The bars for the belly should be the same species as the belly wood. They must be clear, straight-grained, quarter-sawn material. The annual growth rings ought to be as close as the belly grain: tighter grain means a more brittle and nasal tone so use your judgement on the degree of stiffness required. The bars should all be prepared from the same piece of timber. Select the lightest in weight with the growth rings running parallel with the depth of the bar (*see* Fig 48). Bars for the back should also be clear, straight-grained, quarter-sawn material of western red cedar or Brazilian mahogany with the growth rings running parallel with the depth of the bar.

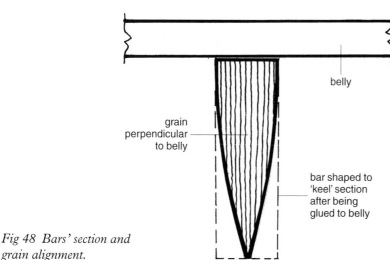

belly

grain
perpendicular
to belly

bar shaped to
'keel' section
after being
glued to belly

Fig 48 Bars' section and
grain alignment.

Linings for the belly connection to ribs should be clear straight-grained, quarter-sawn spruce, willow or poplar. Use spruce linings if at all possible. Linings for the back connection to ribs could be spruce, willow, poplar or Brazilian mahogany. For both the belly and back linings the grain must run in the direction shown (*see* Fig 49).

Tailblock and Back Centre-Join Reinforcement

The tailblock should be close-grained, quarter-sawn spruce, willow, poplar or Brazilian mahogany. It is usual to use a tailblock of the same species as the belly, although I tend to use Brazilian mahogany as I have always had a good stock of this. It is important that the grain of the tailblock runs in the same direction as the grain of the belly; this is doubly important if you use a spruce tailblock (*see* Fig 50).

The back centre-join reinforcement strip should be close-grained, quarter-sawn western red cedar, Brazilian mahogany or spruce with the grain running at 90 degrees to the centreline and grain of the back (*see* Fig 51).

The Fretboard

Ebony, *Diospyros ebenum* or Indian rose-wood, *Dalbergia latifolia* are the preferred woods for fretboards. Rock maple, *Acer saccharum* from the USA and Canada can also be used; all should be quarter-sawn. My preference is for Indian rosewood; it is not as hard to work nor as brittle as ebony, re-frets easier and is not as difficult to glue. Avoid the attractive wavy-grain material, this figure is awful to plane regardless of which direction you try and chunks can be torn out.

Peghead Veneer

A covering is necessary to the peghead face as the angle that reclines the peghead produces emergent grain. A thick veneer is required here – much thicker than standard veneers. You could laminate three or four standard veneers or use an off-cut from the ribs or back material, planed down to about 2mm. Luthiers' suppliers provide pieces thin enough for peghead veneer and all manner of exotic species, colours and figure can be obtained. Suitable woods for this purpose are: Brazilian or Indian rosewood; 'fiddleback' sycamore; kingwood, *Dalbergia cearensis*; cocobolo, *Dalbergia retusa*; American walnut; European walnut; and American cherry.

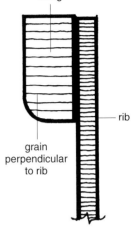

ABOVE: Fig 49 Linings' section and grain alignment.

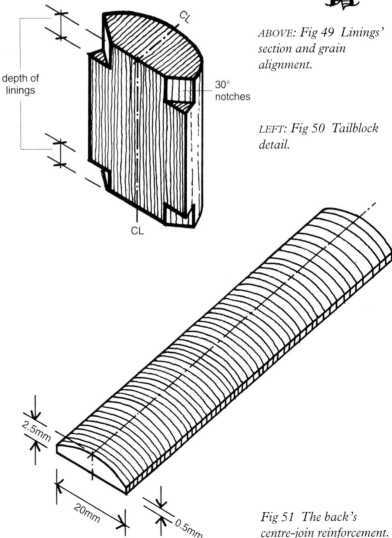

LEFT: Fig 50 Tailblock detail.

Fig 51 The back's centre-join reinforcement.

All the above-mentioned woods look excellent when seen on the radial and tangential faces, but you may also consider the curly 'burr' or 'butt' veneers of hardwoods not usually associated with musical instrument-making, for example ash, elm and European walnut. Plastic or fibre sheet can also be obtained in a 'sandwich' of alternating black and white, giving a striped edge decoration but usually black-faced; I have never been tempted to use it.

Fig 52 Minimum sizes for selected tonewoods.

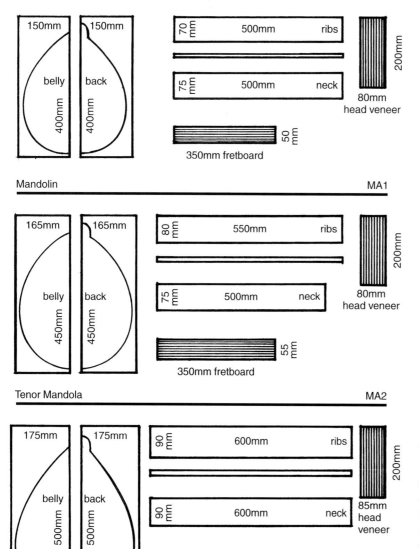

However, if you do desire a black peghead face, then use an ebony peghead veneer.

Edge Bindings

These are let in and glued into rebates cut on the edges of the belly to ribs' join and perhaps the back to ribs' join. They cover the edge or end grain of the belly material and provide a hard edging to protect against bruising or abrasion. Some luthiers claim the bindings improve tone and this may well be true if using ribs' material 'softer' than the binding. If you use a rosewood or sycamore back then binding the back/ribs' join is not so necessary as these woods are naturally hard enough to provide a robust edge. The belly bindings will also help to seal the softwood end grain from absorbing or losing moisture. Select bindings that are a contrasting colour to the belly, ribs and back. Suitable woods for binding are: boxwood, *Buxus sempervirens*; rock maple; holly, *Ilex aquifolium*; ebony; satinwood, *Chloroxylon swietenia*; sycamore and rosewood. Choose the more delicate sections on offer and check out the 'banding' or 'stringing' stocked by the veneer supplier; these can be used to great effect on the back to ribs' edge and there are some standard types about 5mm wide by 1m long. Avoid the composite plastic bindings available as these can degrade from chemical incompatibility with the adhesives and oils used on the instrument: they tend to become very brittle, fracture when bruised and eventually drop off.

SIZES OF TONEWOODS FOR BELLY, BACK, RIBS AND NECK

The minimum sizes of material needed for mandolin, tenor mandola and octave mandola are shown (*see* Fig 52). It is best to buy over-sized lengths of tonewoods as this will aid clamping down and planing to thickness. The 'waste' ends usually get used for something, so off-cuts should not be discarded or used to fuel the fire.

5 THE BELLY'S CONSTRUCTION

Start your instrument by making the belly first. The reason for this is that the belly material is more of a gentle introduction to planing thin boards than the back or ribs and much less daunting than being thrown in the deep end by starting on the neck. Keep your fingernails short as long nails will easily dent the soft spruce. Take the selected thin boards of book-matched spruce and have a really good look at them; they probably look like two old pieces off an orange box and you are wondering how you managed to part with so much money for these. If they are much longer and wider than you actually need, this is good news as it will give you more room to work, so don't think that trimming them down or squaring them off will help you at this stage; you need all that 'waste' to help clamp the boards to the bench while you plane them.

Your first task is to reduce the thickness of the boards by planing them down smooth and level; the outlines do not matter at all until you have glued the two halves together. This material is much too thin to plane against a bench stop: you have to clamp it to the worktop and plane *away* from the clamped ends. Screwing the boards to the bench with well-countersunk screws is possible, but you must first establish which way the plane will cut 'with the grain' otherwise you could end up pulling the plane rather than pushing it. Decide which edges will be at the centre-join: you need the closest grain on the boards to the centreline as shown (*see* Fig 53). Place one board on the hide sheet and clamp it to the bench using two clamps at the

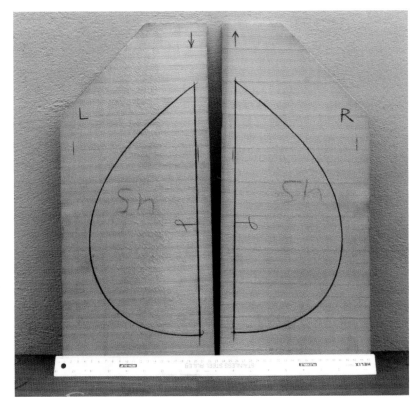

corners. Give the board a light planing (away from the clamps, always) with the plane iron set to the thinnest of shaves to remove saw marks and rough fibres that obscure the grain. You will now have found out whether you are planing with the grain; if the plane starts to snag, undo the clamps and turn it around; plane away from the clamped end again and you should find this is the best direction to plane with the grain on this face. So, in the far corner, chisel on an arrow mark to remind yourself which way to plane in future and then mark on a provisional 'L'

Fig 53 The belly halves centre-join edges.

Fig 54 Book-match the belly grain.

for left half in soft pencil. Turn this piece over to plane the other face – plane in the opposite direction, usually – and clamp this to the bench as before, always lightly planing away from the clamps so the grain is clearly visible and every annual growth ring is obvious. Mark the direction of planing with the grain with an incised arrow in a waste corner to this face as well.

Now take the other half of the belly and repeat exactly as above marking a provisional 'R' for the book-matched right half. It is best to plane these halves first to a reasonable face on both sides before gluing them together, then you will find it easier to establish which line of grain you will plane the centre-join edge to on the shooting-board, so that the centreline will be an exact and invisible glue join with mirror-imaged grain to both halves (*see* Fig 54).

Now is the time to give them close scrutiny: check for defects, stains, cracks and bruising that you may not have noticed in their sawn state. Lay them down on the hide sheet with the centre-joins touching and take the belly template and mark out the outlines to each in soft pencil, allowing about a 4mm waste edge to the actual centre-join. Do any defects in the wood lie within the template area? If they do, then scrub out the original pencil outline, turn them round (180 degrees) and mark on the template outline again. When you are content that the L and R halves are blemish-free, choose which sides will be the belly face (the top of the instrument). This choice is made from the most beautiful grain and once you have decided, mark the face-side with the carpenter's 'F' and then leave it alone!

It is quite likely that having made your choice of which will be the face-sides of the belly halves means that 'L' has now become 'R'! If this is so, then rub off the provisional pencil marks and re-mark correctly before proceeding further. The 'L' half is the bass side of the belly and the 'R' half is the treble side. (If you are making a

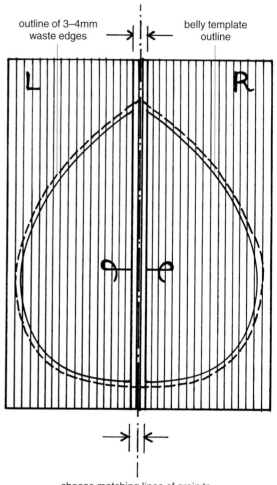

outline of 3–4mm waste edges

belly template outline

choose matching lines of grain to become the centre-join of belly

left-handed instrument, then this rule is reversed.) Make certain that the carpenter's 'F' symbols have been made correctly for denoting the face-sides (top); to mark the wrong face-side on one half at this stage will mean that the two halves when glued together will not be book-matched grain. If this does happen (it has happened to me, but *only* once) then do not despair, the tone will not be impoverished because the grain is not mirror-imaged. Once both halves look less like matchwood and are an even thickness overall, lay them face-sides up on the bench under good lighting and select which line of grain will become the glued centre-join. Mark it at either end of the 'L' half with a fine pencil or nick of the marking knife, then find its corresponding grain line on the 'R' half and mark this similarly. Now use the steel straight-edge to pencil on these lines so it is quite obvious which line of grain you will plane down to on each half. Check everything again. Now, place the 'L' and 'R' halves back to back with the chosen grain lines *exactly* aligned to each other. You will 'shoot' with the plane down to the 'line' on both belly halves at once to achieve a good mating joint (*see* Fig 55). This is preferable to shooting the edges of each half individually.

It is not possible to cut these straight mating edges with a craft knife and a steel straight-edge, so don't attempt to: the grain is rarely dead straight even though it may look it, and a knife cut will either follow along the latewood or cross it and leave a wavy edge. The plane and shooting-board are the tools for this. Clamp the shooting-board in the vice and then place the two halves of the belly with the 'L' face-side up on the shooting-board base, with the pencil line of the centre-join dead on the guiding edge of the fence. If you have adopted the sort of shooting-board I use, by looking straight down over the belly halves you can accurately align the pencil line with the top and bottom fence, so your plane will cut exactly to this. Use a couple of packing pieces or a batten to clamp the workpiece to the shooting-board. Now sight your eye over the fences again to make sure the pencil line is still in the right place (*see* Fig 55 again). With the smoothing plane laid on its side with a low set iron, shave the workpiece with one complete long 'pass'. Is the grain tearing? If it is, then plane in the opposite direction with complete long passes until the sole of the plane meets the fences. Keep planing until no more shavings come off the fences or the workpiece. In theory, you should now have a straight and true edge with the pencil line shaved off as well. If the pencil line is still obvious then loosen the clamps and adjust the position by a whisker,

Fig 55 Shooting the centre-join edges of the belly halves.

and 'shoot' the edge a few more times. Once you are happy that the grain lines chosen have been 'shot', take both halves and place them together, centreline edges touching – as though they were already glued together – across a window or a light box if you have one. Look for gaps showing light – if there are none, well done! If there is a gap then back to the shooting-board, checking the halves constantly until they marry perfectly with virtually no light peeping through.

Do not feel tempted to use abrasive paper on a straight-edge to get the centre-join edges straight: sanding a true, straight edge is very difficult and in any event the abrasive rounds-off the edges and tears up the grain making it woolly and dusty which does not, contrary to popular belief, produce a good gluing interface. If you find that planing off your chosen grain line keeps happening but you are nowhere nearer to achieving two straight, close-fitting edges, then check the fences of the shooting-board for the problem: ensure with the steel straight-edge that they are guiding the sole of the plane in a true, straight run. If the top fence has bowed slightly this will frustrate your efforts till doomsday, so correct it. The reason the belly halves are left with a good deal of 'waste' edge on them will now be apparent: you may need to 'shoot' the edges to the next grain line in, or the next, to get the centre-join as tight as possible. If after several attempts with the plane you are still left with a hair's-breadth gap, then you will be able to close this with the pressure of clamping; spruce will 'give' enough to close the join.

GLUING UP

It is important to glue the two belly halves together immediately you have 'shot' the centre-join edges before they get damaged (or the weather changes and you discover those two perfect edges don't close up tight any more). Find a piece of clean block-board, plywood or MDF board at least 19mm thick and bigger than the belly halves. Tape down a 50mm wide strip of thin paper to the centre of this board on its longest face (see Fig 56). Now place the 'L' belly half, face-side up, with the centre-join edge on the middle of the paper strip. Find about eight 20mm panel pins and hammer these into the board at about 40mm intervals along the outside edge of the 'L' belly half, leaving the heads of the pins about 10mm proud of the board (so you can pull them out easily with pincers, later). Now place the 'R' belly half, face-side up, against the left, as though the two were already

glued; slip a batten – 10 × 25mm in section and a bit longer than the belly halves – directly under the centre-join to lift the two halves up at the centre-join and hammer in another row of eight panel pins to the outside edge of the right belly half, making sure the centre-join edges remain tightly together. You have completed the 'clamp' for gluing up the belly halves.

Get another 50mm strip of thin paper as long as the 'clamp' board and two pieces of clean plywood, blockboard, chipboard or MDF at least as long as the belly halves but about 10mm narrower so they fit in between the lines of panel pins but leave a gap in the middle. You will also need about four house bricks or other similarly convenient-sized weights. You are now ready to glue up. Wipe the centre-join edges of each belly half with a damp sponge and mix up Cascamite powdered resin glue in the recommended proportions with cold water: you will need about a teaspoonful of mixed adhesive. Brush the adhesive on to both mating edges, hold them together and rub them back and forth to squeeze the adhesive into the pores. Now place both halves, face-sides up, in the 'clamp' with the batten still in place underneath on the centreline and apply the other paper strip to cover the glue join, pressing this firmly on so it sticks to the excess glue squeezed out. Feel with your fingers that one half is mating the other flush and then gently withdraw the batten from underneath. The two belly halves will remain 'arched ' over the clamp because of the panel pin restraints compressing them. Now place the two pieces of board on the joined belly halves and press them down to force the belly flat to the clamp's surface. Make certain that the belly halves have gone down absolutely flat and that one mating edge has not risen up or overridden the other: check the gap between the pressure boards to feel the glue line with your finger through the paper strip (see Fig 57). If all is okay then pile on the bricks or weights to keep the belly halves

Fig 56 Gluing up the belly halves in the clamp.

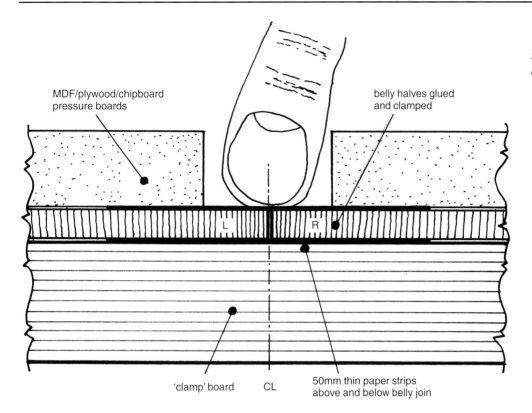

Fig 57 Check that the belly's centre-join lies flush.

MDF/plywood/chipboard
pressure boards

belly halves glued
and clamped

L R

'clamp' board   CL   50mm thin paper strips
above and below belly join

flat whilst the adhesive sets. Leave the belly in the clamp for about six hours.

Later, remove the weights and the two pressure boards, taking care not to scratch, dent or mark the face-side of the now complete belly. The belly should arch up, but if any excess glue has found its way past the paper strip, you will need to withdraw all the panel pins first and tease the belly from sticking to the clamp board with a thin steel rule slid under it until it springs the workpiece free. Try not to gouge any material from the belly if it does get stuck and *never* try to lever the belly free of unintentional gluing. At this stage the belly is, of course, very thin material and prone to snap along the grain should pressure be exerted locally. Place the belly on the hide mat and clamp it firmly to the worktop; now scrape off the paper strips that have stuck to the centre-join areas. *Do not* attempt to plane the paper off as you may be planing against the grain on at least one side of the centreline. The plain steel scraper is the only tool to do this job.

Now you can plane the joined belly to thickness from the underside faces, so clamp the belly down on the hide mat and plane away taking care around the centre-join area for grain that may go against your plane. Aim for a provisional overall thickness of 3mm and use the thickness gauge to ensure there are no thin or high spots being left by the plane's action. You do not need any more thickness on the belly than necessary. Always keep the plane iron razor sharp and low set to avoid tearing out chunks of this precious material and follow rigidly the incised arrow marks for direction of planing. Unclamp and turn around the workpiece 180 degrees to facilitate planing with the grain. Be especially careful not to plane away too much material at the edges as this can easily happen. Keep one eye on the edge thickness, which should be *no thinner than 3mm* at this stage. It is far better to leave the centre-join area over-thick and scrape or rub down to thickness. This thin belly material is now very vulnerable – keep it clean and well away from sharp edges and corners while you are working on it. The use of filler wax to disguise dents and torn-out grain is not good practice and is cosmetically challenging.

With both faces cleaned up, take a piece of medium grit, 'free-cut' aluminium oxide abrasive paper on a cork sanding block and sand the belly *across* the grain; this will show up any small crests and troughs in the surface, so keep sanding until the whole face becomes a uniform colour and texture and is quite smooth and level. You may have sanded off the template outlines of the belly, so reinstate these now as there will be no more rubbing or scraping down of the belly until it is glued to the soundbox.

There is a great temptation – if you are similar to me – to flex the belly to see how good the centre-join gluing is. I can save you the trouble by stating confidently that the glued join rarely fails. The stiffness of the belly material, now the 'L' and 'R' halves are joined, will be apparent and to flex it gently will tell you if the thickness is about right. There is no objective criterion to determine the finished thickness of any belly; the only guidance is that it feels 'right'. You could tap it with your knuckle to find out what it sounds like; even get a chromatic quartz tuner to tell you the belly's resonant frequency, but I don't consider that you can really tell whether it is 'tuned' to thickness until it is fitted to the soundbox. Work to the 3mm nominal planing and then handle it to feel its springiness, taking off a bit more from the underside face with the scraper and abrasive paper if it seems too stiff. It is okay to have the treble side of the belly a bit thinner than the bass. Whatever you do to get the 'feel' of the belly, avoid flexing it into an arch otherwise you could be left with two unequal pieces – one in each hand! If the face-side 'F' mark has been rubbed off, reinstate this in soft pencil, so you cannot fail to distinguish it and keep the face-side clean from this point onwards.

CUTTING THE SOUNDHOLE

Marking and cutting any decorative inlay and the soundhole is the next step. Decide what shape of soundhole you want; circular soundholes are easier to cut and embellish, but an oval soundhole is good enough without inlays, if it is well-shaped and neatly edged. The oval soundhole also fits in with the bars' positions as dimensioned. If you have never executed any inlay work, now is *not* the time to do your apprenticeship – sloppy inlays will ruin the belly and it is best to omit them. The inlays do nothing for the tonal qualities anyway and weaken an area of the belly that is highly stressed. If you must add a soundhole inlay, then keep it simple and delicate: lines of concentric 'purfling' are fine and the 'purfling' cutter can accurately slice the edges of the channel on the face of the belly, then a 'toothpick' chisel is used to excavate the channel to inset the curved strips. You will need to soak the purfling in very hot water for one to two minutes to make it pliable, then form these to shape on an off-cut of MDF board, cut and channelled as a soundhole 'mould' to prepare the shape as a 'dress rehearsal'. *Do not* try to stuff unformed purfling into the actual groove(s) cut on the belly.

Before you cut out the soundhole, mark on the underside of the belly the outlines for bars B1, B2 and B3 as taken from your full-scale plans. These will help you to establish the position or centre of the soundhole. Make a template from an old plastic credit card to give you the soundhole shape you want, then stab a hole through it to mark the very centre and scribe on two intersecting lines for the long- and short axis at 90 degrees to each other. You can buy elliptical templates from drawing office suppliers; if they are not big enough, you can get them enlarged on a photocopier then glue the paper shape to an old credit card and cut the outline with a craft knife and sand the edges smooth.

If you choose a circular soundhole a 'soundhole cutter' will cut this out (and the channel edges for the inlays). The method is: cut channel and inlays first, then cut out the hole. The inlaid material is glued and inserted in the channel so it is proud of the belly material and then (when the glue has set) is scraped down flush. I have made my own purflings from 1.5mm strips of sycamore, set in concentric bands to show the alternate polarized cell aspects of the grain; when scraped clean and oiled, this white wood flares like mother-of-pearl. With this purfling I embellished the round sound-hole of a simple, plain, steel-strung folk gui-tar (the last instrument I built in the twentieth century) and it surprised me how excellent it looked. This detail is shown on a photograph of the guitar's belly (*see* Fig 58).

If you have marked your oval soundhole shape to both faces of the belly, choose a spot about 5mm inside the soundhole out-line on the centreline at the top and bot-tom of the hole and drill 2mm diameter holes through which to pass the blade of the fret saw. Because the belly is so fragile it is important to use a fret saw with a cut-ting board to support the workpiece. Any piece of ply or blockboard about 19mm thick will do with a 30 degree 'V' cut into it. Clamp this board to your bench with the 'V' end overhanging and hold down the workpiece over the 'V' with one hand, using the fret saw to cut the curved hole about 1mm inside the soundhole pencil outline (*see* Fig 59). Use the whole length of the blade, avoiding jerky or snagging motions that may stampede down a line of soft earlywood into the belly material, not the waste. It is best to cut from the centre-line pilot holes outwards for each curve, meeting at the long axis. It is very tricky to cut the soundhole to the template outline using a craft knife or scalpel; I do not rec-ommend it. You could, if you possess curved carving chisels, chop out the sound-hole shape. The best method is to chisel out or fret saw undersize and trim to the line as

ABOVE: *Fig 58 Sycamore three-band purfling soundhole inlay.*

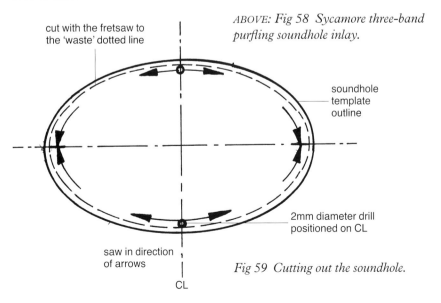

cut with the fretsaw to the 'waste' dotted line

soundhole template outline

2mm diameter drill positioned on CL

saw in direction of arrows

CL

Fig 59 Cutting out the soundhole.

Fig 60 Reinforce underside of soundhole inlay.

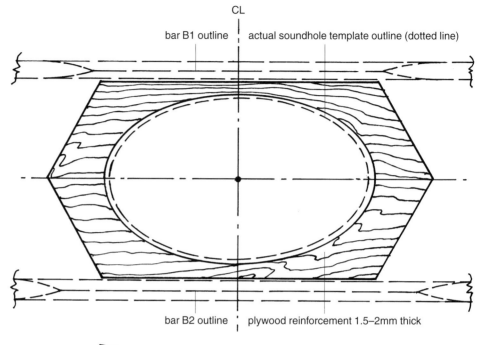

CL

bar B1 outline | actual soundhole template outline (dotted line)

bar B2 outline | plywood reinforcement 1.5–2mm thick

direction of saw cuts

Fig 61 Cut out belly's outline allowing waste edges.

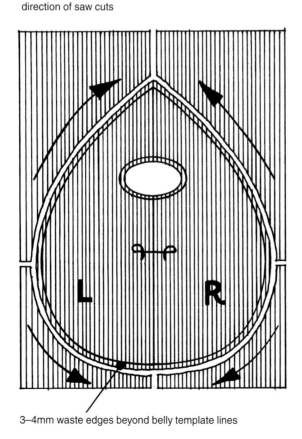

L   R

3–4mm waste edges beyond belly template lines

follows: get a piece of broomstick about 100mm long and glue on, or use double-sided adhesive tape to stick on a wrap of the medium grit, 'free cut' abrasive paper. Use this like a round 'spokeshave' to trim the soundhole edges smooth to the line. This is better than a half-round file and will not rag the edges. Do not profile the edge yet, this comes later – just dress it square-edged to the even radii of the pencil outline. It must be a smooth, continuously curved shape. If you have inlaid decorative material to the soundhole, then you should reinforce the underside of the belly, using the lozenge-shape backing of 1.5 to 2mm birch ply glued on with C3 PVA as shown (*see* Fig 60).

CUTTING OUT THE BELLY OUTLINE

Cut out the belly shape with a coping saw or scroll saw. Always use fine-toothed blades to avoid ragged edges. The blades generally sold in DIY stores are too coarse, so select carefully. I do not recommend jig saws or band-saws for this operation as they can be rather brutal and tear out ear-lywood along the grain. Hold the belly face-side up onto the 'V' board, so the material is well supported. Using the coping saw vertically, cut the belly outline on a line about 3 or 4mm *outside* the actual template pencil line, all the way round (*see* Fig 61). You must leave this much waste margin, which will be trimmed off later, only after the belly has been glued to the soundbox. Cut in the directions as shown in Fig 61 to prevent the saw blade wandering into a line of soft earlywood. Avoid stressing the workpiece: cut with slow and deliberate strokes using the whole blade length, but don't push the blade. When the belly outline is cut out, save the triangular off-cuts to make the internal back-join centreline reinforcement strips.

Lay the belly on the hide mat – you now have something that looks as if it belongs to a musical instrument. If what you see before you is a pure white, silky smooth, pear-shaped, very thin board, with beautifully book-matched grain, an invisible centre-join and a neatly cut soundhole you can congratulate yourself. Don't be too depressed if there happens to be a grubby mark, smallish dent or torn out piece of grain, the provisional 3mm thickness will allow for some cleaning up later on before the bindings get glued on. As long as there are no deep gouges or thin areas, you have done very well. If you have got this far, then don't stop now: it doesn't get any more difficult.

If the pencil outlines for the bars on the underside of the belly have become lost or shaved off, then reinstate them and put the belly somewhere warm, dry and safe while you prepare the transverse bars.

THE BARS B1, B2 AND B3

The bars are prepared from the selected piece of quarter-sawn spruce and cut to size in the rectangular sections with the grain parallel to the depth of the bar as shown. Cut them over-long to the sizes shown (*see* Fig 62). Plane them to finished thickness and square, but ensure they are

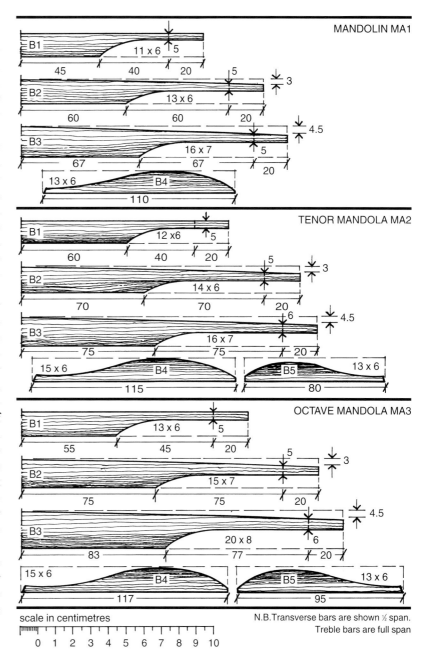

scale in centimetres

0 1 2 3 4 5 6 7 8 9 10

N.B. Transverse bars are shown ½ span.
Treble bars are full span

planed over-deep as a waste margin must be allowed to plane the cambers to bars B2 and B3. Mark on the centreline to each bar and pencil on 'B1', 'B2' and 'B3' to the respective bars. Use the camber template with the 3mm rise to give the camber profile for bar B2 and then the 4.5mm rise on the other edge of the template for the

Fig 62 Details for the belly's bars B1, B2 and B3.

camber profile to bar B3, both marked on with a hard, sharp pencil.

You must now plane the camber to bars B2 and B3 down to the pencil lines. This is not as difficult as it may seem: clamp the bar, camber face uppermost, in the vice with about 6 to 7mm proud of the vice jaws and plane *away* from the centreline with the block plane until you are level with the pencil line. Do this on both bars. If you are not confident about getting the camber to a good, low convex arc, then use the sanding block to smooth the profile, and ensure this edge remains at a true 90 degrees to the sides of the bar. It is best to sight your eye down the length of each bar – you will soon detect the odd lump or hollow spot. Be conscious that the cambered edges of the bars B2 and B3 do a very special job and their mating surface to the belly must be smooth, true and perfect. The bars' fashioning, as stated before, must be executed with great diligence. They are what will make (or break) a good soundboard. Bar B1 does not need any camber, but ensure that its mating surface with the belly is as good as B2 and B3.

Now mark on the profiles for the scalloping to the bars, exactly as the plans show but *do not* cut the scalloping yet: this comes later when it is relatively easy to chisel-pare the scallops when the bars have been glued onto the underside of the belly. Store the bars with the belly for a few days so they reach an equal low moisture content. In the meantime, you can start on constructing the two halves of the back, which is essentially the same as the belly you have just completed, but with two differences: you will be using hardwood that will be more effort to plane and 'shoot' to two good mating centre-join edges and you must allow the extra material to form the 'button' where the back overlaps the neck heel. But don't be discouraged, if you've succeeded in getting the belly and bars complete, then turn to Chapter 6 until you are content that the belly and bars are dry and stable enough to be glued together.

GLUING THE BARS TO THE BELLY

For this operation you will need to prepare a simple clamp from two 300mm lengths of 38 × 19 planed pine batten. Drill an 8mm diameter hole through them both about 100mm in from one end (*see* Fig 63). You will need a 6mm diameter bolt about 100mm long, two steel washers and a

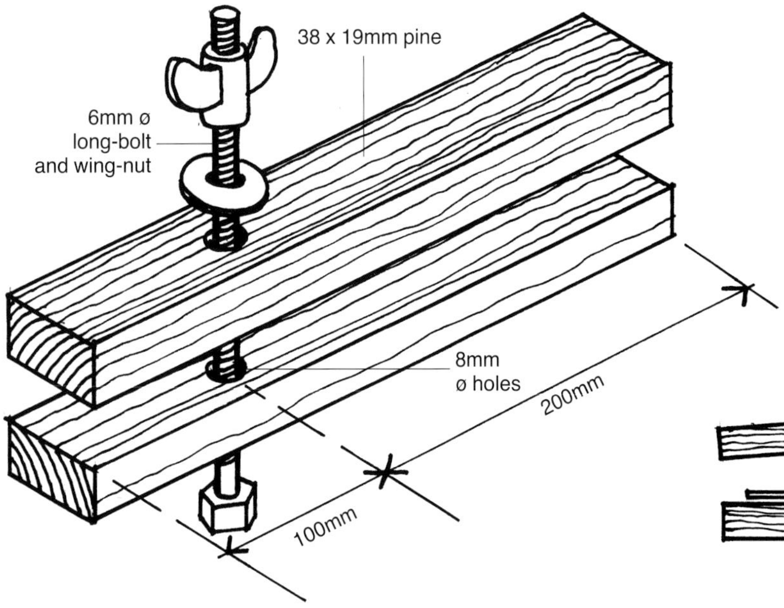

Fig 63 Clamp detail for centre of bars.

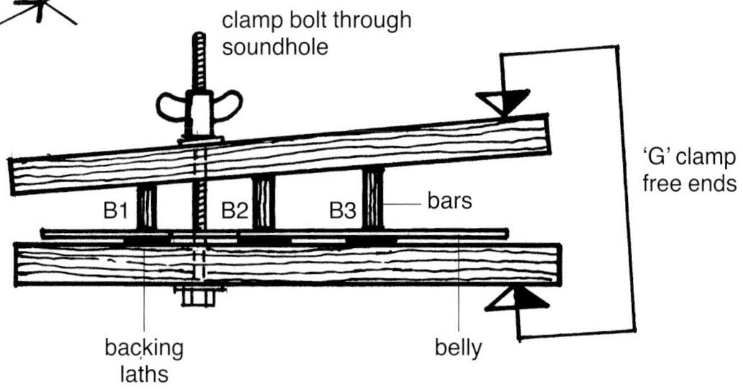

6mm diameter wing-nut to complete the clamp. Other helpful items will be three thin strips of planed softwood lathing about 20 × 5mm (as long as each of the 'untrimmed' transverse bars B1, B2 and B3); 6 mini-sized 'G' clamps and an ordinary 'G' clamp. A few slip wedges or off-cuts of cowhide should be within arm's reach as well, in case you need them.

Clamp the belly vertically in the soft-jaw vice, tail uppermost with the face-side away from you, and brush on a thin film of C3 PVA or Titebond adhesive to the cambered edge of bar B3. Do not apply too much glue as it will only be wasted excess. Place the bar B3 onto the pencil outlines precisely to the underside of the belly and press this on. The adhesive may hold it in place until you get the clamps on, but I have never found this to be the case and the bar normally drops off into a pile of dirt on the floor! So, hold bar B3 in place with one hand and pick up the backing lath corresponding to B3 and a mini 'G' clamp with the other. With the lath backing onto the face-side of the belly, clamp one end of bar B3 to the belly, but not over-zealously (see Fig 64). Note the backing laths for B2 and B3 are inadvertently transposed in this photo – this can easily occur in the haste to clamp; it is not so serious as long as it is not the actual bars as well! Now clamp the other end of bar B3 with a mini 'G' clamp ensuring the backing lath is aligned with the bar. Check the bar has not wandered away from the pencil lines – they do have an annoying habit of slipping around on the glue – and if you can enlist a third hand to help you, do so. Do not tighten the mini-clamps too much, just enough to keep the bar in place.

Do exactly the same to glue on bar B2, including the backing lath. You will need to remove the workpiece from the vice (to glue on bar B1) and turn it over so that the tail gets clamped in the bench vice. Do not omit the backing laths just because they make this task even more fiddly: they will

ensure the bars will be firmly pressed to the belly and prevent the clamps' jaws from bruising the belly's face-side. Once all three bars are on and clamped securely at the ends you may notice that the centre span area of the bars has not squeezed out as much glue as the ends. You must correct this to achieve the thin glue join so necessary for 99 per cent efficiency. This is where the clamp featured in Fig 63 comes in: pass the long-bolt through one half of the clamp and then through the sound-hole, place on the other half of the clamp on the bolt end the other side of the belly, then the washer and wing-nut and clamp up making sure the clamps align along the

Fig 64 Gluing on the bars using 'G' clamps, batten and laths.

belly's centreline. The method in Fig 75 in Chapter 6 shows two simple battens being clamped together (because there is no soundhole to pass the bolt through) but the clamping principle is the same. Screw up the long-bolt until the glue is squeezed out consistently across the span of each bar, then clamp the batten ends with a 'G' clamp to ensure that bar B3 gets firmly pressed to the belly as well. The bead of glue seen either side of the bar is the best indicator that the bar is evenly clamped on. You should now clamp up the mini 'G' clamps at the bars' ends more firmly. *Do not* clamp up so tightly that you start to crush or bruise the bars' material: this will weaken their structural properties.

Place the workpiece face-side down on the worktop and using a 200mm long spill of wood rake off the excess glue from the belly/bar joins: this is tricky because the clamps get in the way, but dollops of excess glue are not needed as ballast! You can then check that the bars are still aligned with the pencil outlines. Now place the clamped-up workpiece into a warm cupboard or heated room and leave for two hours for the glue to set firm.

I must emphasize again that the gluing of the bars to the belly is one of the most important assembly tasks. The woods must be as dry as possible before you assemble and even if you have been storing them in a warm cupboard, do not attempt this particular job on a grey, damp, cold day. Bottled butane or propane gas heaters are about as welcome in your workshop as an unreliable fire sprinkler: they give out a lot of moisture into the air. Use electric heaters or central heating radiators only, if your workshop, garage or shed is cold.

Having allowed time for the glued bars to set, remove all the 'G' clamps, the long clamp with the bolt withdrawn through the soundhole, and then the backing laths will fall away. The next operation is to cut the scalloping to the bars and shape them to the finished 'keel' section. Using the

hide mat to cushion the face-side of the belly, place the belly on the mat and clamp the mat so it cannot move; but do not try to clamp the belly down as it is now domed and will not lie flat. Great care should be taken during this exercise to avoid a slip of the chisel gouging into the belly material or shavings finding their way between the mat and the belly that can bruise or scratch the face-side. It is best to hold the belly firmly with your left hand (the hide mat will prevent it from wandering around) and work with the razor-sharp 25mm chisel, bevel *downwards*, over your left hand and away from it to avoid an unscheduled visit to the nearest hospital. Start at the top of the scallop as shown (*see* Fig 65), paring off the waste in layers, *always* towards the ends of the bars. Adopt a diagonal slicing motion with the chisel; this method cuts cleanly without having to use too much force. On no account use a mallet: elbow and muscle power only!

Once you have pared off to the pencil outlines of the scalloping on all the bars you can then shave them to the 'keel' profile with the block plane. Use a low set plane iron and hold the plane on its side, almost vertically to plane along each side of each bar, gradually tilting it over towards the bar to fashion it as shown (*see* Fig 66). You should not experience any difficulty in planing against the grain on the bars as these side faces are quite tangential if the sections you selected and originally planed were true and straight-grained. Do not trim off the over-long ends of the bars yet: this happens much later, but prepare the spruce treble bar(s) B4 (and B5) according to the dimensions and details given and glue on using the C3 PVA or Titebond adhesives, clamping up firmly using two 'G' clamps and a caul and cowhide off-cut to protect the face-side of the belly and treble bar(s) from bruising; ensure there are no 'dry' glue lines. Allow two hours for the adhesive to set and then use the 9mm chisel, bevel downwards, and

Fig 65 Chisel-cut scallops to bar ends.

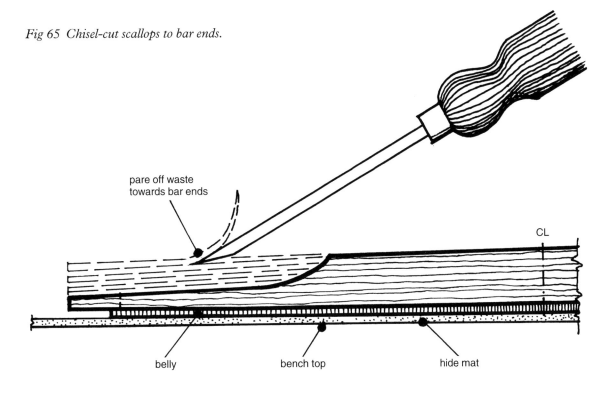

pare off waste
towards bar ends

CL

belly

bench top

hide mat

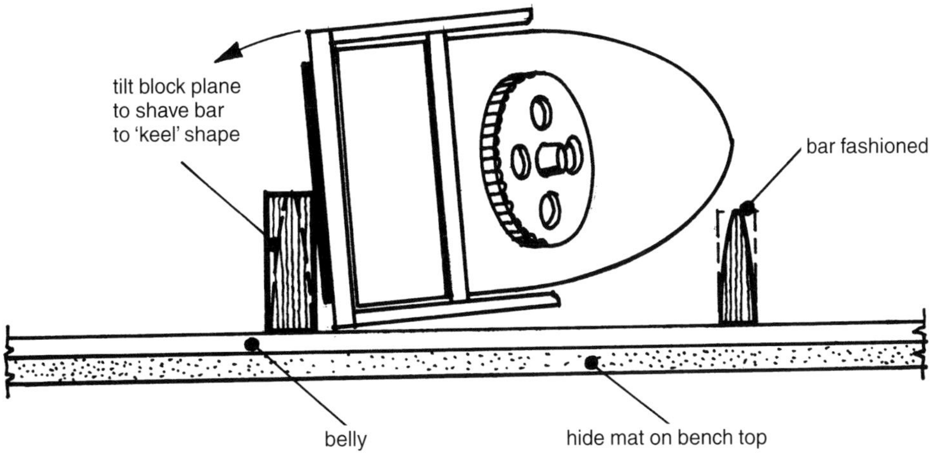

tilt block plane
to shave bar
to 'keel' shape

bar fashioned

belly

hide mat on bench top

*Fig 66 Plane bars to keel-
shaped profile.*

use an old credit card to mask the belly from any slip of the chisel. Now fashion the treble bar(s) to the 'keel' sections and 'whale-back' profiles (*see* Fig 62 again).

Finish off all the bars with a rub down of the medium grit, 'free-cut' abrasive paper to remove pencil marks, grubby glue stains and to round off the sharp edges of the 'keels'. It is the mark of a well-made, hand-built instrument to be just as well finished on the inside. The belly construction is now complete and you should store it somewhere warm, dry and clean until you will need to glue it on to the soundbox in the procedure detailed in Chapter 9. Now you are ready to construct the back.

6 THE BACK'S CONSTRUCTION

The method for constructing the back is identical to the belly and the belly template is used to mark the outlines, but include the extra material at the neck end for the 'button' as shown (*see* Fig 67). The back halves will be hardwood: probably mahogany, rosewood or sycamore, quarter-sawn perfect mirror images of each other. The grain on the diffuse-porous tropical hardwoods may not be that obvious, so clamp each half to the worktop on the hide mat and give them both a light planing. You will soon discover any lurking wild grain that will trip up your plane iron, so try every direction before deciding which one will give you less hassle. I have to mention to you that whatever species you have chosen, planing the back will not be a breeze. Aim for the lines of least resistance with the plane and if the block plane shaves better than the smoothing plane, then use the block plane diagonally – like a guillotine blade – straight, or even across the grain, to avoid ripping up the material. Doing this will make you appreciate why you started off on the belly! If you are working on 'flamed' sycamore, then you must plane *across* the grain. You may have to sharpen the plane iron frequently when using rosewood; it is a bit like planing cast iron. Again, leave the back halves as long and as wide as possible, just

Fig 67 Template outline on back's halves.

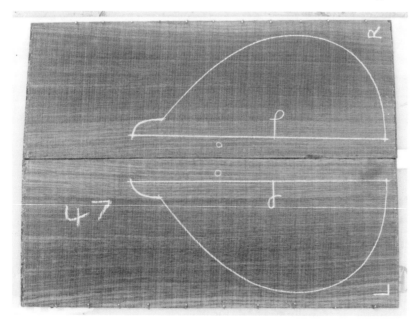

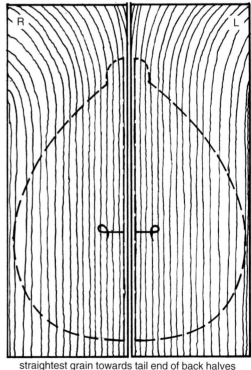

divergent grain to head towards waste areas

straightest grain towards tail end of back halves

Fig 68 Divergent grain should head toward neck.

concentrate on planing them to a fair face both sides; don't worry about the outlines or thickness yet.

Once the plane has exposed enough of the grain on each face, lay them on your bench worktop under good lighting and have a close look at them. Choose the closest grain to be at the edges that will form the centre-join; if the grain does not run straight with the edge or length of the boards then make a grain line obvious with the pencil and straight-edge. If any grain tends to fan out, widen or curl, then make sure this heads for the neck end of the back (*see* Fig 68) so most of it will become 'waste' for peghead veneers or truss rod covers; these features on rosewood and sycamore can be a little risky especially on the wider boards. The back of the octave mandola shown (*see* Fig 69) is flamed sycamore, and very beautiful the figuring is, but what a horror it was to clamp down evenly to the ribs.

tightest grain to centre-join edges

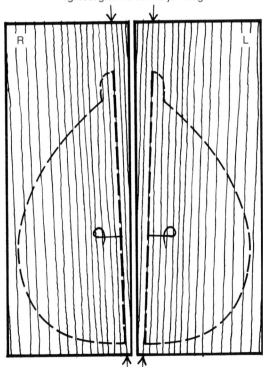

the centreline should follow the length of the matching grain on each back half

Scrutinize the two halves and choose the grain line you want to be the actual centre-join. The waste margin may not be quite so accommodating as the straight-grained spruce, so ignore parallel lines at this stage. Select your grain line and mark it in white crayon if necessary, then mark its twin on the other half. Mark on 'L' and 'R' and the carpenter's 'F' symbol for chosen face-sides (*see* Fig 70). From here on I can save wear and tear on my word processor and save paper, as the techniques are the same as preparing and gluing together the belly halves. You may wish to have a stripe of contrasting material in the centre-join and I recommend this to help you get a tight and perceived clean join. I suggest this because 'shooting' true straight edges on the back's tonewoods and clamping the glue join up tight is not so easy. The hardwoods do not

Fig 69 'Flamed' sycamore mandola back.

Fig 70 Centre-join grain alignment.

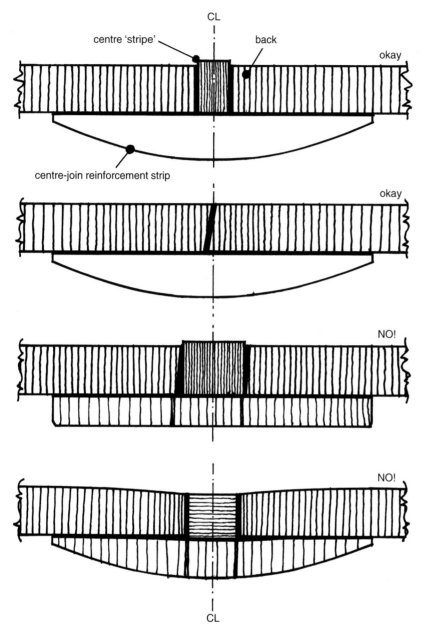

Fig 71 Centre-join sections: good and bad practices.

no more than 2mm. The centre-stripe should be prepared over-depth before gluing up to the back halves, so it is proud of the face-sides to allow it to be scraped down flush with them for a good, smooth join.

You may find that 'shooting' the centre-join edges tends to repeat the problem of wild or divergent grain preventing the plane cutting cleanly in either direction. Rosewood can be very obstinate and lead to ragged edges; sycamore can be tricky and mahogany very occasionally goes a bit feathery. The block plane may cut cleaner, so if you do experience difficulty when 'shooting' the back halves, by all means use the block plane. At the risk of corrupting your best intentions, should you find that 'shooting' the centre-join edges never brings the mating surfaces anywhere near a nice, tight, invisible join, then where the back is concerned, you can resort to levelling the edges with some medium grit, 'free-cut' abrasive paper stuck to a straight-edge (the business side of an aluminium spirit level is fine). Be aware that this abrasive paper cuts down remarkably quickly. The back centre-join gets reinforced internally with the transverse-grain strips, so a good structurally sound join is possible if the glued edges are a little woolly. Once you have achieved the tightest join possible, clean the mating surfaces with a clean non-lint rag, dampened (with cigarette lighter fuel if you are using rosewood) to remove fine dust from the pores.

Glue up the back halves immediately. If you are inserting a centre-stripe then do not forget to place this between the back halves when hammering in the panel pins to form the 'clamp'. Use Cascamite powdered resin glue, mixed with clean cold water – you will need about a teaspoonful mixed up. Clamp up as you did for the belly halves (*see* Chapter 5) using: baseboard, panel pins, thin paper strips, 25 × 10mm raising lath and the half-size pressure boards, two boards being used again so the gap between them will allow the glued centre-join to be felt

'give' as much as spruce, so a 'stripe' of sycamore, for example, will help you glue up a good centre-join. Do not use the centre-stripe, however, to disguise a sloppy joint, and take note of good (and bad) practices (*see* Fig 71). Suitable centre-stripe materials are: rosewood, boxwood, sycamore, rock-maple, holly, satinwood or ebony and they should have a face width of

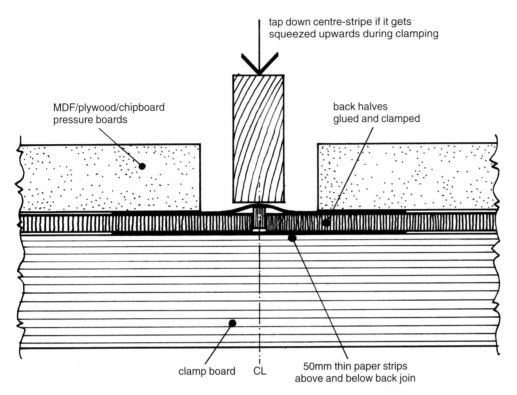

tap down centre-stripe if it gets
squeezed upwards during clamping

*Fig 72 Centre-join
section: join and stripe
must lie flat.*

MDF/plywood/chipboard
pressure boards

back halves
glued and clamped

clamp board   CL   50mm thin paper strips
above and below back join

beneath the paper strip – double check before piling on the bricks or blocks that the centre-join edges are lying absolutely flat to the baseboard, and the centre-stripe (if you are using one) is not being squeezed either upwards or downwards out of the compressed join. A finger end is sensitive enough to feel through the thin paper whether the two halves are mating level with each other. Cascamite does not set quickly, so you can take time and trouble to avoid the sort of problems that might occur as shown (*see* Fig 72). If necessary, tap down the centre- stripe with a thin block of softwood and a light hammer. Leave the two halves evenly weighed down for at least six hours. Once the glue has set firm, remove the weights, pressure boards and panel pins and 'G' clamp the whole back to the worktop and shave off the paper strips and excess glue with the steel scraper. Scrape the centre-stripe absolutely flush.

Now aim to plane and scrape down the joined back to about 2.75mm overall thickness for rosewood, but allow 3.25mm for mahogany and 3mm for sycamore. You will find the scraper does a far better job than the plane. Scraping takes longer but you will achieve excellent faces by this method. Use the thicknessing gauge to ensure that you are not hollowing out any particular areas and take especial care not to shave down too much off the edge areas. Just like the belly, it is best to leave the thickness at the centre-join area a little thicker than the rest of the back.

Now cleaned up, give both faces a rub down with the medium grit, 'free-cut' abrasive paper on the flat cork block *across* the grain to smooth out the surfaces level to a uniform colour. Scrutinize both faces and make your final choice for the face-side. Mark on the template outlines again, allow for the 'button', mark the face-side with the 'F' and from the grid-scale plan dimensions, mark on the outlines for bars BB1, BB2 and BB3 to the underside face. You may now cut out the shape of the back

RIGHT: Fig 73 Cut out the back's outline allowing waste edges.
BELOW: Fig 74 Details for the back's bars BB1, BB2 and BB3.

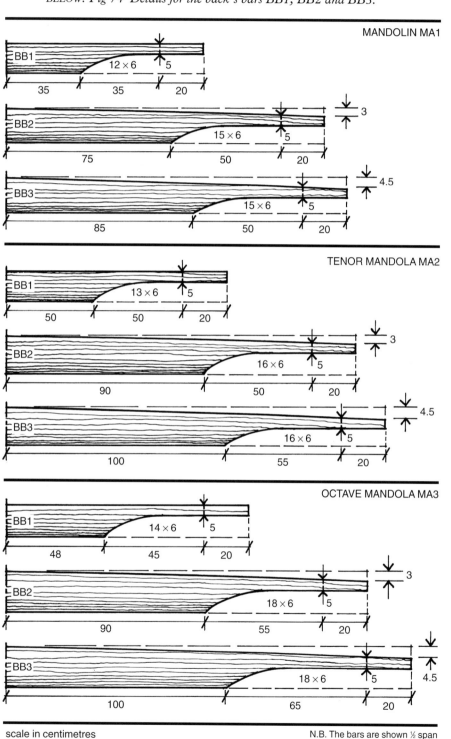

MANDOLIN MA1

TENOR MANDOLA MA2

OCTAVE MANDOLA MA3

scale in centimetres

N.B. The bars are shown ½ span

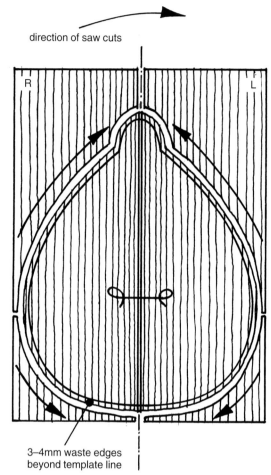

direction of saw cuts

3–4mm waste edges
beyond template line

on the 'V' board with the coping (or scroll saw) leaving a 3 to 4mm waste edge outside the actual pencil outline – all the way round. Cut in the directions as shown (*see* Fig 73). The back, being a thickness – by this stage – of somewhere between 2.5 to 3mm is very thin and very brittle, so saw carefully, steadily and keep that waste margin even; you will notice how easily the saw blade wants to follow the earlywood and avoid the latewood. Place the back somewhere warm and dry while you prepare the transverse bars BB1, BB2 and BB3.

Prepare the bars as before (*see* Fig 74). You may use selected, clear western red cedar or mahogany, close-grained and quarter-sawn with the grain parallel to the depth of the bar and in every respect the same as the belly bars: no camber for BB1, 3mm camber for BB2 and a 4.5mm camber for BB3. Cut them over-long, mark on the scalloping outlines with a sharp, hard pencil but do not fashion the scalloping until they have been glued to the back. Gluing and clamping on the bars is a little trickier on the back because there is no soundhole to utilize the long clamp previously shown in Fig 63, Chapter 5. If you possess long-jawed clamps that will reach the centre-span area of the bars this will aid gluing up; if you don't have these, then adopt the method shown (*see* Fig 75). Use slim wedges or cowhide off-cuts to pack out any gaps. Glue the back bars on with C3 PVA or Titebond adhesive. Ensure that the glue beads squeezed out are even and consistent to give an accurate indication that the bars are compressed firmly to the back for that superior thin glue join. Remove excess glue with the 200mm spill and place the clamped-up workpiece in a warm place for at least two hours.

Before you dash off to Chapter 7, you might as well fashion the centre-join reinforcement strips. These are fashioned from the triangular off-cuts from the belly (or just buy them as ready-profiled stripwood in western red cedar, maple or mahogany). Mark these in strips about 20mm wide *across* the grain; the grain has to be at right-angles to the centre-join (*see* Fig 76) otherwise it has no strength and therefore cannot reinforce. Some luthiers do not trouble to plane on the convex profile, after all this is an internal fitting, however, there is a good reason for the convex section: its thickest part lies across the actual centre-join, giving greater stiffness and support, then tapering away to prevent a sudden stress line that does occur with an unprofiled strip. The convex surface also looks better as it can be seen through the soundhole. Planing the strips is not easy: they are thin, fragile and narrow. Holding these

Fig 75 Glue and clamp on the bars.

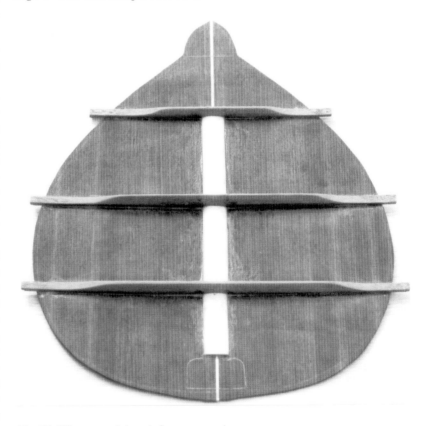

Fig 76 The centre-join reinforcement strip.

Fig 77 Fashioning the reinforcement strip's profile.

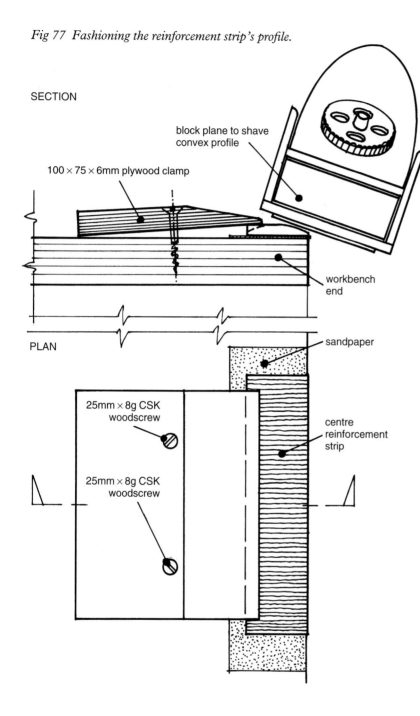

SECTION

block plane to shave convex profile

100 × 75 × 6mm plywood clamp

workbench end

PLAN

sandpaper

25mm × 8g CSK woodscrew

25mm × 8g CSK woodscrew

centre reinforcement strip

paper stuck onto the underside to improve the grip. A piece of 6mm thick plywood about 100 × 75 with a tapered edge as shown is fine. Use some double-sided tape to stick a strip of abrasive paper to the worktop end as well to grip from below. The clamp is screwed down to the worktop's end to hold the strip. The block plane is then used in long passes tipped at an increasing angle to cut across the grain. Once the plane has shaved the approximate convex profile, use a flat file and the medium grit, 'free-cut' abrasive paper on the cork block to finish it silky smooth. You will only achieve fashioning short pieces of this transverse-grained strip, which is fine as they fit in between the back bars and are not required to be a continuous strip from neck to tailblock. Prepare three such strips about 100mm long and then store them somewhere warm and dry for fitting later to the inside of the back (*see* Chapter 7).

The next stage is to scallop and shape the back bars BB1, BB2 and BB3, so remove the clamps once the glue has set firm and place the back, face-side down, on the cowhide mat. The methods for paring the scalloping and shaving the bars to a 'keel' profile are the same as you used for the belly (*see* Figs 65 and 66 in Chapter 5 again). The centre-join reinforcement strips are not glued in at this stage as they would obstruct the shaving and final shaping of the bars. The razor-sharp 25mm chisel is used, bevel side downmost in diagonal slicing cuts and then each bar planed to 'keel' profiles with the block plane. Then clean them up with the medium 'free-cut' abrasive paper to remove sharp edges and grubby glue marks; be aware that the inside of the back will be visible through the soundhole: if someone looks at your maker's label, they will see the bars and centre-join strip as well. Do not trim off the over-long bar ends yet. The back is now complete and is to be stored on one side somewhere warm and dry while you progress to the ribs and linings in Chapter 7.

strips down on the bench while you plane or file them is very tricky. The plane iron is always too horribly close to the ends of the fingers so I use a clamp (*see* Fig 77) made from an off-cut of ply with some abrasive

7 THE RIBS AND LININGS

It is usual to select the material for the ribs from the same tonewoods as the back. It may be from the same log, with the same grain pattern and you will be fortunate if this is the case. Tonewoods for the back and ribs are usually sold as a set: whilst this may mean they are of the same species and perhaps from the same tree they are not necessarily from the same part, as economic conversion of the log does not always closely match pieces of different sizes. Timber merchants of the kind that supply tonewoods do not take kindly to customers dismembering and swopping around their 'package deal' of ribs and backs, but you can be choosy and find a set that is closely matched for figure, grain and colour unless you want a visual contrast between ribs and back.

Avoid mixing species together for the back and ribs – this can lead to coupling together tonewoods of very different properties and movement. Mixed tonewood species are more suited to the narrow ribs of the segmental bowl-backed instruments, where alternating and contrasting timbers can be used. I have seen a lute with a bowl back made of pine ribs, that has proved quite stable.

Reject tonewood for the ribs if it has been supplied sawn too thin. This problem can be common with sycamore and if it has well-flamed figuring the saw will have left the surfaces very woolly: by the time you have planed both faces of these smooth and rubbed them down then they will probably be too thin and will be useless. The rib material should be supplied sawn about 4 to 5mm thick. It is always better to buy sawn material too thick and plane it to thickness yourself – this does mean more work but at least you will have more control over quality.

Presuming you have obtained two book-matched, quarter-sawn pieces, leave them long and wide but 'G' clamp one on the hide mat with a short piece of batten. With the razor-sharp plane iron set low, lightly plane *away* from the clamp. If the plane snags against the grain turn the rib around and try planing in the opposite direction. Rather like planing the back halves in Chapter 6, you may meet wild or divergent grain and as the rib material is not very wide it is not possible to plane across 'ribbon' or 'flamed' figure. Make sure you do not plane off too much material from the area near the edges – keep an eye on the edges' thickness. You can try planing with the plane held diagonally – so the blade cuts like a guillotine – or if that proves just as difficult try the block plane; this *should* shave cleaner. The steel scraper is certainly the best tool to thickness the ribs to about 2mm while achieving a smooth and level surface on both faces, and then use the medium grit, 'free-cut' abrasive paper on the cork block to produce a final thickness of about 1.75 to 2mm. If you are using sycamore or mahogany, which can sometimes feel rather soft and pliable at this stage, then do not thickness it less than 2mm.

Do the same thicknessing, scraping and rubbing down of the other rib until you have a perfect set of twins with fair faces to both, showing the grain clearly. Place them on the worktop together and book-match the grain. Decide which faces are best and

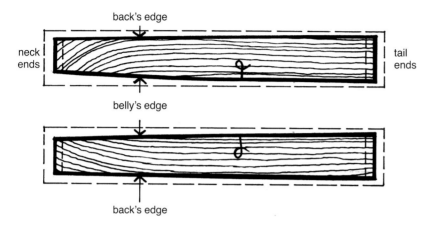

Fig 78 Ribs' profile for grain and cambered edges.

Fig 79 Reinforce the ribs' ends prior to bending.

outside the pencil outline. When they are both cut out, hold them together back to back and use masking tape on the ends to keep them together; you can also tape the bottom edges to ensure that that they do not slip about when executing the following: place both ribs together in the bench vice with about 6 to 7mm projecting above the jaws. Now use the smoothing plane to plane down to the pencil line, taking care not to plane 'into' any emergent grain at the gentle curved edge between the middle of the rib and the neck end. Keep the plane dead true so the edges are cut at right-angles to the face-sides. You should now have an 'L' and 'R' rib with precisely the same top (belly) edges. Mark this top edge to both with a pencil or crayon arrow to make absolutely certain no confusion between the top and bottom of the ribs can occur. This is very important, otherwise the designed longitudinal doming for the belly will be on the back!

Now tape together these top edges, turn the ribs over, peel off the tape to the bottom edges, clamp in the vice again and then plane these edges down to the pencil outline. You will now have two identical ribs. Mark on another arrow to denote the top (belly) edges, just to be certain! By now the ribs will have razor-sharp edges, so be careful.

Before preparing to bend the ribs on the hot iron, it is wise to reinforce the waste ends with off-cuts of lining, glued on to the face-side (*see* Fig 79). Use C3 PVA adhesive; this precaution will prevent splitting down the grain as you bend the ribs around the iron. Rosewood is especially prone to split during this exercise, so *don't* omit the temporary end reinforcements; they chisel off cleanly when bending is complete.

Cut out the linings from one piece of spruce, poplar or willow to the sizes specified (*see* Fig 80); the grain must be quarter-sawn and run as shown, that is, parallel with the grain of the ribs. You will need to prepare six linings although only four are

mark them with the 'F' for face-side. Also decide which edges will be the top (belly's edge) and bottom (back's edge). Mark on 'L' and 'R'. If the grain tends to wander off the straight or curl, ensure that this feature will be at the neck end of the ribs and the divergent grain runs towards the top (belly) direction (*see* Fig 78). Use the rib template to mark on the outlines, choosing a specific line of grain on each so the two ribs are identical twins when cut out in profile. This will mean the grain will match exactly at the tail-join on the centre axis: the sign of a carefully made instrument.

Cut out the ribs with the coping saw (or scroll saw), keeping the blade about 2mm

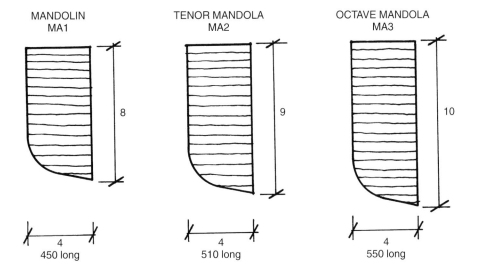

MANDOLIN
MA1

8

4
450 long

TENOR MANDOLA
MA2

9

4
510 long

OCTAVE MANDOLA
MA3

10

4
550 long

Fig 80 Detail of the linings for back and belly.

needed (two for spares in case the bending process breaks a couple). You can use Brazilian mahogany for the linings to the back/ribs' join; this wood is much preferred here as you will be coupling together two hardwoods with little movement. Some luthiers use 'kerfed' linings that are slotted with wide saw cuts almost through their thickness at about 5mm intervals to enable bending to the curve of the ribs without heating them. Kerfed linings are usually fitted to steel-strung acoustic guitars, but as the mandolin family is smaller and has a single, simpler curve, then light-section, one-piece heat-bent linings are ideal: they are certainly easier to prepare, glue in and clamp.

BENDING THE RIBS AND LININGS

A bending-iron is needed for this next procedure and you can obtain an electrically heated one from a luthiers' supplier or make up your own that can be heated by a gas torch or burner from a LPG bottle. This can be fabricated from a 100mm diameter mild steel pipe about 175mm long, capped off at one end and mounted very securely over a gas burner or blow-lamp torch, that will have a tap or valve to adjust the intensity

of flame. The steel pipe section is commonly used for gateposts or highway signs, so it is not difficult to find an off-cut and get a metal fabricator to press it into an egg-shaped section and weld a cap on. You will need to drill about twelve 3mm diameter holes in the cap to allow the gas burner to work properly (*see* Fig 81). Inside the

Fig 81 The home-made bending-iron.

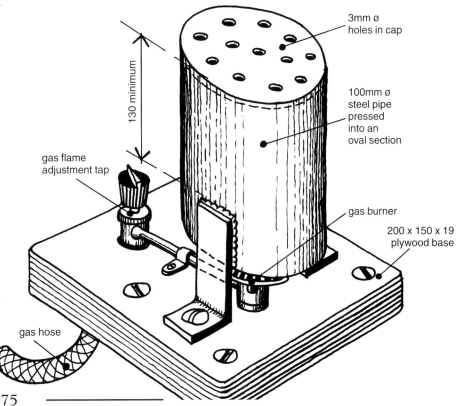

3mm ø holes in cap

100mm ø steel pipe pressed into an oval section

130 minimum

gas flame adjustment tap

gas burner

200 x 150 x 19 plywood base

gas hose

hollow pipe, squeeze in some crushed-up plasterer's expanded metal lathing (or chicken wire) to provide a 'heat-sink' to dissipate the burner's heat to the walls of the pipe more efficiently. The other details of the home-made bending-iron can be fabricated from scrap metal. Make sure that whatever you scrounge or cobble together is safe and can be clamped firmly in the vice or screwed to the bench top when in use.

It is not absolutely necessary to have the pipe pressed into the egg-shaped section. I had this done to simulate the various radii, but then there was a blacksmith in the next village who liked a challenge – most of you won't be so fortunate. Clean up the outside of the pipe with abrasive paper until it is clean bright metal and then polish it with a metal polish. Experiment with the assembly to ensure that the burner combusts correctly within the bottom of the pipe and mount the pipe higher up on the angle-iron legs if 'popping' of the flame occurs or the flame keeps expiring. The gas tap will give you a fine adjustment for the flame and you will not require much of a flame as the steel pipe does not need to get red hot. You will need to access the on–off valve on the gas bottle as well – in case of an emergency.

If you choose to fabricate your own bending-iron for economic reasons then *do not* utilize old electric fire elements as a heat source; the bending process requires lots of water and damp wood: electricity with water does not form a healthy alliance. Remove volatile liquids from your work space and sweep up wood shavings if using a gas torch or burner. Our ancestors used cast bronze or iron vessels filled with charcoal or coal, but you will find bottled LPG is more convenient and controllable.

The method for bending the ribs is basic (and ancient) in principle. I mentioned wooden clinker-built boats in Chapter 3, and the planks and bent frames ('ribs') of these use the agents of heat and water to make them pliable to fit a curved profile. Heat is the prime agent for bending; the

water (as steam) aids heat penetration of the cellular structure making the fibres 'plastic' for as long as the material is hot. Dry heat alone is no good as local shrinkage will occur too readily, damaging the cellular integrity and causing irreversible distortion and splitting. The ribs and linings will need to be soaked in very hot water for ten to fifteen minutes for rosewood or five to ten minutes for mahogany and sycamore immediately before using the bending-iron.

When you are ready to bend the ribs, you will need a bowl of clean cold water and an ordinary paintbrush about 50mm wide. Once you have turned on the bending-iron watch the burner for a couple of minutes to ensure that it is burning steadily, but not roaring away – the sort of flame you would use to simmer a pot of soup. It may take some time for the iron to heat up, but when a droplet of water 'spits' on the cap of the iron, then this is almost hot enough. It is a good idea to wear an old pair of leather gloves for this exercise as the workpiece gets hot and accidentally touching the hot iron with your hand is too easy. Remember to have the 'F' face-side of the ribs as the outside of the curve, in other words, the ribs get pressed up to the hot iron on their inside face, otherwise the carefully matched mirror-imaged grain will have been a futile exercise. Be certain also, that the tail end of the rib is round the right way when you are bending the workpiece and offering it to the body mould to check curvature. It is easy not to notice such details amongst the sizzling and steam, so be obsessive with the pencil markings – the widest part of the rib *always* goes towards the tail and to avoid the remotest chance of getting the curve wrong, mark the tail ends and 'F' face-sides conspicuously.

Take the 'L' rib, for example, from its hot soaking; grasp each end and holding its face-side ('F') towards you with its inside face across the face of the bending-iron, rock it backwards and forwards at the tail end to heat it, but do not force it against the iron yet. As the rib starts to sizzle and steam, exert a little pressure to feel it 'give' around the iron slightly. Remove and wet it with the paintbrush on both faces and hold up to the iron again, with slightly more pressure this time, until it bends a little more. You will perhaps only have bent about a length of 50 to 60mm, so continue to the next area, wetting the rib and working gently but firmly until the rib curve looks a little like the mould shape. Take care not to bend in segments so the gentle curve becomes faceted like the sides of a 50 pence piece. If you slide and rock the rib around the iron's profile, this heats up a larger area so the curves should remain smooth (*see* Fig 82).

As soon as the steam and sizzling stops, wet the ribs both sides again. *Do not* exert pressure if the ribs are dry. Bending to the full and correct curvature will not happen in one attempt: plenty of water, heat, patience and gentle pressure is the trick here. You will get a 'feel' for the right amount of force to apply; certainly by the time you start on the second ('R') rib. When the 'L' rib is a passable imitation of the body mould, clamp it into the mould while still warm and damp; the turn-buttons will force the still pliable rib into the exact curve of the mould, so when cool and dry it will maintain the shape.

Repeat the wetting process to the 'R' rib piece and bend this on the hot iron as successfully as you did the 'L'. Offer it to the mould when you are close enough to the curve and making sure the tail end of both ribs are overlapping 5 to 6mm, clamp the 'R' rib with the turn-buttons and allow to cool and dry off by natural evaporation. Now you have got the knack of bending on the hot iron without breaking the workpiece, you can turn your attention to bending the linings – the iron will be hot enough, so you might as well do all the bending in one go. Take one lining from the hot soak and use the same sliding and rocking technique across the iron's face. The linings

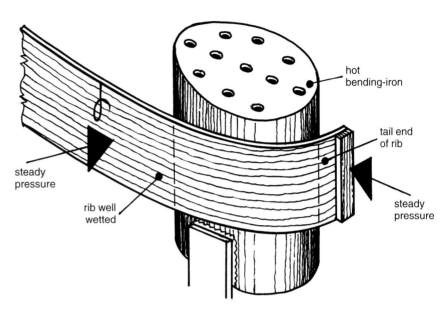

must be kept well-wetted, but as they are of thicker material you must be even more gentle when applying pressure to bend them. They can buckle or crease easily or even fracture, so you need to have them steaming wildly and make several attempts to get the tighter curvatures right. If you do fracture a lining when bending it, the force is too great or the wood is not wet enough. You may think that several days' prolonged soaking of the linings prior to bending them will make them more co-operative – I am afraid this is not the case. Once you have bent two linings approximately to the curves, clamp them to the inside of the ribs (still locked in the body mould) using the clothes-pegs clamps (*see* Fig 83). Then bend the other two and clamp them to the ribs as well. On cooling and drying, the linings too, once unclamped will keep their curved shape. Place the linings somewhere warm and dry as you will not need them yet; they need to be quite dry before gluing them onto the ribs. Turn off the bending-iron and let it cool down. Then give the iron a wipe with an oil-soaked rag to prevent it rusting and store it somewhere safe. (You will need it again in good condition when you build your second, third, fourth … instrument!)

Fig 82 Bending the ribs around the hot iron.

steady pressure

rib well wetted

hot bending-iron

tail end of rib

steady pressure

Fig 83 Gluing and clamping the linings to the ribs.

Slacken all the turn-buttons and remove the two ribs from the body mould and with the ribs lying on their edges on the worktop pare off with the chisel those glued-on off-cuts of linings to the waste ends. It will be necessary now the ribs are bent, to mark out the tail-join on each one. Some luthiers use a gradual wedge-shaped cut like a 'dovetail' and insert a corresponding (but often contrasting material) angled graft to achieve a close-fitting central tail-join: you push in the graft until it is a tight fit. As the method I adopt to glue the ribs together at the tail-join incorporates the gluing on of the tail-block simultaneously, then a straight, square-cut join on the centreline is preferred. You may, with this method, fit the centre-join with a contrasting stripe to match and correspond with that of the back's stripe: this feature enables visual accurate alignment when the back bars are finally trimmed and the back is to be glued up to the ribs.

To mark up the ribs' tail-join, use the try-square to scribe on with the marking knife a line perpendicular to the bottom edge of the ribs about 5 or 6mm in from the waste end; the grain on either rib should mirror-image match either side of the lines. Using the razor saw and holding one rib's tail end on a block of scrap wood, securely clamped

in the vice, cut to the knife line, squarely and cleanly: the razor saw is the only tool to do this. Now repeat to trim the end-join of the other rib. When you have cut the ends true, place them together as if they were already glued; are there any gaps? Are they a good fit? Improve the mating edges if necessary with the medium grit, 'free-cut' abrasive paper on the flat cork block. Put aside the ribs and fashion the tailblock.

THE TAILBLOCK

Select your material for the tailblock; if possible use the same species as the belly so the nature and degree of moisture movement will be the same. The material *must* be quarter-sawn, close-grained and the grain running in the direction shown, in other words the same as the belly grain. Mark out the tailblock slightly oversize in height from the sizes given (*see* Fig 84). Plane it true and square to width and thickness as specified. Do not plane or chisel the convex profile, this is finally shaped only after it has been glued to the ribs. Mark on the 30 degree shouldered notches and then cut them out with the razor saw; these will house the lining ends scribed to them. The tailblock should not be too large; you may consider that a good chunk of wood here will give the tail of the instrument greater strength and stability and so it would, but it would also inhibit the dynamics of the belly. It must be substantial enough to join the tail ends of each rib and provide the 'meat' for anchoring the strings' tailpiece, that imparts great stress to the tail from the tension of the strings. The tailblock is a component that is probably never seen (unless your clients are curious and have a dentist's mirror and 12-volt Lilliputian inspection lamp) but its design, selection of suitable wood and gluing up cannot be treated in a slapdash way. Mark on the profile of the convex face and the centreline to the end grain to aid positioning, gluing up and clamping.

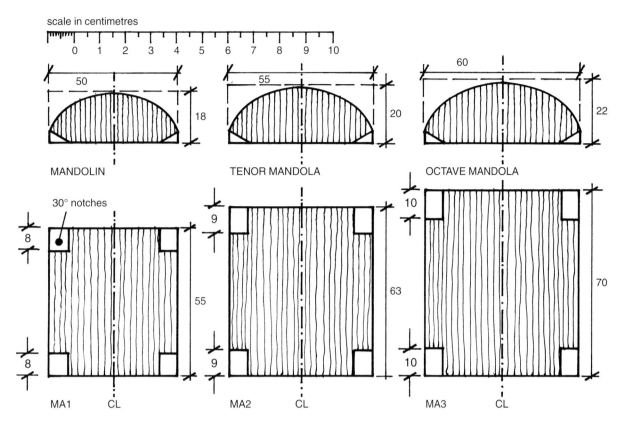

scale in centimetres

0 1 2 3 4 5 6 7 8 9 10

50 / 18 — MANDOLIN

55 / 20 — TENOR MANDOLA

60 / 22 — OCTAVE MANDOLA

30° notches

8 / 55 / 8 — MA1 CL

9 / 9 — MA2 CL

10 / 63 / 10 — MA3 CL

70 — MA3

Fig 84 Detail of the tailblock.

With the ribs ready bent and the tailblock ready cut square, glue up the tail centre-join and the tailblock in one exercise. If the ribs are rosewood then de-oil the surfaces to be glued with cigarette lighter fuel on a clean rag. Place a square of greaseproof paper or thick Cellophane about 100 x 75mm on the body mould at the centre-join area of the tail and tape it down to the mould's base board. Place both ribs in the mould with their bottom edges downmost and lock them up lightly with the turn-buttons, so that the tail-join edges are just about 2 to 3mm apart. (If you are going to infill the join with a centre-stripe to complement the back's, then prepare a matching piece of this ready for gluing in, cut over-long but with the ends cut square and true.)

Mix up standard Araldite epoxy resin adhesive – about half a teaspoonful – and with the spatula supplied, wipe the adhesive liberally on the back face of the tailblock and the tail-join ends of the ribs. Place the tail-block against the ribs and (insert the stripe now) push together the ribs to close up the join, locking the turn-buttons firmly. With your fingers still pinching the tailblock in place, dead on the centreline, use another piece of grease-proof paper or Cellophane about 75 x 75mm to cover the tail join and a caul to 'G' clamp the tailblock tight to the ribs. Use two 'G' clamps if they will fit on (see Fig 85). The adhesive will act as a lubricant initially so the tailblock has a tendency to wander about as you clamp up. Make sure the centrelines remain aligned. Araldite is deliberately chosen for this application as it takes ages to set, so you have plenty of time to get this right. This adhesive also produces an almost indestructible join. Now place the body mould with ribs and tailblock clamped in, somewhere warm for at least sixteen hours. In the meantime, turn to Chapter 8 and make a start on planing the neck timber true and square and mark on from the template: the face and side profiles;

Fig 85 Gluing and clamping tailblock to ribs.

zero-fret and 12th (or 14th) fret lines; and slot with recesses for the truss rod. By the time you have done that, you will be able to continue to work on the ribs and linings.

GLUING ON THE LININGS

Remove the complete ribs/tailblock assembly from the mould, peel off the grease-proof paper or Cellophane from the glue lines and turn it over so the back (bottom) edges are uppermost and align the centre-line of the tailblock dead on the mould's centreline – now clamp up the turn-buttons to hold everything firm. Place an old credit card between the tailblock and the baseboard of the mould – this will prevent the mould from being chopped up by the chisel in the next operation. Fashion the convex face to the tailblock with the 25mm chisel, paring down vertically using your weight, not a mallet. Trim it as smooth as you can achieve; it is not necessary to rub the convex face down with sandpaper as the sharp chisel will cut cleaner. Pick out any rogue bubbles of adhesive which may have found their way into the 30 degree shouldered notches for the linings.

Take two of the bent linings (the mahogany ones perhaps, as this is the back/ribs' join) and cut the tail ends to a 30 degree angle with the razor saw to fit into

the tailblock's shoulder rebates. It is not necessary at this stage to scribe or cut the neck end of the linings; these remain over-long until the sequence of shaving them down to the ribs' edges. Mix up about a tea-spoon of Cascamite powdered resin glue and get the clothes-peg clamps ready, about forty of them. If the ribs are rosewood, then de-oil the surfaces to be glued as described before. Take one lining and brush on a lib-eral film of adhesive to the outside curve of the lining, then fit it into the tailblock notch, pushing it well in until the glue squeezes out, whilst using clothes-pegs to clamp the lining to the rib as well. Work progressively around the curve of the rib towards the neck end, pinching the lining tightly to the rib with your thumb and forefinger as you apply the clothes-pegs in turn (*see* Fig 83 again).

The lining must be glued on just proud of the edge of the rib as it will be shaved down to form a good flush jointing face later on (*see* Fig 86). When you have fin-ished gluing and clamping in one lining, do exactly the same as above to fit the other lining. Do not worry about cleaning off any excess glue that has squeezed out as this will get shaved off, but do wipe off any drib-bles of glue that have run down the inside face of the ribs. Now place the mould with ribs and linings clamped somewhere warm for at least six hours.

Fig 86 Plane linings' top edges to a slight angle.

FITTING THE BACK AND NOTCHING THE LININGS

Restore the mould to your bench and remove all the clothes-pegs. You will need to fit a block tailored to hold the free ends of the ribs. A method of doing this is shown (*see* Fig 87). The block is then screwed directly onto the baseboard of the mould. You will need to trim back the over-long linings at the neck end with the razor saw so they are exactly as long as the ribs. *Do not* trim off any 'waste' ends of the ribs yet, the amount to be removed will only be determined and scribed when the neck is fitted. (If you cut the ribs short now, you may not have adequate material to house into the shoulder slots of the neck.) Once the neck ends of the ribs are secured by this method, use the block plane around the edges of the ribs to shave down the linings flush, but at a slight angle as shown previously in Fig 86. This feature is necessary to correspond with the doming of the back and provide a broader gluing joint. Make certain that the block plane does not remove too much of the ribs' material but just enough to give that slight angle. The tailblock's end grain face may need to be cut down to be level with the ribs/lining edges; do this carefully to avoid stressing the tail. I suggest the medium grit, 'free-cut' abrasive on the flat cork block rather than the block plane for this operation.

The ribs and linings, including the tail-block, are now ready to have the back glued on. The positions of the back bars BB1, BB2 and BB3 will need to be marked on to the linings so they can be notched to house the ends of the bars. This is not a simple

Fig 87 Use fashioned block to hold the ribs' free ends.

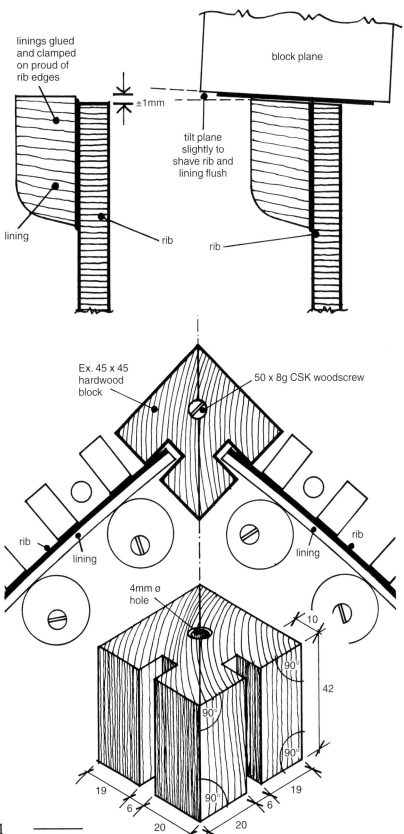

task as there is not a single straight surface to the assembly you see locked up in the body mould. Place the body mould on your bench so that the tail end is facing you. The bars on the back are still over-long and need to be for the marking out. Place the back on to the ribs as though it was already glued on. Now align the centre-join of the back to the centre-join of the tail. (If you have used a centre-stripe then this is easy.) Allow about 4mm of the back's waste mar-

Fig 88 Mark the bars' positions on to the linings.

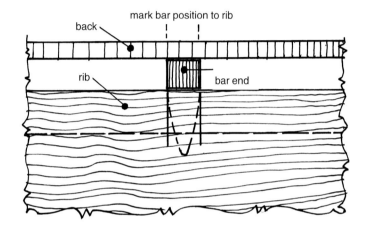

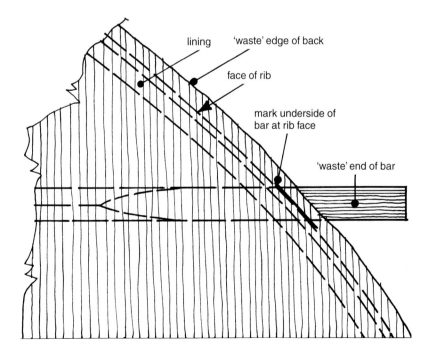

gin to overhang the ribs' face at the tail and tape this down with masking tape. You will need a house brick or similar weight, with a cork tile glued to cushion it from scratching the back's face-side. Now use the small set-square to align the centre-join at the 'button' (neck end) absolutely perpendicular to the centreline marked on the baseboard of the mould. Place on the weight to hold it down: it will want to spring back up as the ribs' edges are slightly curved. Check that the centre-lines are still spot on; the ability for the back to wander off this axis alignment is truly amazing! Use a bit more masking tape to make sure that the back remains in place and that at least 3mm of the back's waste edge is overhanging *all* the way around the ribs.

Now you need to mark the positions where the bars lie across the ribs; this means kneeling on the floor to see clearly. Use a very sharp white crayon if the ribs are dark coloured. Mark a line each side of the bar BB3 on to the rib (*see* Fig 88), then with a hard pencil, mark the underside of the bar at the point where it projects beyond the face-side of the rib. Mark the bar/rib positions for BB2 and BB1 similarly. This is very fiddly, but accuracy is a must. When you have established these positions, cast your eye over the centreline axis alignments at button and tail centre-joins. Are they still spot on? If they are not, then suspect that your bar position markings might be unreliable and start the marking-up again. When you are certain all is well, remove the weight and masking tape and place the back somewhere safe while you proceed to mark the lining notches from the crayon lines on the ribs.

Leave the ribs clamped up in the mould and span a steel straight-edge across to transfer the bars' positions and thickness to the top face of the linings. Use the marking gauge to scratch on the depth of each bar to the lining and the small set-square to mark the vertical sides of the notches. As shown (*see* Fig 89), razor saw

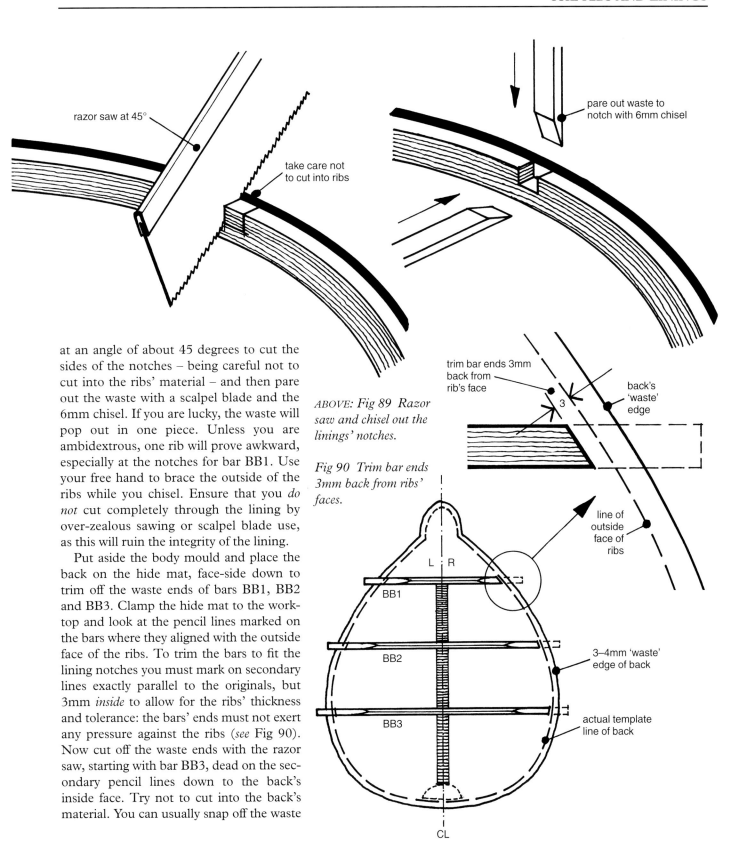

at an angle of about 45 degrees to cut the
sides of the notches – being careful not to
cut into the ribs' material – and then pare
out the waste with a scalpel blade and the
6mm chisel. If you are lucky, the waste will
pop out in one piece. Unless you are
ambidextrous, one rib will prove awkward,
especially at the notches for bar BB1. Use
your free hand to brace the outside of the
ribs while you chisel. Ensure that you *do
not* cut completely through the lining by
over-zealous sawing or scalpel blade use,
as this will ruin the integrity of the lining.

Put aside the body mould and place the
back on the hide mat, face-side down to
trim off the waste ends of bars BB1, BB2
and BB3. Clamp the hide mat to the worktop and look at the pencil lines marked on
the bars where they aligned with the outside
face of the ribs. To trim the bars to fit the
lining notches you must mark on secondary
lines exactly parallel to the originals, but
3mm *inside* to allow for the ribs' thickness
and tolerance: the bars' ends must not exert
any pressure against the ribs (*see* Fig 90).
Now cut off the waste ends with the razor
saw, starting with bar BB3, dead on the secondary pencil lines down to the back's
inside face. Try not to cut into the back's
material. You can usually snap off the waste

ABOVE: Fig 89 Razor saw and chisel out the linings' notches.

Fig 90 Trim bar ends 3mm back from ribs' faces.

ends now they are sawn through, but any remaining bar material still glued down can be pared off with the 25mm chisel. Now trim off the waste ends of bar BB2 and then bar BB1; the back with the bars trimmed to size is now ready for gluing and clamping to the ribs (*see* Fig 91).

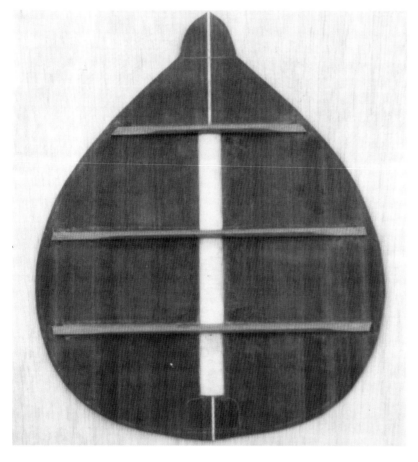

Fig 91 Inside of back with bars scribed to notches.

GLUING THE BACK TO THE RIBS

With the ribs still locked into the body mould, offer the back to see how it fits. Place the back's centre-join in line with the tail centre-join and use a strip or two of masking tape to hold this alignment steady, while gently pressing the back down so that the bars BB3, BB2 and BB1 fit into their respective notches in the linings. If any bar end seems reluctant to seat in a notch, then

do not use force: take off the back and find out why. Perhaps the back is not centred to the tail centre-join correctly or the notch is slightly misaligned, not wide enough or a piece of waste material is still in the notch. Remedy as necessary and try the fitting again. When you are sure that each bar has seated snugly into each notch, use masking tape on the tail and a weight near the button to hold the back down, flexing it to the longitudinal doming as though it was already glued to the ribs.

You will need to kneel down to view the back/ribs' join as you rotate the mould on the worktop to scrutinize the whole of the workpiece. Are there any places where the back does not meet the ribs tightly? Press down with your fingers at points where a gap is seen; if the gap does not close up with light pressure, then investigate – it may be the bar is slightly deeper than the notch, so shave off a bit more of the bearing surface of the notch. Try again until the whole join is a straight and tight line, from shoulders to tail. It is now time to glue the back to the ribs.

You will need to use about twenty of the 6mm diameter long-bolts, the loose wooden spindles and 6mm diameter wing-nuts to clamp the back on when glued up. The method of clamping is carried out on the body mould (*see* Fig 92). Leaving the ribs firmly locked in the mould with the turn-buttons, the long-bolts are then passed through the holes (previously drilled) from the underside of the mould, so that they stick out of the face of the baseboard on the outsides of the ribs. The bolts should not fit tightly in the holes as a bit of sideways play in them is necessary (an 8mm diameter drill bit was recommended). It is easier to clamp the neck end of the body mould in the vice so it stands vertically while you insert the long-bolts, then hold a piece of thin board against the underside of the mould until you transfer it to a horizontal position. Once the mould is laid flat on the worktop, slide out the board, these bolts then stay in place! You will need to insert some thin slip

Fig 92 Gluing and clamping back to ribs in mould.

wedges between the ribs – only towards their neck ends – and the mould baseboard as the ribs' low-curved profile will prevent them from resting on the baseboard.

If the back and ribs are rosewood, then de-oil the areas to be glued with cigarette lighter fluid. Mix up about two teaspoons of Cascamite powdered resin glue with clean cold water and apply an even bead of adhesive with the small artist's brush to the top of the lining/rib edges and into the notches for the bars. *Do not* apply glue to the lining/rib edge between bar BB1 and the neck ends; this area gets glued up *only* after the neck is fitted. Apply a liberal coating of adhesive to the end grain face of the tailblock as well. Now offer the back to the ribs, pressing the bar ends into the notches and clamp up the tail end first, using 2 'G' clamps and a caul; *see* Fig 92 again. Now you place a weight on the button area to flex it down to the longitudinal doming and now – as fast as you can

– slip on the wooden spindles to each long-bolt, leather face downwards, working from the tail around to the neck end, screwing on a wing-nut and clamping down just finger-tight to each. Too much pressure from the spindle clamps will distort the ribs or may fracture the overhanging waste margin of the back, so just clamp until the back/ribs' joins are closed up tight, with a consistent glue bead squeezed out. Remember, a thin glue joint is the strongest. Do not worry about the excess glue line, it gets shaved off later. Now place the mould with the back/ribs' assembly somewhere warm and dry for at least six hours.

Once the glue has set firm, slacken off the spindle clamps, withdraw the long-bolts, remove the 'G' clamps, cauls and slip wedges. The complete back/ribs' assembly can now be removed from the mould, but exercise care as the turn-buttons are still locked 'on'. *Do not* pull the assembly out of the mould, as you could fracture the glue join or overhanging waste edge or a rib. It is best, as previously described in Chapter 1, to gently lever up the workpiece with a 9mm chisel between the ribs and baseboard until the ribs are clear of the turn-buttons. Once free of the mould, the back should have its centre-join reinforced with the transverse-grained strips you have already prepared.

GLUING IN THE BACK'S CENTRE-JOIN REINFORCEMENT

The internal reinforcement strips for the back's centre-join must now be cut to size and glued in. Because the transverse bars BB1, BB2 and BB3 are keel-shaped in section it will be difficult to measure the exact dimension between them, unless you possess calipers that measure internally. You can use thin paper strips about 125mm long to press into the spaces between the bars with a fold one end pushed into place with a fine pencil point; then use these paper templates to transfer the sizes to the

Fig 93 The back/ribs' assembly complete.

strips. Thus mark the lengths and square a line across with the try-square to scribe the ends; now cut them to size. Because the grain on these strips is transverse, a chisel cut will tend to follow the latewood line, which may not be square, so use the razor saw cutting just undersize. It is important that the strips are scribed to fit the bars neatly – they should give the appearance (when fitted) that the bar is notched over them; these reinforcement strips can be seen through the soundhole on the finished instrument, so execute this particular fitting with great care (*see* Fig 93).

Fit the strip between the tailblock and bar BB3 first. Align it so it lies dead on the centreline and stick some strips of masking tape each side of it to guide it in place when it gets glued in. Do this for the strips between bars BB3 and BB2 and between bars BB2 and BB1. Use the C3 PVA glue applied in an even coat to the flat underside of the strips and press them into place with a piece of off-cut softwood by their ends – not their middles – or they may snap on a grain line. The moisture in the adhesive will make the reinforcement strips swell slightly and bow up, losing the adhesive join, so have some suitable small, heavy objects ready to hold them down until the adhesive grabs (the head of a 2kg club hammer is useful). Leave the back/ribs' assembly somewhere warm for one hour, after which the reinforcement strips should have stuck firm. Pick off any unwanted bubbles of adhesive with the 25mm chisel before it hardens. Peel off the masking tape either side of the reinforcement strips and clean up the back. The work to complete the back/ribs' assembly is now complete, and nothing further needs to be done until the neck has been fashioned and is ready for fitting and gluing to the body. The neck ends of the ribs are still over-long for a very good reason, so leave them like that. The body mould can be put aside as it will not be required until you reach the stage where the bindings need to be heat bent and clamped into the mould.

8 THE NECK AND FITTING

aving selected your material for the neck as described in Chapter 4, lightly plane each side and block plane the end grain, so every line of grain can be scrutinized. The grain direction on the cut ends must be as shown (*see* Fig 94) and check the run of the grain for best 'figure' lengthwise. If the end grain is not parallel to the sides, then choose the face with the best radial grain for the side of the neck that will be facing the player (*see* Fig 95). If you are constructing a left-handed instrument, then the best radial face grain should be chosen for the opposite side.

The neck material will need to be planed with the smoothing plane until straight and true, with the sides squared to the face. Set the plane iron low so that there is less chance of tearing out divergent grain and the awkward 'flaming' and 'ribbon' figure

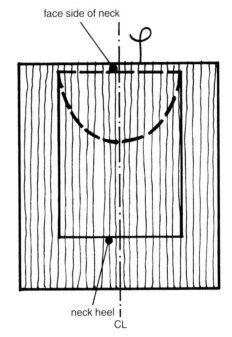

Fig 94 The neck's end grain alignment and section.

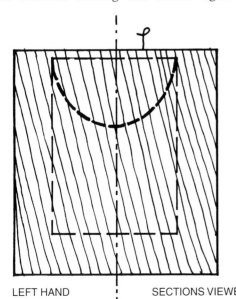
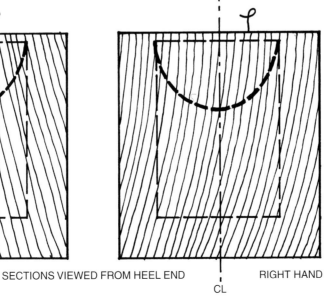

LEFT HAND   SECTIONS VIEWED FROM HEEL END   RIGHT HAND

Fig 95 The radial and tangential grain appearance.

often encountered with sycamore and mahogany. Check each face with the straight-edge and try-square as you proceed to plane; this is no mean task and it may take you quite some time. The face-side (top) of the neck material – the surface that will have the fretboard glued to it – must be absolutely straight and level.

Once you are content that the planing has done the best job it can, the face-side of the neck should be checked for 'winding'. For this operation you will need two winding sticks, which can be made from a machined square section, for example, 150mm long pieces of 9 × 9mm mahogany. Dye one stick with black ink. Now mark onto the neck's face-side (from the neck template) the positions of the zero-fret and 12th (or 14th) fret

with the marking knife and try-square, then place the neck material on the bench, face-side up, so the end grain of one end is facing you. Now place on a black winding stick at the zero-fret line and the other plain one at the 12th (or 14th) fret line as shown (*see* Fig 96). Ensure that they are lying square across the neck with a check from the try-square. Now position yourself about one metre away from the bench and kneel or bend down to bring your eye-line about level with the face-side of the neck, viewing the workpiece as shown (*see* Fig 97). Do the pair of winding sticks appear to have their top edges parallel with each other? If they do then you are either lucky or a natural born craftsperson. If the winding sticks indicate a 'wind' by not aligning parallel, then it's back

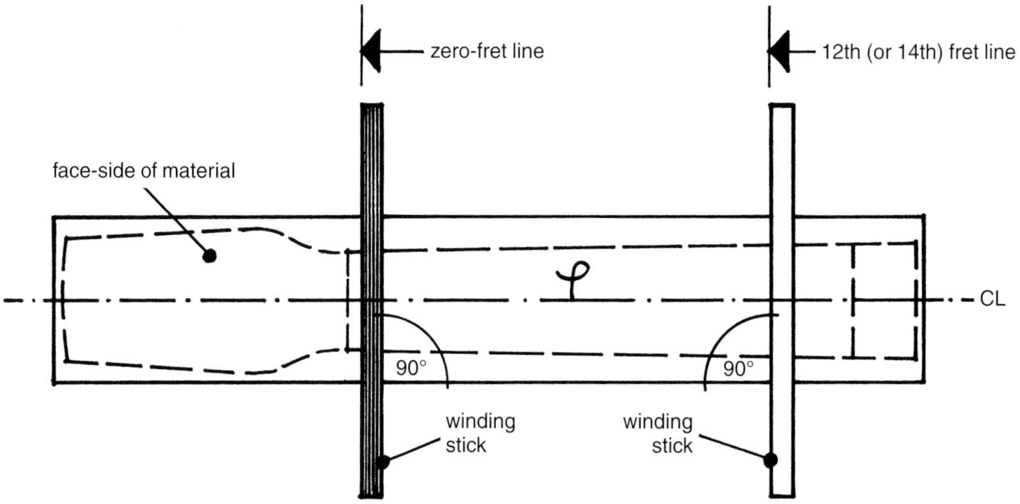

Fig 96 Align the winding sticks square on the neck's face.

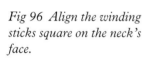

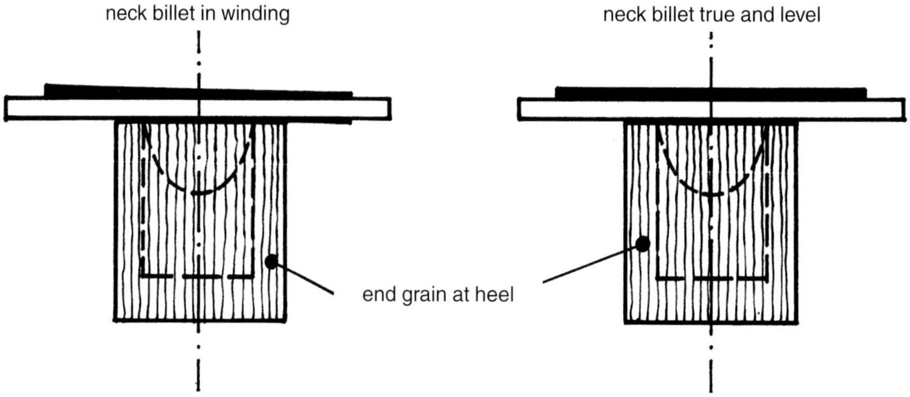

Fig 97 Sight across winding sticks for a true and level face

to some light planing with the smoothing plane again to remove the high spots to achieve a truly level face. Keep checking progress with the winding sticks and straight-edge: you may get rid of the 'winding' to discover the face-side is no longer straight! This can be a little frustrating, but persevere, the neck material has enough depth to permit you to plane off enough to get it square, level and straight. Do not trouble too much about the bottom face (underside) of the neck material; it does not need to be level or square as it becomes waste – you planed it initially to be able to view the run of grain to select the best grain aspect and check for any defects.

If you are making an octave mandola with a much longer neck than the mandolin, then it is doubly important to ensure there is no 'wind'. Optimum action for the strings will not be achieved if a wind is not corrected. If the zero-fret and 12th (or 14th) fret lines marked with the knife have been planed off, then reinstate them. Now you can mark on the actual neck profiles from the template to the sides of the neck, aligning the zero-fret and 12th (or 14th) fret positions exactly: use a fine, black, felt-tip pen. Measure and mark the centreline position along the length of the face-side (top) and score this line with the marking knife. The next stage is to cut the slot and fit the truss rod; this *must* be done now before any further fashioning of the neck material takes place.

FITTING THE TRUSS ROD

The truss rod is a very necessary addition to the neck. It will enable the neck to be slim in section to assist comfort of fingering and playability. It can also be adjusted to permit optimum action to be maintained, always. You can buy ready-made adjustable truss rods from luthiers' suppliers, or make up your own to the simple design as described below. The design of truss rod detailed is quite reliable and its reaction for the whole length of the neck is completed by the compressive element of the rosewood or mahogany cover fillet that takes on the role of a spine. No other woods will suffice as an alternative in this position. The truss rod itself acts as a 'tie', while the cover fillet acts as the 'strut': as the 'tie' is tensioned the 'strut' is compressed into bending, but it can only bend towards the 'tie', hence the neck will be pulled away from the bending moment caused by the other 'tie': the tensioned strings.

As stated in Chapter 2, the use of a truss rod can be the subject of argument: it adds weight to the neck, makes the neck less springy and may (or may not!) affect the acoustic qualities of the instrument. You may wish to omit a truss rod if you use hard sycamore and fashion the neck's cross-section deeper than specified. Sycamore will certainly resist the bending from string tension better than mahogany, but you risk making a neck that *may* take on a permanent set and its playability and action will deteriorate with time.

To fit a truss rod, mark out on the neck's face-side the slot width, length and recesses' centres according to the dimensions shown (*see* Fig 98). It is important to drill the recesses no deeper than shown and the slot for the truss rod to be excavated no deeper than dimensioned. Clamp the neck material horizontally in the bench vice, face-side uppermost, about 40mm proud of the worktop and drill out the peghead recess first with the 18mm diameter flat bit, using a depth gauge (if your drill has one) or by sticking some masking tape or a collar to the bit as a depth guide. Then drill out the neck heel recess using the 10mm diameter clean-cut bit. You must keep the drill bits perpendicular to the face-side by using mirrors set up on the bench or by use of a pillar drill or drill stand. If you are to use a hand-held electric drill, then beware of the sudden power kick as this may cause the bit to jump off the centre and chew up that immaculately planed face you have taken great pains to achieve. I do not recommend

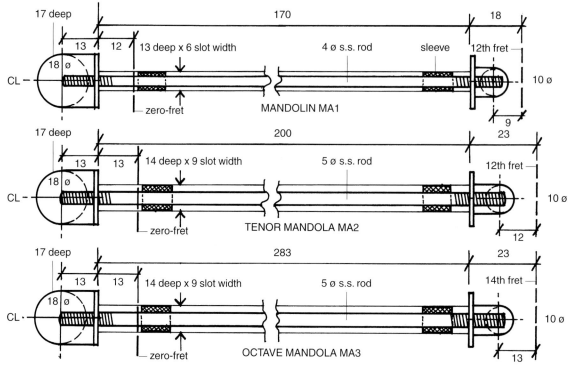

Fig 98 Details for the truss rod.

a hand-held electric drill unless it has a trigger-action variable speed control.

It is likely that the centre point of the 18mm diameter flat-bit will cut deeper than the recess depth needed. You will not discover this until the sequence where the underside of the peghead is cut out from the neck material (this hole can be drilled out to 5mm diameter and be filled later with a mother-of-pearl or abalone fretboard marker dot).

To cut out the slot for the truss rod you can use a power router, which is the easiest and most accurate method. The slot sizes specified are standard for 6 or 9mm diameter straight-cut router bits, obtainable from any DIY store. If you hire or borrow a power router and are unused to it, then get some practice trying it out on a few lengths of scrapwood to obtain and set the plunge depth required and get the knack of holding the router's fence firmly against the side of the trial workpiece as it cuts the slot.

It is always best to take several 'passes' with the router, locking the plunge depth a little more on each 'pass'. When you are confident you can handle the router, check that the fence is set so that the slot will be cut dead centre on the neck face and then cut out the truss rod slot, starting at the peghead recess and stopping at the neck heel recess. Stop the router motor when you have run one shallow pass *exactly* when the cutter is in the neck heel recess and *do not* remove the router for a second or subsequent pass until the cutter has stopped revolving. This is not just for your safety, but will prevent the cutter from chewing into a part of the neck it shouldn't. When you have reached the full plunge depth, measure to check the slot is deep enough and exactly to the dimension specified. The power router is the most suitable horse for this particular course and do not be afraid to have the revolution speed set fast: this cuts cleaner. It is important that the slot is straight and neat as the inserted hardwood truss rod cover fillet – to be fitted later – must be a good close fit before gluing in.

The next step is to cut out the two anchor plate slots that lie at each end of the truss rod slot. Use a 1.5mm diameter twist drill, boring a line of holes perpendicular to the neck's face, to the depth specified – use the masking tape wrapped around the drill bit to ensure you do not drill too deep – then 'burr' out to excavate the waste with the same drill bit, then use the 6mm chisel to pare the recesses' shoulders perpendicular.

Before you cut out the neck's profile, you must first fit the truss rod. This sequence is preferred as it strengthens the neck and it is easier – while still in block form – to fit the truss rod and glue in the hardwood fillet. Refer again to the previously mentioned Fig 98 for the truss rod dimensions and diameters. Use stainless steel (S.S.) rod or threaded studding (available from yacht chandlers if all else fails) with S.S. washers and hexagonal nuts. Brass hexagonal nuts are recommended for the adjustable peghead end of the truss rod as these cannot strip the rod's thread when being tightened. Fashion the S.S. washers into the shapes and sizes required for the anchor plates with hacksaw and file (see Fig 99). Then file or hacksaw a small slot in the top edge of

the anchor plates, so you can ensure they can be identified before being fitted in the slots the correct way up.

You will need to sleeve the truss rod with four 10mm lengths of polythene or rubber tubing to isolate it from the sides and bottom of the slot, otherwise it can rattle against the neck timber when strings are vibrating. The sort of tubing used for fuel line or aquarium ventilator apparatus is fine, although you may need to 'square off' the round rubber hose with a scalpel to make it fit snugly. Screw on two S.S. hexagonal nuts to one end of the rod and turn them against each other with spanners to lock them tightly together: this neck heel end must not come undone! Slide on an anchor plate, the four sleeves, another anchor plate and apply petroleum jelly (Vaseline) to the peghead end of the threaded rod, then two brass hexagonal nuts to complete the assembly. It is now ready to be inserted in the neck.

Mix up a teaspoonful of Araldite adhesive and apply this to the recesses' shoulders and into the anchor plate slots, then fit the truss rod, tapping in the anchor plates with a light hammer until the truss rod rests via its sleeves on the bottom of the slot. Clean off any excess squeezed-out adhesive with a 'cotton bud' to ensure no adhesive has contaminated the adjustable peghead

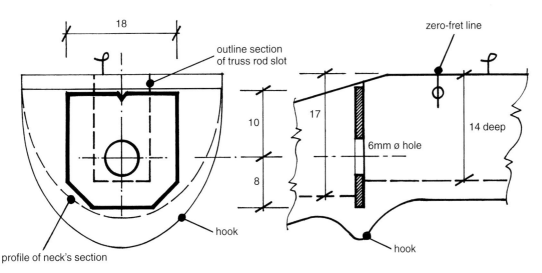

Fig 99 Details for the truss rod anchor plates.

end of the threaded rod. With the remainder of the adhesive, fill the neck heel recess fully to lock this 'fixed' end of the truss rod firmly to the neck timber. Now place the neck assembly somewhere warm for sixteen hours for the Araldite to set rock hard. In the meantime, prepare the rosewood or mahogany cover fillet from either a 6 or 9mm square machined section, according to the slot's width. This wood must be quarter-sawn, with the grain perpendicular to the face-side of the neck – otherwise it will not prove effective (*see* Fig 100).

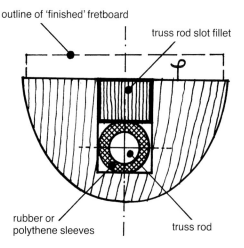

Fig 100 Section through neck.

outline of 'finished' fretboard

truss rod slot fillet

rubber or polythene sleeves

truss rod

BELOW: Fig 101 Open-ended spanners to fit brass hexagonal nuts.

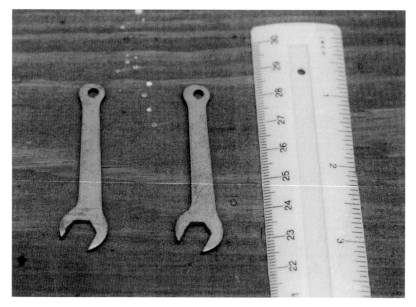

Once the adhesive locking the anchor plates in their slots has set, tighten the two brass hexagonal nuts until slight resistance is felt. The range of tiny spanners sold in car accessory shops will reach into the peghead recess (*see* Fig 101). The truss rod cover fillet should now be cut to length and glued into the slot. It must be a tight fit between the two anchor plates, so do not cut its length allowing any tolerance fit. If the fillet is rosewood then de-oil it with cigarette lighter fuel. Mix up a teaspoon of Cascamite adhesive and apply this to the sides of the slot with the small paintbrush, avoiding getting any on the actual rod; also apply adhesive to the tangential grain faces of the fillet. Now tap the fillet into the slot with an off-cut of softwood and a light hammer until it 'hits bottom'. Now leave the neck assembly in a warm place for at least six hours for the adhesive to set.

The fillet will, once glued in, need planing down to make it flush with the face-side of the neck; stop planing before you reach the actual neck material: the remainder of the proud fillet can then be scraped flush or be rubbed down level with the medium grit, 'free-cut' abrasive paper on the cork block. Check the face-side for straightness and winding again. The truss rod assembly is now complete and the side and face profiles of the neck can be cut out.

CUTTING OUT THE NECK PROFILES

The side profile of the neck is cut out first. If you have a band saw then this will make the next task quick, clean and trouble-free; otherwise a bow saw must be used to cut by hand, but this will take some time and great care, especially if sycamore is your chosen neck material. Always cut about 2mm *outside* the template outlines to leave enough waste material to be shaved off later for the final shaping. If using hand saws, clamp the neck material in the bench vice at whatever angle will aid you to always cut vertically;

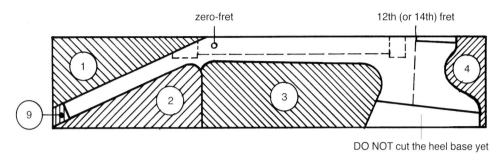

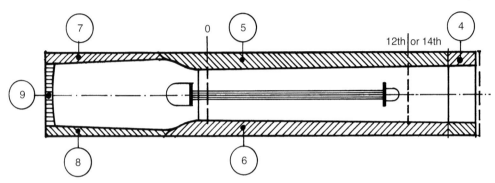

Fig 102 Cut out the neck's profiles in the sequences shown.

the eye prefers this alignment and you will always have gravity on your side.

Use a tenon saw to cut the peghead face first. The bow saw will cut out the remaining curved profiles. Keep the blades perpendicular to the sides of the neck as you cut to ensure the profile on both sides is identical. Check frequently that the blade is not running into the template outline on the side facing away from you. You can mount a mirror on the bench top so you can see both sides at once.

The advantage of the band saw is that it cuts quite perpendicular to the sides of the workpiece and quickly. It is important to cut out the profiles in the sequences shown (*see* Fig 102) otherwise you will be stressing the neck material unnecessarily.

As soon as you have cut out the reclining peghead face (1) then plane it down to the actual outline, true and level, using the block plane, then smooth with the medium grit, 'free-cut' abrasive paper on the flat cork block. Now you can cut out the back of the peghead (2). Once you have cut out the peghead, continue and cut out the back

of the neck from hook to heel (3) and then the instep (4). *Do not* cut or trim down the heel's base yet, nor the shoulder rebate for the belly – this is done later on. The side profile will now be completely cut out roughly as shown (*see* Figs 103 and 104).

BELOW: Fig 103 Side view: neck profile cut out on the band saw.
BOTTOM: Fig 104 Face view: neck profile cut out on the band saw.

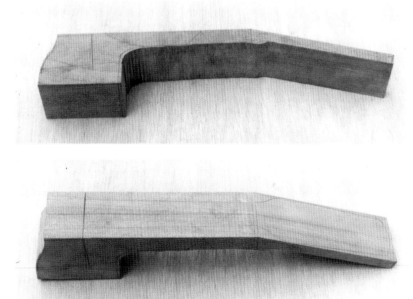

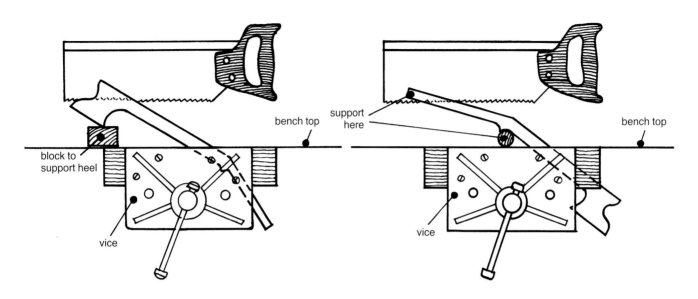

*ABOVE: Fig 105
Cut out the face profile:
heel to peghead.*
*ABOVE RIGHT: Fig 106
Cut out the face profile:
peghead end to neck.*

*BELOW: Fig 107 Final
neck shaping on 'arm'
clamped in vice.*

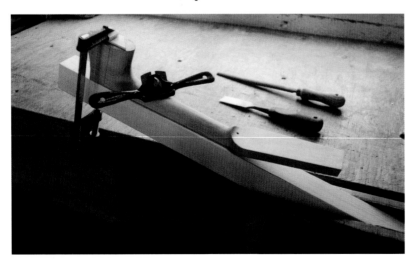

You may now cut out the face profiles of the neck. Clamp the neck in the bench vice and support with off-cuts of wood as shown (*see* Figs 105 and 106). Cut with the tenon saw and bow saw, in the sequences shown, again about 2mm *outside* the actual template outlines: use the tenon saw for the straight runs (5) and (6) and the bow saw for the curves at neck to head (7) and (8) and end of peghead (9) (*see* Fig 102 again). It is not advisable to cut out the face profiles with the band saw: there is no useful flat surface to the neck now to keep the workpiece level on the band-saw table.

The neck is now ready for final shaping using the spokeshave, chisel, block plane, and half-round file to remove the sawn edges down to the actual template outlines. The underside of the peghead does not get veneered so you need to do a neat job to achieve a level, finished surface. You will find the half-round file and 25mm chisel the most useful tools and they are the least likely to over-cut the neck material. The fashioning of the neck is not the easiest of tasks (some luthiers fashion the back of the neck when it is fixed to the body, but I recommend you do this while it is a separate workpiece). It is no longer a regular shape to clamp securely in the vice, however, so you must adopt a piece of pine, about 700mm long with a square, planed section of about 45 × 45mm, clamped in the vice at an angle of between 0 to 20 degrees to the horizontal, whichever gives you greater ease and access (*see* Fig 107) and 'G' clamp as shown on the heel. This will allow you to work on the back of the peghead, neck, hook and heel areas with two free hands. You will be rather surprised how quickly you can carve and file to shape; the heel of the neck will prove to be the most difficult area to carve. The use of an anglepoise lamp strategically placed to cast shadows

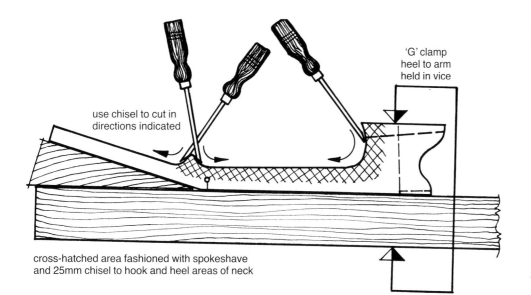

Fig 108 *Chisel carve these areas in directions shown.*

'G' clamp
heel to arm
held in vice

use chisel to cut in
directions indicated

cross-hatched area fashioned with spokeshave
and 25mm chisel to hook and heel areas of neck

BELOW: Fig 109 Side profile: neck fashioned to shape.

across the back of the neck will help you chisel, spokeshave and file this to an even 'D'-shaped cross section. Use the 25mm chisel in the cutting directions shown (*see* Fig 108). One useful tip: if you dampen the wood to the heel and hook areas, you will find the chisel cuts easier across this emergent grain; sycamore is so difficult in these areas, you need a little assistance to soften it up. Be careful with the spokeshave, especially with mahogany: it can tear out material rather too deeply if meeting divergent grain or areas where the hook and heel start to curve; use it for initial shaping but not for the final outline. The file is then used to dress the curved surfaces smooth, but they are not rubbed down yet.

The 'hook' should be well-finished and generous in its projection from the back of the neck: it makes an otherwise unattractive change of angle most pleasing and also forms the natural 'stop' for the player's hand in the first position. The thickness for the peghead needs to be about 14mm for all the instruments, with a finished thickness of about 16mm when the peghead veneer is applied. The best tools to finish the underside of the peghead are the spokeshave, half-round file, medium grit, 'free-cut' abrasive paper wrapped around a piece of broom-stick and on the flat cork block (*see* Figs 109 and 110). The sides of the peghead can be shaved straight with the block plane and the very end grain of the peghead filed and sanded down till silky smooth.

Fig 110 *Back view: neck fashioned to shape.*

The sides of the neck and heel should be sanded straight and smooth to the pencil lines, then protected with masking tape. The instep of the neck heel that fits inside the soundbox should be filed and sanded to a smooth surface, showing off the quarter-sawn end grain. The finished width of the neck at the heel *must* be complete before the shoulder slots are marked on and cut. The next job is to prepare and fit the peghead veneer as this will protect the face edges of the peghead from bruising or splintering; it is also easier to drill out the holes for the tuning machines while the neck is yet to be fitted and glued to the soundbox.

THE PEGHEAD VENEER

Select a head veneer from attractive quarter-sawn material as suggested in Chapter 4. Plane it to about 2mm thickness by clamping it to the bench top, *see* Chapter 2, Fig 35 again, and rub it down on both faces with the medium grit, 'free-cut' abrasive paper on the flat cork block. Use the peg-

head template to mark out the shape using a white crayon if the wood is dark (*see* Fig 111). Leave plenty of waste on the nut end of the veneer as this will be scribed and cut off only when the fretboard has been fitted. Cut out the shape, allowing about a 2mm waste margin outside the template outline, using the fret saw on the 'V'-shaped cutting board (*see* Fig 112). Also mark on the cut-out for access to the truss rod recess: trace the actual recess from the peghead and transfer this to the veneer and cut out with the fret saw and dress the edges with the half-round file. If using rosewood as a peghead veneer then de-oil it with cigarette lighter fuel before gluing on.

To glue and clamp up, you will need two off-cuts of MDF board cut to the approximate shape of the peghead; these will act as pressure plates (cauls) to spread the action of the 'G' clamps to ensure the veneer is glued evenly and tightly to the peghead. Mix up some Cascamite adhesive – about 1 teaspoonful – and brush it thinly on to the face of the peghead and the underside of the veneer. Clamp the neck in the vice

Fig 111 The peghead template.

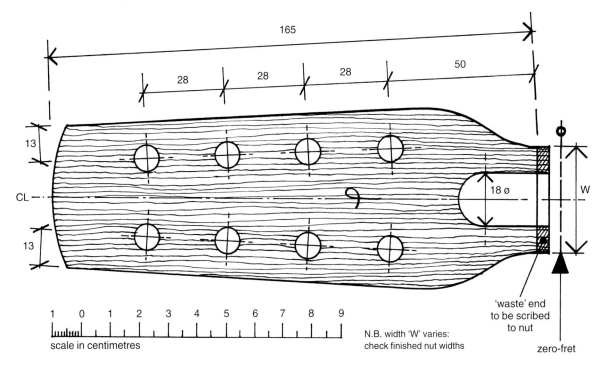

Fig 112 The peghead veneer marked and cut

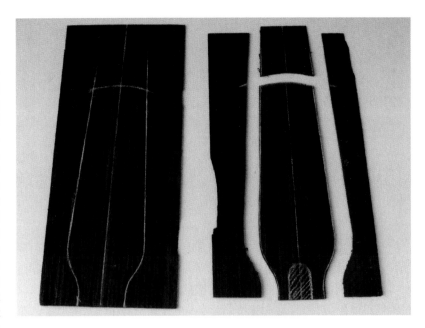

vertically and apply the veneer to the peghead and hold it in place until you succeed in placing the MDF cauls either side of the peghead and get two 'G' clamps on to hold the whole assembly together (*see* Fig 113). Check, before you tighten up the clamps, that the waste margin of the veneer is overhanging the peghead edges all the way around and then clamp up using as many 'G' clamps as you can fit on the peghead and tighten them up very tight, until excess adhesive is squeezed out. Wipe away the adhesive oozing out of the edges with a 'cotton bud' – this is tricky because the clamps get in the way, but any adhesive left on will get planed off once it is set without staining the woods. Now leave the neck with its veneered peghead clamped up, somewhere warm, for six hours.

When the adhesive has set rock hard the next task is to remove the clamps and cauls and trim the waste edges off the veneer so they are flush with the sides of the peghead. Clamp the peghead in the bench vice to expose the edges you need to plane. A block plane is perfect for the long straight edges and the 25mm chisel for the curves, shaving or paring with the grain always until you are on the template outline – but do not 'finish' these edges yet: the final rub down takes place later. Now is the time to mark on and drill out the holes for the tuning machines.

DRILLING THE HOLES FOR THE TUNING MACHINES

If you have chosen to fit the individual, high-quality tuning machines, then the peghead template hole centres are correct; do

Fig 113 Gluing and clamping on peghead veneer.

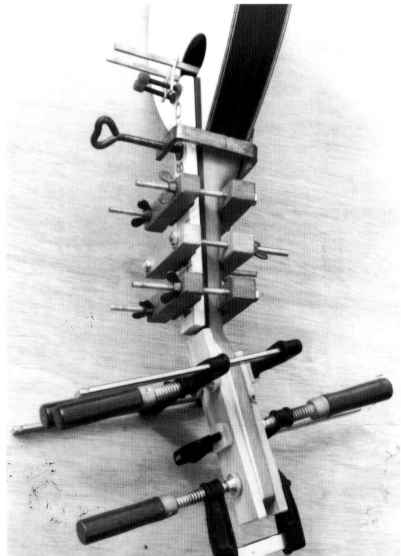

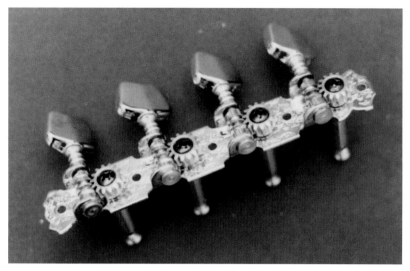

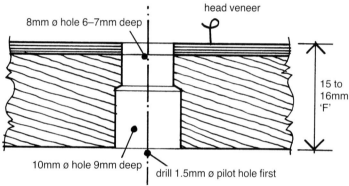

head veneer

8mm ø hole 6–7mm deep

15 to 16mm 'F'

10mm ø hole 9mm deep

drill 1.5mm ø pilot hole first

TOP: *Fig 114 Four-on-a-plate tuning machines.*
ABOVE: *Fig 115 Detail for drilling peghead for fitting 'minis'.*

the vice jaws. Mark on the four hole centres to each half of the head veneer with a bradawl point or centre-punch, so there is no chance of the drill bit wandering. Now use a 1.5mm diameter 'clean-cut' drill bit to make a pilot hole all the way through the peghead. If you do not have a pillar drill or a drill stand, then use two mirrors placed on your bench to view the drill: it must be held quite perpendicular to the peghead face. Now, according to the type of tuning machines you will fit, use a 'clean-cut' drill bit to the actual diameters specified (*see* Fig 115). Start with the drill in *reverse*, on a low revolution speed to score a clean edge to the hole, then drill out in forward gear, slowly, until you are about halfway through the peghead; *do not* drill completely through as the emerging bit will tear the underside face to shreds. Turn the peghead over and now drill from the back face to complete the holes. With the individual tuning machines the holes need to be 'shouldered' so you will have to drill different diameter holes from each face to meet as dimensioned. If your drill does not have a depth gauge, then wrap a piece of masking or insulating tape around the shank at the depth required.

If you are to fit the four-on-a-plate type, then the holes must be drilled for the diameters of the bushes or collars, not the string posts. Do not omit the collars as these prevent the string posts from wearing the holes in the peghead into an oval shape, which allows the worm gears to get slack and cause tuning difficulties. Having drilled out the holes, then rub down the peghead veneer and the underside of the peghead with the medium grit, 'free-cut' abrasive paper (on the flat cork block) to silky smoothness so the holes have good, neat edges (*see* Fig 116). Some luthiers do not drill the holes in the peghead until the neck is fitted to the body and the finish applied, but it is easier and more convenient to drill while the neck remains separate: it can be clamped in the vice so that it is steady and secure, leaving two hands free. This means

not make them any closer. If your choice is the four-on-a-plate type, then purchase these *first* and check the centres of the string posts – they are usually around 25mm centres, but not always! (*see* Fig 114). Do not be mean when it comes to selecting tuning machines: the cheaper ones wear fast and will not hold the strings in tune, which is a common grumble among mandolinists, and if you replace them later with something better you may find the hole centres will not accommodate the new string-post centres. A handmade instrument deserves good tuning machines: *see* Chapter 13 for types which are suitable and recommended.

To drill out the holes, clamp the neck, peghead face upmost and horizontal, in the bench vice. You will need a scrap of MDF to place under the peghead to rest on top of there is less chance of unintentional vandalism occurring and the advantage of having the holes drilled prior to finishing will permit a rod or bar to be passed through the peghead to hang up the complete assembled instrument when the finish is applied: in one full coat, all over, which saves much time and effort. *Do not* fit the tuning machines until Chapter 13.

FITTING THE NECK TO THE BODY

The neck is now ready to have the shoulder slots, heel angle and the shoulder rebate for the belly marked on and cut in this sequence before gluing to the body (soundbox). The measuring and cutting must be undertaken with great care and great accuracy. Follow the template angles and allow a good margin for waste: the design of the 'through-neck' connection is simple and robust but the jointing surfaces must be absolutely accurate for neck angle (tiller) and finished dimension. The process is best

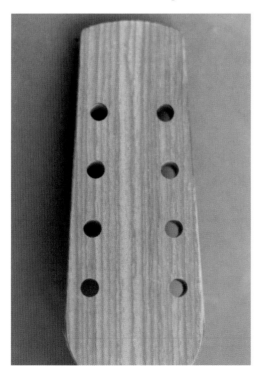

done on the principle of 'take a little off and offer it up for fit'. There is a margin for slight adjustment in this designed joint and true alignment to the centre axis is quite achievable as the gluing and clamping up of the neck heel to the body permits a final check. Do not assume the neck template will give you the exact depth for the neck heel; every instrument will differ slightly at the shoulder's depth and will test your skill.

Before you mark on the shoulder slots on the neck heel, remove the masking tape that protected the rubbed down 'finished' width. Take the sliding bevel and adjust the angle to correspond exactly with the angle of the slots given on the template in relation to the face-side (top) of the neck. Mark these angles on to the side faces of the neck so they correspond precisely with the 12th (or 14th) fret position and score them on with the marking knife (*see* Fig 117). Repeat this angle to mark the width of the slots so you know exactly where the saw-blade will cut. The shoulder slots are deliberately cut over-wide so that the ribs can be glued and wedged tight up to the 12th (or 14th) fret line to create a fine join where the neck meets the shoulders of the body. Use the razor saw to cut these slots as follows (*see* Fig 118): clamp the neck in the bench vice so the peghead is pointing to the floor at an angle of about 45 degrees with the vice jaws holding the heel area, with at least one slot accessible for cutting. Hold the razor saw vertically and you will be about the right angle. Mask the outside of the 12th (or 14th) fret line on the sides of the heel with two or three layers of masking tape; this not only protects the finished side of the neck from an unwelcome slip of the saw but will help guide the saw-blade into the scored line until you get the saw 'going'. *Do not* over-cut the depth of the slots: 8mm is enough, otherwise you will weaken the neck here.

Once you have successfully sawn down both cut lines, use the fret saw or piercing saw to insert down the slot and cut across

Fig 116 Peghead drilled for string posts.

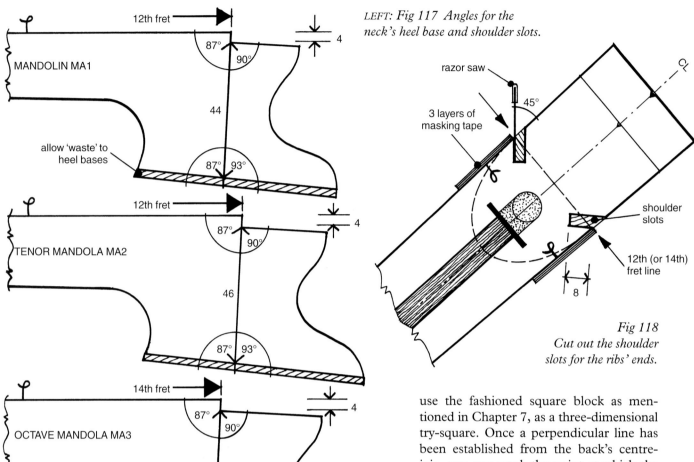

LEFT: *Fig 117 Angles for the neck's heel base and shoulder slots.*

MANDOLIN MA1

allow 'waste' to heel bases

12th fret

87° 90° 4

44

87° 93°

TENOR MANDOLA MA2

12th fret

87° 90° 4

46

87° 93°

OCTAVE MANDOLA MA3

14th fret

87° 90° 4

53

87° 93°

10 0 10 20
millimetres

razor saw

3 layers of masking tape

45°

CL

shoulder slots

12th (or 14th) fret line

8

Fig 118
Cut out the shoulder slots for the ribs' ends.

the base to remove the waste. Now remove the neck and re-clamp it in the vice so the peghead points towards the floor at about 45 degrees again, with the heel held firm to make the other slot accessible for cutting. Once both shoulder slots are cut you must scribe the waste ends of the ribs to fit into these slots, so the neck will fit onto the body by sliding down over the ribs' ends. The best method, to avoid any guesswork, is to use the fashioned square block as mentioned in Chapter 7, as a three-dimensional try-square. Once a perpendicular line has been established from the back's centre-join, you can mark the point at which the neck's finished width 'W' at the 12th (or 14th) fret will coincide with the ribs, using the corner of the block as aligned (*see* Fig 119). Half the dimension 'W' can be pencilled to the belly's edge of the ribs, which will be the actual line of the shoulders. It is important, once you have established the finished neck width/rib join, to mark a line at 90 degrees to the top (belly) edge of the rib and then add 7mm, which will give you the amount of rib to fit (allowing for tolerance) into the shoulder slots, *see* Fig 119 again. Now you may trim off the waste end of the ribs with the razor saw with the body (back downwards) on the hide mat, holding steady the ribs with one hand to prevent them from being stressed as you cut. The next step is to trim the neck's heel base to the template angle but allowing a waste

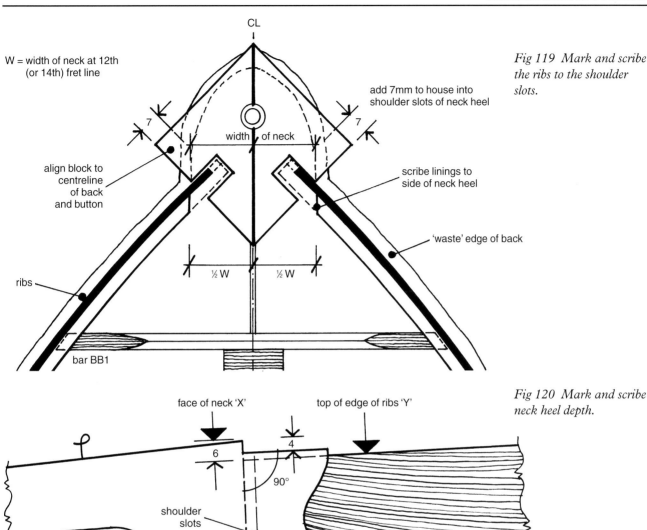

W = width of neck at 12th (or 14th) fret line

CL

add 7mm to house into shoulder slots of neck heel

7   7

width of neck

align block to centreline of back and button

scribe linings to side of neck heel

'waste' edge of back

ribs

½ W   ½ W

bar BB1

Fig 119 Mark and scribe the ribs to the shoulder slots.

face of neck 'X'   top of edge of ribs 'Y'

6   4

90°

shoulder slots

'waste' to heel base

2

back

trim off 2mm to 'fit' heel to ribs' depth

Fig 120 Mark and scribe neck heel depth.

margin to be removed to scribe and fit the heel's depth to the exact depth of the ribs.

Mark on with sharp pencil, the heel's base angle as shown (*see* Fig 120) which will be the template line given. Now mark on a line parallel, about 2mm outside, to allow for waste. Clamp the neck in the vice so the heel end points upwards and the line you have marked is vertical. Saw to this line using the tenon saw – you have now cut the correct angle of the heel, but you will need to 'fit' it. Remove the neck from the vice and offer the neck to the body by sliding the heel's shoulder slots over the ribs' ends until the neck heel base sits on the back's linings. Mark this width of the neck heel to the linings with a sharp pencil and scribe the linings so that they fit to the sides of the neck heel accurately: the razor saw and the 6mm chisel are best for this fiddly detail. The heel base should now slide down to fit to the inside of the back. There should be a little play so that you can align the 'V' cut on the centreline of the heel's base with ease, with just a millimetre or two of sideways play. If one trimmed rib end pushes the neck off the centreline then remove the neck and trim a little more off that rib's end to allow an accurate axis alignment.

Clamp the neck to the body using a caul and 'G' clamp, as if the two were glued up, and measure the distance between the top edge of the rib 'Y' and the top edge of the neck face 'X', that in the example shown on Fig 120 is 6mm. Now subtract 4mm for the belly's shoulder rebate and you have the exact dimension of waste to trim off the heel (2mm in the example) to make the heel 'fit' the shoulders. Now trim off the waste of the heel's base, using the block plane, adhering religiously to the original template angle; so clamp the heel, base uppermost in the vice and plane down to the 'fit' line – then rub flat and smooth the heel's base with the medium grit, 'free-cut' abrasive paper on the flat cork block. Now you can cut out the 4mm deep shoulder rebate, which has its belly face at 90 degrees to the shoulder slots:

clamp the neck heel in the vice so you always cut vertically and use the tenon or dovetail saw, then finish with the 25mm chisel, bevel uppermost, to clean off the saw marks and get the faces true and flat; the rebate edge must have a neat, straight cut dead on the 12th (or 14th) fret line: use the square-edged flat file to achieve a good face here. File a small 'V' notch to the neck centreline at the heel end and shoulder rebate end: these are register points for axis alignment. The next task is to glue on the neck to the back of the soundbox.

GLUING THE NECK TO THE BODY

Check the 'fitted' neck angle (tiller) to the body before mixing up the adhesive. The method shown (see Fig 121) will allow you to establish that the required bridge height can be achieved, so clamp the neck heel to the body using two 'G' clamps and a caul: the fixed jaws of the clamps should hold the flat area of the shoulder rebate (see Fig 122). Before tightening the clamps, align the neck's centreline at the heel base with the back's centre-join and check the ribs are tight up to the slot edge on the 12th (or 14th) fret line, in other words, as though

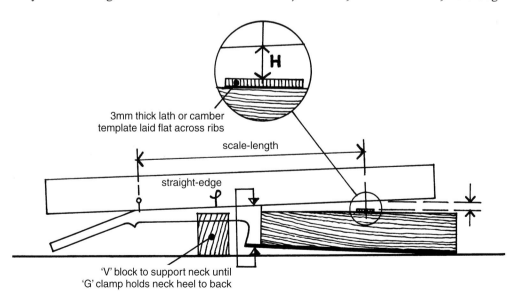

Fig 121 Checking the neck's angle (tiller) to body.

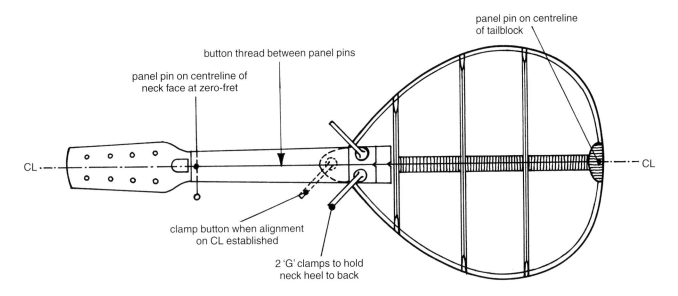

panel pin on centreline of tailblock

button thread between panel pins

panel pin on centreline of neck face at zero-fret

CL

CL

clamp button when alignment on CL established

2 'G' clamps to hold neck heel to back

already glued and clamped up. You may now hold the handle of one of the 'G' clamps in the bench vice and rest the neck in the 'V' block near the heel as shown on Fig 122. Next, clamp a straight-edge to the face-side (top) of the neck so the straight-edge continues to overhang the body past the bridge position (scale-length) and span the body width with the camber template – laid flat – so it simulates the belly at the bridge's position. Mark on the scale-length to the straight-edge with a pencil or piece of tape. Measure the dimension 'H' perpendicular between the straight-edge and 'belly'; if the neck angle is correct then the following dimensions will prove satisfactory: Mandolin 'H' 7 to 8mm; Tenor Mandola 'H' 8 to 9mm and Octave Mandola 'H' 10 to11mm. (These 'H' dimensions allow for the 4.5mm doming, fretboard thickness and string action.) If the dimension actually measured does not lie within the recommended range, then you will need to trim the heel base angle a little more: less angle to reduce 'H', or more angle to increase 'H'.

The last procedure before gluing on the neck is to arrange an easy way to get the centreline aligned so that the body and neck are glued together exactly on the long axis of the instrument. The method shown on

Fig 122 is simple and adequate: drill a 1mm diameter hole in the tailblock's top on the centreline and another in the truss rod fillet at the zero-fret position. Insert a 25mm panel pin about 10mm deep into each hole and tie a length of red button thread tightly between the heads of the panel pins – you will now see if the alignment is correct by checking whether the 'V' notches to the shoulder rebate and base of the neck heel lie under the red thread; if they don't then slacken off the 'G' clamps holding the neck to the body and adjust as necessary. Now you have completed the 'dress rehearsal', you are ready to glue on the neck. Remove the thread, clamps and neck.

Mix up about half a teaspoonful of Araldite adhesive – de-oil the area to be glued up on the inside of the back if the back is rosewood, using cigarette lighter fuel on a clean rag. Apply the adhesive to the base of the neck heel and fit it to the body, sliding it via the shoulder slots over the ribs' ends. Clamp up the neck to the back using the 'G' clamps and a caul – see Fig 122 again – and tie on the red thread between the pins and check the centreline axis. Ease off the clamps and adjust, as required – you have plenty of time to get the axis alignment spot on, as Araldite takes

Fig 122 Aligning the neck/body to the long axis.

Fig 123 Glue and wedge the ribs into the shoulder slots.

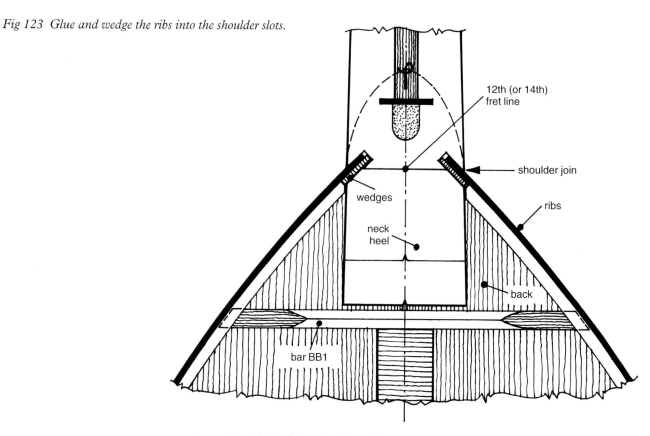

some time to 'grab'. You may find the adhesive will cause the neck/back join to slip about, so leave the red thread in place until you have the clamps tight and the adhesive has squeezed out. Now remove the thread and get another 'G' clamp and two cauls and clamp the neck tightly to the button area of the back. Hang the assembly up by the peghead somewhere warm and dry for at least sixteen hours for the adhesive to set rock hard and be careful that you do not knock the body when hanging it up: this could put the neck off the centre alignment! You will no doubt be wondering why the ribs' ends have not been glued and wedged into the neck's shoulder slots as well: this particular task is best done separately.

Remove the clamps and cauls and lay the instrument on its back on the hide mat, with the peghead overhanging the end of the bench and the neck supported by the 'V' block. Fashion two off-cuts of the ribs' material into slim wedges, as shown (*see* Fig 123). The grain *must* be perpendicular to the ribs' grain. Using a small amount of Araldite adhesive, slide a scalpel or thin knife blade to open up the (previously unglued) join of the back and ribs between the bar BB1 and the shoulder slots and brush in the adhesive here, also into the join between the lining ends and neck heel and into the shoulder slots either side of the loose ribs, then tap the small wedges into the shoulder slots with a light hammer, forcing the ribs tight against the slot edges coinciding with the 12th (or 14th) fret line. The Araldite will aid the insertion of the wedges as it is slippery before setting. When the adhesive has been allowed to set for sixteen hours, use the razor saw and 6mm chisel to trim the wedges flush with sides and face of the neck heel and clean off any bubbles of excess adhesive. Now the linings and belly can be fitted.

9 FITTING THE LININGS, BELLY AND BINDINGS

The linings for the belly/ribs' join should now be scribed to the tailblock's notches and the sides of the neck heel. The method is identical to the fitting of the linings to the back/ribs' join as described and detailed in Chapter 7. Offer the lining with the 30 degree angle cut end into the tailblock shoulder and then mark and scribe the angle to the neck's side face; trim this a little over-long and offer it to the neck's side: it must be a good tight fit. If it will not fit, then razor saw a little off until it does fit snugly (*see* Fig 124). Do exactly the same for the other lining. Now you can glue in the linings with Cascamite adhesive; if the ribs are rosewood, then de-oil the gluing surfaces first, as mentioned before. Allow the top edge of the linings to be glued on just proud of the ribs' edges as you clamp up from tail to neck with the clothes-peg clamps (*see* Fig 125) and place the instrument somewhere warm and dry for at least six hours for the glue to set hard.

Follow the same procedure as in Chapter 7. *See* Fig 86 again, to shave down the jointing surfaces to the linings and ribs' edges with the block plane to the slight

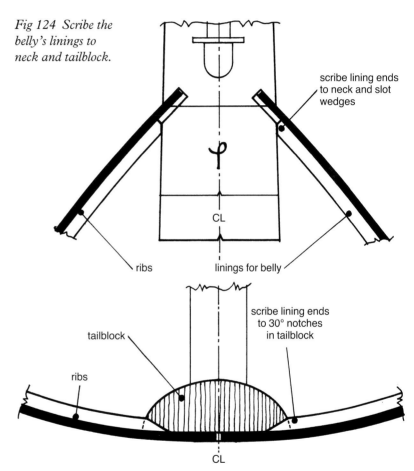

Fig 124 Scribe the belly's linings to neck and tailblock.

scribe lining ends to neck and slot wedges

ribs

linings for belly

scribe lining ends to 30° notches in tailblock

tailblock

ribs

CL

Fig 125 Glue and clamp on the belly's linings.

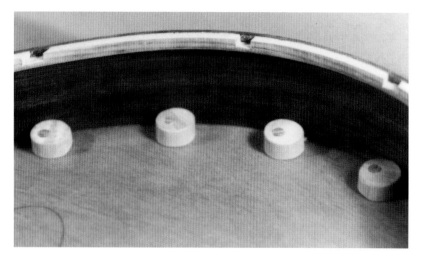

angle required to accommodate the belly's doming. The linings will need to be marked up and notched for the belly's bars B1, B2 and B3 (*see* Fig 126). In all respects the method of marking and notching are identical to the back's bars BB1, BB2 and BB3 so refer back to Chapter 7. Ensure that you align the centre-join of the belly with the centreline of the neck and tail, and position the belly's waste edges at least 3mm overhanging the ribs' faces all the way round when you mark on the bars' positions.

Once the notches are cut, trim back the over-long ends of the bars 3mm inside and parallel to the line of the ribs' faces (*see* Fig

Fig 126 Notch the linings for the belly's bar ends.

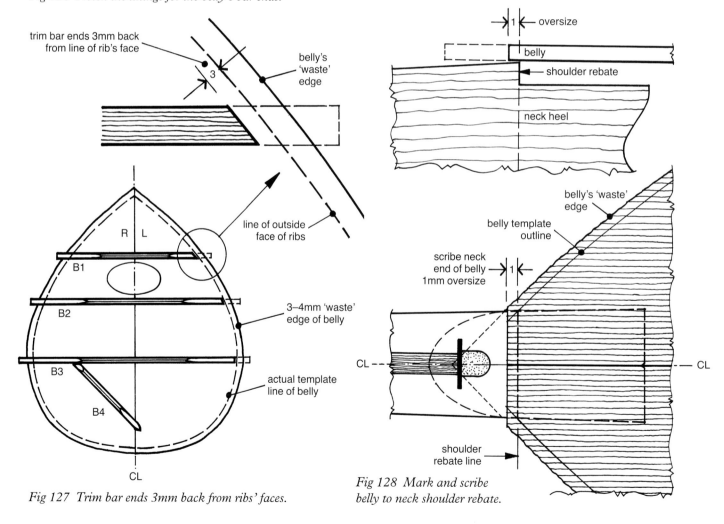

Fig 127 Trim bar ends 3mm back from ribs' faces.

Fig 128 Mark and scribe belly to neck shoulder rebate.

127). Now offer the belly to the body and check the bars' ends seat perfectly into the linings' notches and the join between belly and ribs is good and tight all round; check the tailblock/belly area to ensure this join is good: take a little material off the tailblock's end grain with the medium grit, 'free-cut' abrasive paper on the flat cork block if necessary to effect a tight join. Bar B1 will not seat into its notches as the shoulder end of the belly has not yet been scribed into the shoulder rebate. This must be done now, so mark on in sharp, hard pencil a line on the belly parallel to the shoulder edge but 1mm beyond it (*see* Fig 128) and mark this line with the knife. Remove the belly from the body and place it on the hide mat and put a waste block of wood about 13 to 15mm thick under the belly's shoulder end to support it while you razor saw to the knife line. Take note that the cut edge should be 90 degrees to the belly's face. The belly's length must be 1mm oversize to make it a tight compressive fit into the shoulder rebate to maintain the longitudinal doming and brace the neck. Offer the belly to the body again, fit in the bar ends and now press down the neck by the zero-fret position to flex the body (gently) until the newly scribed shoulder end of the belly drops into the rebate. Take the pressure off the neck and check the fit. If it is OK, then you are ready to glue the belly to the body. If the scribing is not tight, then remove the belly and use the medium grit, abrasive paper on a wooden block to dress the cut end until it fits perfectly. *Do not* cut this shoulder joint short as any piece infilling the gap will be visible even when the fretboard is glued on. Now remove the belly and place it out of harm's way.

It is this moment when the inside of the soundbox should be cleaned up: pick off rogue glue lumps and brush out the shavings and wood dust. Now you may glue in your maker's label – use C3 PVA to stick this in and allow one hour for the adhesive to set. You have a choice of two internal sealers: lemon oil, or water-based clear

matt varnish. Apply just one coat of whichever sealer you prefer to the inside of the back, the centre-join reinforcement strip, the bars, linings and convex face of the tailblock. Once this has dried, you can prepare to glue the belly to the soundbox.

GLUING AND CLAMPING ON THE BELLY

Use C3 PVA or Titebond adhesive for the belly/soundbox joint. Apply the adhesive evenly with the small artist's brush around the top of the linings and rib edges, into the linings' notches and to the shoulder rebate and shelf and to the end grain of the tailblock. Ensure there are no 'dry' joints, or the belly will rattle or buzz when played. Now fit the belly – flex the neck down gently so the scribed shoulder fits in the rebate – and clamp up from tailblock to neck with the cello clamps (*see* Fig 129). Do the clamping up quickly and evenly; not too much pressure otherwise you may bruise or split the waste edges of the soft spruce: just enough to close the joint and squeeze out a consistent line of glue. Place the instrument in a warm dry place for at least two hours.

To trim off the waste edges of the back and belly, use the foam mat folded into a 'U' shape to cushion the vice jaws and hold the soundbox lightly in the vice, with just enough pressure to stop it slipping about;

Fig 129 Use cello clamps to glue belly to instrument.

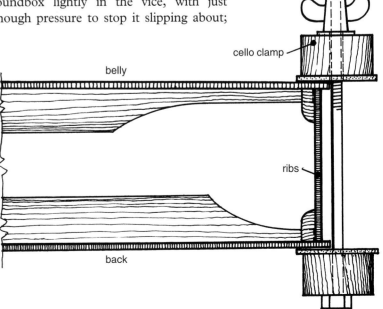

belly

cello clamp

ribs

back

you will need two free hands to pare off the waste edges with the 25mm chisel. Start with the back, paring in the directions shown with the grain always (*see* Fig 130) and keep the sole of the chisel flat to the ribs' face. Now trim the belly's waste edges off as well. Where the belly is concerned, it is advisable to pare down with the chisel *almost* to the ribs' face, then finish with the flat cork block and medium grit, 'free-cut' abrasive paper; this is because the edge grain of the spruce tends to lead the chisel to trimming a 'washboard' effect, that can show up on the ribs' face as well.

The 'button' of the back will still be ragged with waste edges ready for trimming

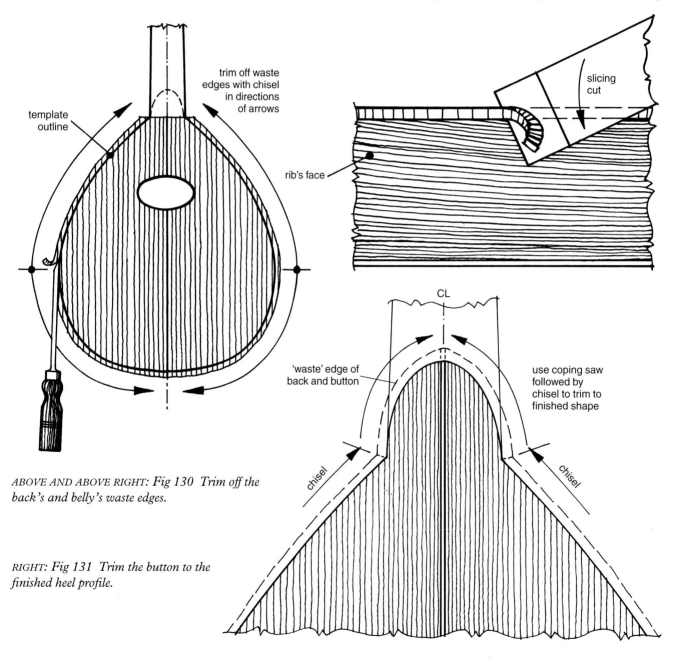

ABOVE AND ABOVE RIGHT: Fig 130 Trim off the back's and belly's waste edges.

RIGHT: Fig 131 Trim the button to the finished heel profile.

to the neck heel. This area is a little difficult to work, although the 25mm chisel, used bevel downmost, is the tool for this task. You may find the coping saw will get into the internal angles of the shoulders and the chisel will pare off the remainder as shown (*see* Fig 131). You may wish to fashion the button and neck heel to a lancet-shaped point – similar to the classical guitar – as shown (*see* Fig 132) or round it off to the shape of half an ellipse, using the soundhole template's small radius.

Once all the waste edges have been trimmed off, give the belly, back and ribs a light rub down with the medium grit, 'free-cut' abrasive on the cork block. Rub down *across* the grain of the belly and back, but *with* the grain on the ribs. It is now you must aim for the finished thickness (F) of the belly and you can do this by taking complete long passes with the sanding block to avoid 'dishing' the material in the centre: do not rub back and forth as though you are scrubbing a table top. Keep an eye on the end and edge grain of the belly to gauge progress. The final thickness (F) should be at 2.75mm to the bass side (left) and 2.5mm for the treble side (right). *Do not* rub down the neck or peghead areas yet, but get the soundbox smooth, with neat edges and any excess glue patches removed, as the next step is to mark and cut the rebates for the bindings to belly/ribs' join and, if you wish, the back/ribs' join.

REBATING AND GLUING ON THE BINDINGS

Having selected the bindings you wish to use, measure them for depth and width; the rebates to be cut to house the bindings will be cut undersize to the actual bindings, as the best technique is to fit on the bindings so they project beyond the finished faces of the belly, ribs and back; they can be scraped down flush once the glue is set, that is just like normal inlay work as in Fig 133. You may use any of three alternative methods to cut the rebates, depending on how well

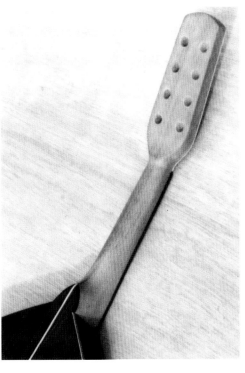

Fig 132 The button, neck and back bindings finished.

equipped your workshop is. I recall reading an excellent book on Spanish guitar-making that stated at this juncture '... now pare out and glue in the bindings ...' but neglected to instruct: 'how?' Well, you can use: (a) the purfling cutter adjusted to score on the right depth and width, then pare out to line with the 6mm chisel and dress with

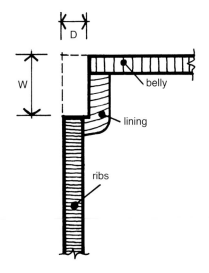

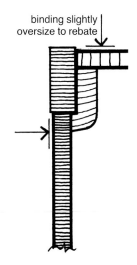

Fig 133 Detail of the bindings' section and rebate.

the edge of a flat file; or (b) the home-made scratch-stocks made from off-cuts of mahogany, a couple of stainless steel nuts, bolts and washers, and broken pieces of hacksaw blade ground square (*see* Fig 134); or (c) the electric hobby drill with a small milling cutter and shouldered collar, which is a standardized rebate fence for guitar bindings, but not necessarily correct for anything else. The scratch-stocks (b) work well, once you have fine-tuned the position of the blades to cut the rebate size exact – practise on some straight runs of waste material and offer the binding for fit: it only needs to be a little proud.

Whichever tools you use, the shoulder's area will be the most difficult to rebate consistently: use the 6mm chisel to shape the rebate where the scratch-stock will not aid you at the junction of neck to ribs. Keep the scratch-stock or purfling cutter fences tight to the body as you draw the cutting blades

around the curves *with* the grain always, as you did with the chisel; *see* Fig 130 again for directions of cut. *Do not* use any abrasive paper on a hardwood block to fashion the bindings' rebate: it rounds off the sharp edges making an invisible glue join between the body and bindings difficult.

The rib ends in the shoulder slots of the neck heel will need to be cut out just enough to fit in the end of the bindings, so they effectively scribe into the slots for a depth of about 2mm (*see* Fig 135). This is a tricky area to work on as it is easy to damage the sharp edge of the slot. The neatest method is to use the scalpel to cut into the ribs' material for the thickness of the binding and then excavate the waste with a twist drill the same diameter as the binding's thickness, 'burring' the waste out.

You will need to cut the bindings to the length of the rib template and soak them in scalding hot water for 10 to 15 minutes

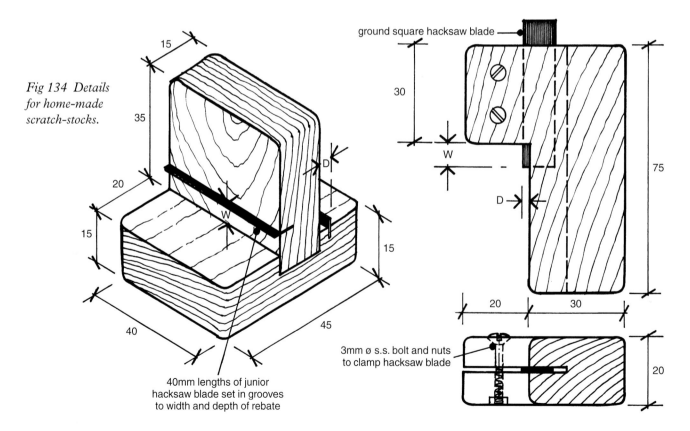

Fig 134 Details for home-made scratch-stocks.

ground square hacksaw blade

40mm lengths of junior hacksaw blade set in grooves to width and depth of rebate

3mm ø s.s. bolt and nuts to clamp hacksaw blade

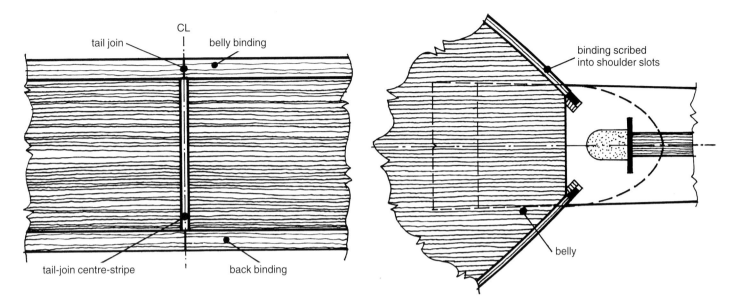

before you can bend them to the ribs' pro-file: when still hot and pliable, lock them in the body mould with the turn-buttons, allow them to dry out and then remove them: scribe one end of each binding square and true with a vertical chisel chop or the razor saw. Prepare about forty strips of masking tape about 50mm long and stick them on the steel rule by one corner and lay the rule on your bench within easy reach; you are now ready to glue in the bindings. Start with the belly rebate: glue in these two first as they will protect the soft spruce edges.

Mix up Cascamite adhesive – you will need about two teaspoonfuls – and apply the adhesive liberally to the inside faces of one binding, then push the square end of the binding into the shoulder slot and hold it tightly in place with a piece of masking tape; continue to fit the binding around the curve of the belly, squeezing it into the rebate as you stick on the tape, working around to the tail. Do not scribe the tail-join end yet. Glue and tape on the other belly binding and when you reach the tail-join then scribe accurately, with the razor saw, both meeting ends dead on the centreline as shown, *see* Fig 135 again. If the masking tape tears as you wrap it around the edge

between belly and rib, then just ignore it and apply another piece of tape over it.

Scribe and glue on the bindings to the back (if you are going to bind the back) as you have done for the belly. Make a good job of the centre-join of the bindings at the tail – this detail does not get hidden by the tailpiece! When all the bindings are glued in leave the instrument to hang up by the peg-head in a warm dry place for at least six hours. The next task is not so simple – you have to remove the masking tape without ripping the soft earlywood from the face grain of the belly: peel off the tape from the ribs first and then peel off diagonally on the belly spruce (or at right-angles across the grain) *gently* – don't pull upwards, pull backwards – as you would a 'Band-aid' sticky plaster on the back of a hairy hand! Now use the plain steel scraper to remove the excess glue and shave down the bind-ings flush with the belly, ribs and back faces. Now give the belly, ribs and back a gentle rub down with the medium grit, 'free-cut' abrasive on the flat cork block to remove all glue stains, grubby marks and to round off slightly the sharp edges of the bindings. Hang up the instrument by the peghead and proceed to Chapter 10 to fashion the fretboard shim and fretboard.

Fig 135 Scribing the bindings at tail-join and shoulders.

10 THE FRETBOARD AND SHIM

The fretboard material requires a fair amount of planing from the sawn strip of ebony, rosewood or rock maple you have chosen. It is necessary to plane it to thickness before any face-side (top) is dimensioned. You can, if the material is supplied large enough for a classical guitar, saw off the edges that can later be used as material for truss rod slot fillets, but leave the long edges absolutely parallel to each other and the face width wider than the finished fretboard at the 20th fret position.

When both long edges have been planed straight and parallel the fretboard needs to be thicknessed, but the cross section is not rectangular: the bass side of the fretboard is thinner than the treble side, as shown (*see* Fig 136). The reason for this seemingly inconsiderate detail is to compensate for the strings' varying gauges, thicker on the bass side and thinner on the treble – to allow for the correct action to be maintained the fretboard is planed thinner on the bass side. The alternative compensation would be to have a higher bridge saddle on the bass side; this is usual on factory-produced instruments and steel-strung guitars, but the increase in bridge height one end creates a greater 'break' angle for the bass strings, that increases the pressure on the bass foot of the bridge. Paradoxically, this extra pressure is not desirable as it attenuates the belly dynamics for the bass range; as we know from Chapter 3, the low notes need all the help they can get. It is not difficult to hand-plane the tapered thickness.

Use a bench stop and plane with the block plane as it will not tear up any wild or wavy grain as much as the smoothing plane. Make sure the plane iron is razor sharp. The thickness should be reduced to the dimensions shown on Fig 136; keep the face of the fretboard straight – check with the straight-edge constantly as you work down to finished thickness. Utilize the cabinet scraper for final dressing: this will give you smooth and level faces, so you can decide which is best for face-side and underside. Now rub both faces lightly with the medium grit, 'free-cut' abrasive paper on the flat cork block until the colour and surface is even. Leave the fretboard overlong. Mark on in crayon or pencil the centreline (long axis) and the finished width of

Fig 136 Details for fretboard widths and sections.

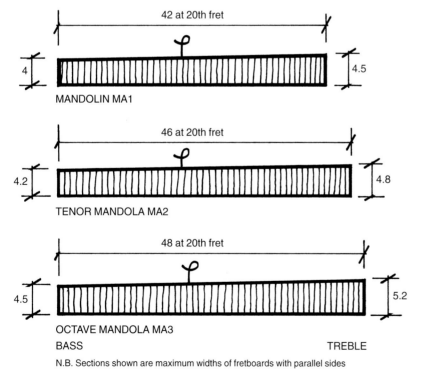

N.B. Sections shown are maximum widths of fretboards with parallel sides

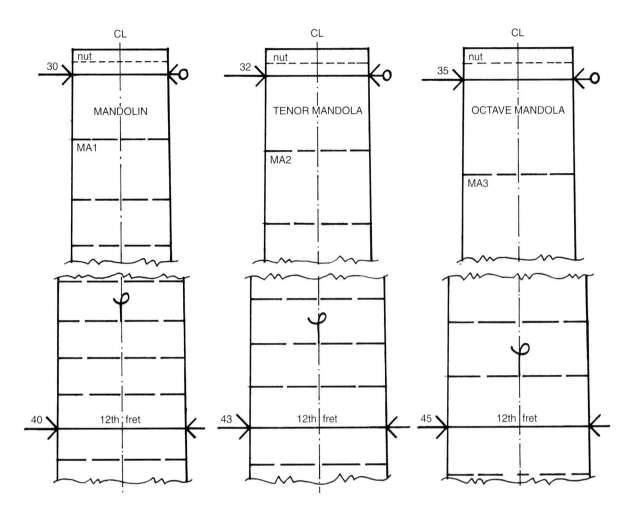

Fig 137 Fretboard face widths at nut and 12th fret.

the fretboard from the dimensions shown at zero-fret and 12th fret positions (*see* Fig 137). Score on the finished width lines with the marking knife. Now you must decide whether you will use the scale-lengths recommended or increase them slightly; if you do desire a longer scale to aid playability then you may calculate your fret positions from the formula: 1.059463 for twelve tones of equal temperament to one perfect octave.

As the '1.059463 formula' gives the distance from theoretical bridge to fret, this can be a problem as the fret positions are marked on and slotted before the fretboard is fitted and glued to the neck. The method recommended for greatest accuracy is to measure the fret positions from the zero-fret always; so to calculate the spacings for your own desired scale-lengths, use the following formula: scale-length divided by 1.059463 = distance from bridge to 1st fret, then: distance from bridge to 1st fret divided by 1.059463 = distance from bridge to 2nd fret and so on. Once you have calculated each fret dimension from the bridge, then subtract each of these figures from the scale-length to give you the zero-fret to fret dimensions. For example: scale-length 352.99mm divided by 1.059463 = 333.18 mm, then: 352.99mm minus 333.18 = 19.81 mm, being the distance from zero-fret to 1st fret.

See Figs 138, 139 and 140 for fret spacing tables for instruments MA1, MA2 and MA3.

MANDOLIN MA1
FRET SPACING TABLE   SCALE – LENGTH 353 mm
ACTUAL SCALE-LENGTH FOR CALCULATIONS IS 352.99MM FOR A 20-FRET MANDOLIN

Fret	Dot mark between	Distance from bridge in mm	Distance from zero-fret in mm	Individual space between frets in mm
0		352.99	00.00	00.00
1		333.18	19.81	19.81
2		314.48	38.51	18.70
	*optional			
3		296.83	56.16	17.65
4		280.17	72.82	16.66
	★			
5		264.45	88.55	15.72
6		249.60	103.39	14.84
	★			
7		235.59	117.40	14.01
8		222.37	130.62	13.22
9		209.89	143.10	12.48
	★			
10		198.11	154.88	11.78
11		186.99	166.00	11.12
	★★			
12	join at body/neck	176.49	176.49	10.50
13		166.59	186.40	9.90
14		157.24	195.76	9.35
	★			
15		148.41	204.58	8.82
16		140.08	212.91	8.33
	*optional			
17		132.22	220.77	7.86
18		124.80	228.19	7.42
	*optional			
19		117.80	235.20	7.00
20		111.18	241.81	6.61

Fig 138 Fret spacing tables for mandolin MA1.

TENOR MANDOLA MA2
FRET SPACING TABLE   SCALE – LENGTH 420mm
ACTUAL SCALE-LENGTH FOR CALCULATIONS IS 419.78MM FOR A 20-FRET TENOR MANDOLA

Fret	Dot mark between	Distance from bridge in mm	Distance from zero-fret in mm	Individual space between frets in mm
0		419.78	00.00	00.00
1		396.22	23.56	23.56
2		373.98	45.79	22.24
	*optional			
3		352.99	66.78	20.98
4		333.18	86.60	19.81
	★			
5		314.48	105.30	18.70
6		296.83	122.95	17.65
	★			
7		280.17	139.61	16.66
8		264.45	155.33	15.72
9		249.60	170.17	14.84
	★			
10		235.59	184.18	14.01
11		222.37	197.40	13.22
	★★			
12	join at body/neck	209.89	209.89	12.48
13		198.11	221.67	11.78
14		186.99	232.79	11.12
	★			
15		176.49	243.28	10.50
16		166.59	253.19	9.90
	★			
17		157.24	262.54	9.35
18		148.41	271.36	8.82
	★			
19		140.08	279.69	8.33
20		132.22	287.56	7.86

Fig 139 Fret spacing tables for tenor mandola MA2.

The fret positions should now be marked on using the spacings according to your instrument's scale and calculations or to the tables given herein for scale-lengths. The zero-fret to fret dimensions are less likely to permit an accumulative error creeping in and creating havoc with the intonation: a wrongly cut fret slot results in the fretboard becoming material to be used to make cover plates for truss rod recesses. There are two ways to mark on the fret lines: mark directly to the fretboard edge, or make up a template from rosewood with the slots cut in one long edge with the razor saw (*see* Fig 141); the template is much preferred and will save time when you make more instruments: it is clamped to the fretboard and then a knife nick transfers the slot in the template to the fretboard face or edge. Whichever method you choose, mark on the nut face line and fret lines with great accuracy using the steel rule and a nick in the edge of the template (or fretboard) with the scalpel. Now measure everything again, precisely, checking zero-fret to fret dimensions and individual fret-to-fret dimensions to double-check – I give all these on the fret-spacing tables – and use the try-square to score on the lines across the fretboard at 90 degrees: this is more accurate in achieving frets that are quite parallel to each other, rather than by trying to use the sliding bevel on the finished edges of a tapering fretboard. At some stage you need to hold the fence of the try-square to the other long edge when you reach about the 12th fret position. *Do not* cut the fretboard to finished length yet, or fashion the soundhole end.

CUTTING THE FRET SLOTS

You will need a fretting saw blade that will cut the slots so they are a good grip to the tangs of the frets. Refer to Chapter 11 for the recommended sizes of fret-wire for the

OCTAVE MANDOLA MA3
FRET SPACING TABLE   SCALE – LENGTH 530mm
ACTUAL SCALE-LENGTH FOR CALCULATIONS IS 528.90MM FOR A 21-FRET OCTAVE MANDOLA

Fret	Dot mark between	Distance from bridge in mm	Distance from zero-fret in mm	Individual space between frets in mm
0		528.90	00.00	00.00
1		499.21	29.68	29.68
2	*optional	471.19	57.70	28.01
3		444.75	84.15	26.44
4	★	419.78	109.11	24.96
5		396.22	132.67	23.56
6	★	373.98	154.91	22.24
7		352.99	175.90	20.98
8		333.18	195.71	19.81
9	★	314.48	214.42	18.70
10		296.83	232.07	17.65
11	★★	280.17	248.73	16.66
12		264.45	264.45	15.72
13		249.60	279.29	14.84
14	join at body/neck ★	235.59	293.30	14.01
15		222.37	306.53	13.22
16	★	209.89	319.01	12.48
17		198.11	330.79	11.78
18	★	186.99	341.91	11.12
19		176.49	352.40	10.50
20		166.59	362.31	9.90
21		157.24	371.66	9.35

Fig 140 Fret spacing tables for octave mandola MA3.

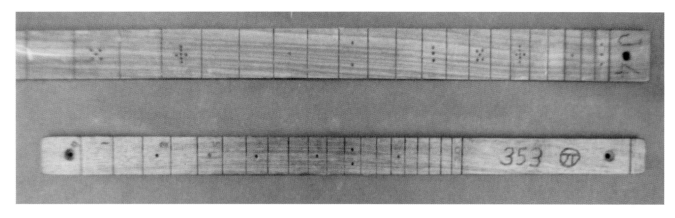

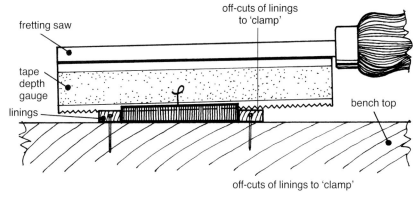

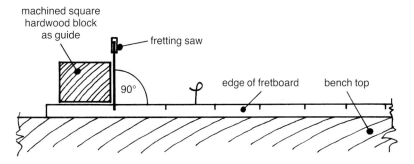

off-cuts of linings to 'clamp'

TOP: *Fig 141 Fret spacing templates made from off-cuts.*
ABOVE: *Fig 142 Cut the fret slots with the fretting saw.*

sides of the slots. When you are satisfied the slots' width and depth match the tangs of the fret-wire, then make up a clamp from the two lengths of linings that you didn't use (or break) to hold the fretboard to the bench top as shown (*see* Fig 142) while you cut the slots. Stick on a strip of masking tape to the saw blade's sides to give you an accurate line to indicate the depth of the cut that should be *just* a little deeper than the depth of the fret's tang. Try this as a 'dress rehearsal' before you slot for the zero-fret proper. Find a piece of machined-square block of hardwood about 50mm long: this will be used as a guide to hold against the side of the fretting saw blade to keep the blade perpendicular to the face of the fretboard, but only when you have got the saw cut 'going'. The fret slots *must* be kept perpendicular to the fretboard face. *Do not* use a junior hacksaw or coping saw to cut the fret slots, even if they do slot the width perfectly – the fretting saw is 'hard-backed' for a good reason: it cuts the slot true and its base even and level.

Start the saw cuts with the razor saw following in the knife-scored lines using the try-square blade edge as a guide; this initial cut will aid the wider fretting saw blade to keep to the line. A saw blade leaping out of the line and cutting into the face of the fretboard is disastrous: you cannot disguise a saw cut that shouldn't be there; you may be able to scrape off minor scuffs from the fretboard face, but saw cuts are, I am afraid,

range of instruments covered in this book. Try a waste-end of the fretboard to slot and tap in a length of fret-wire – it should tap in with short, light hammer blows but not be so loose that the fret springs out of the slot. If hammering violently is required to get the fret to seat in, then the fretting saw blade is not wide enough: try a wider gauge blade.

Do not use candlewax or any lubricant to ease the saw blade in the slots: this will pre-vent the frets from being gripped by the permanent. Use the fretting saw with firm, long strokes, cutting more with the 'pull' of the saw rather than the 'push'. Lift the blade out frequently and remove dust and any oily resins from the slot with a broken piece of junior hacksaw blade: the edge without the teeth. Any dust or grit left in the slots may prevent the frets from seating in properly. Once the twenty-one (or twenty-two) slots are cut, clamp the fretboard in the bench vice and you can now plane down the long edges of the fretboard to the finished width lines, straight and true. The fretboard must be fashioned to finished size *before* it is glued to the neck and shim, so cut the nut's face line perpendicular to the fretboard's face, true it up to a clean line with the flat file and offer the fretboard to the neck and body so the zero-fret and 12th (or 14th) fret positions align to the neck mark and shoulders

THE FRETBOARD SHIM

This particular thin wedge-shaped spacer fits between the underside of the fretboard and the belly. Because the neck angle – and fretboard – does not lie in the same plane as the belly, the fretboard would not be supported if it were not for the shim. The shim also permits the fretboard to be removed (when it has worn) and replaced without damage to the belly's soft spruce; this is another advantage of the raked angle (tiller) of the neck.

The shim is not the easiest component to fashion, so you will need to make up a simple block with a 'stop' (*see* Fig 143) to plane the shim to the wedge shape. Shims are best made from Brazilian mahogany because it is a stable, lightweight wood and its moisture movement is small. Select a quarter-sawn

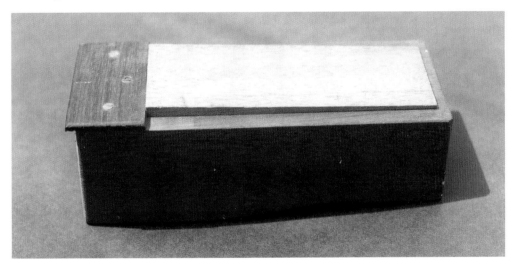

Fig 143 The shim planed to size on the shim block.

respectively; then scribe the soundhole end of the fretboard to the soundhole's finished edge, cutting the curve to the end grain with the fret saw and filing smooth with the half-round file. This exposed end has got to be neat and well-finished, so finish it with the medium grit, 'free-cut' abrasive paper. Do not be mean with the 'spare' length of the fretboard beyond the zero- and final fret: this must be not less than 4mm at any point, and no more than 7 mm.

off-cut: the grain direction must be radial to the face-side of the shim, in other words, the same as the belly and fretboard end grain. Plane the shim to the angle of the tiller, taken from the neck template, and plane it over-size long and wide but to about 1mm thick at the 'thin' end. Clamp the fretboard into its correctly aligned position to zero-fret and shoulders; offer in the shim between the gap between the underside of the fretboard and belly. You will need to scribe the 'thin' end until it fits the shoulder rebate: according to theory the 4mm shoulder rebate has been partly filled with a belly material now about 2.6 to 2.5mm thick, so the 'thin' end of the shim will need to be scribed square and true to a thickness of about 1.5 mm, so the fit is tight when the fretboard is glued down. Mark on in hard, sharp pencil the lines of the long edges of the fretboard and the soundhole end to establish the face profile of the shim and plane or rub down these edges exactly to the fretboard; the shim *must* be fully fashioned in face profile before gluing onto the belly: it is impossible to finish these edges when the fretboard has been glued on. Now unclamp and remove the fretboard.

To ensure the shim does not distort the straight line of the fretboard – by being either too thick or too thin – it is strongly recommended you dowel and glue on the shim first, as shown (*see* Fig 144). Use

masking tape to prevent excess glue from staining the belly and aid accurate alignment, then glue it on with C3 PVA or Titebond adhesive and clamp up using cauls and two 'G' clamps to the neck heel area and two mini 'G' clamps to the soundhole end, the fixed jaws bearing via a strip of cowhide through the soundhole onto the underside of Bar B1 to avoid crushing the bar. Leave clamped up for at least one hour for the glue to set firm and then remove the clamps and cauls, pick off the squeezed-out glue bubbles with the scalpel and level the shim's face using the medium grit, 'free-cut' abrasive paper on the flat cork block, checking with a steel straight-edge that the finished face of the shim is dead level with the face of the neck. Your next task is to glue on the fretboard, but leave the masking tape in position around the shim to protect the soft spruce belly at the vulnerable margins of the fretboard end.

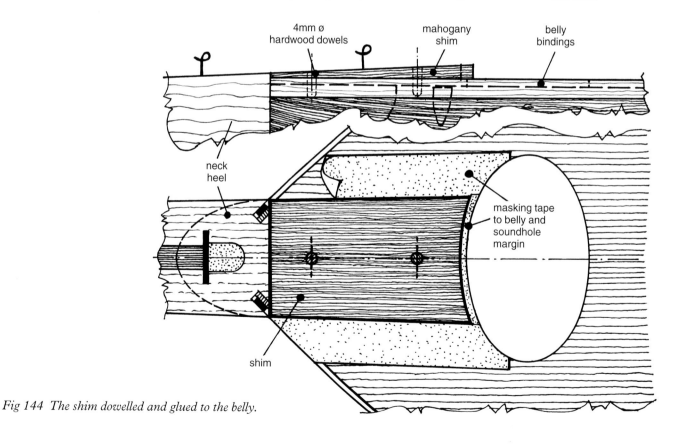

Fig 144 The shim dowelled and glued to the belly.

GLUING ON THE FRETBOARD

Before you glue the fretboard on, decide whether you wish to inlay dot position markers to the face of the fretboard. Traditionally, concert instruments have no position markers but dot markers are useful to the edge of the fretboard facing the player. If you are to fit position markers to the face then check out the various types from luthiers' suppliers – they come in all manner of shapes and inlays, with the simple circular mother-of-pearl or abalone dots being the most popular and easiest to inlay: you just drill a hole! The markers are placed between the frets to indicate the 3rd, 5th, 7th, 10th, 12th, 15th, 17th and 19th frets. Sometimes the 3rd is omitted. Fit the markers before gluing on the fretboard. Mark out their centres accurately and bradawl prick the centre to prevent the drill bit from wandering. Use 4 or 5mm diameter dot markers and the 'clean-cut' drill bits. Drill in reverse first to score the edge of the hole and then drill to cut the blind hole about 1mm deeper than the depth of the marker (they are usually no more than 2mm depth). Glue them in place with a dab of C3 PVA or Titebond to all positions, tapping them in with a light hammer, until they are *just* proud of the face of the fretboard. The fretboard is now ready to glue on.

Take great care when you glue on the fretboard as the wet adhesive does allow the mating workpieces to slip about until the clamps are firmly in place and the adhesive starts to grab. De-oil the underside of the fretboard with cigarette lighter fuel if it is rosewood. *Do not* fit the frets until the fretboard has been glued on; there are two good reasons why: the fret tangs will force open the slots and compress the top of the fretboard making it bow upwards, and secondly, the fretboard may not glue on absolutely flat to the neck, so some frets may be more proud than others, which is

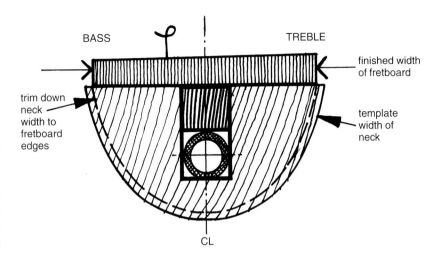

highly undesirable and will lead to unnecessary filing and redressing.

Use Cascamite powdered resin adhesive to glue on the fretboard: mix up enough with clean cold water and apply fairly liberally – there must be no hollow 'dry' areas. Then offer to the neck, aligning zero-fret and 12th (or 14th) fret positions and clamp up as previously shown in Chapter 8, Fig 113, including a piece of planed batten about 18 × 38mm and as long as the fretboard to act as a caul. Re-check the alignment to neck edges and fret lines once the clamps are tight. Now place the instrument in a warm dry place for at least six hours for the glue to set. Remove all the clamps and caul and now trim the width of the neck down to the finished edges of the fretboard, removing the excess glue squeezed out. The best tool is the 25mm chisel, bevel downmost, followed by the medium grit, 'free-cut' abrasive paper on the flat cork block to reach the section profile shown (*see* Fig 145). Be careful you *do not* trim off any of the fretboard edges whilst you fashion the neck to finished width – the fretboard was 'finished' when you glued it on (*see* Fig 146). Pick off any excess glue around the shim and soundhole area with the scalpel, and now carefully tease up the masking tape around the shim and sound-

Fig 145 The fretboard fitted and neck finished to width.

ABOVE: Fig 146 The fretboard rubbed true and level.
BELOW: Fig 147 A 'mask' to protect the belly when fretting.

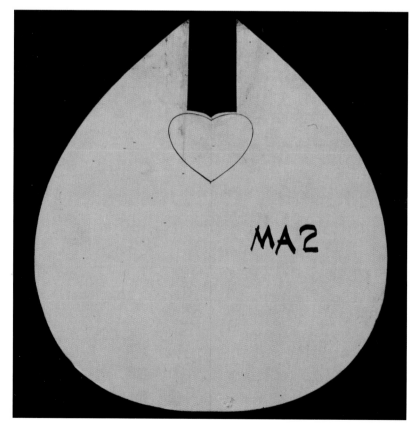

hole, pulling up backwards and diagonally across the grain to avoid tearing out any soft earlywood.

Before you progress to give the face of the fretboard a final rub down to ensure it is flat and level to the steel straight-edge, you will need to make a mask that will fit over the belly (to protect it from the fine oily dust of the rosewood, perhaps) and prevent the occurrence of any damage, scratches or dents to the white spruce while you fit and tap in the frets. The mask can be made from thin cardboard or thick paper, and scribed so it fits around the shim perfectly (*see* Fig 147). Tape the mask on with masking tape pieces about 50mm long stuck over the mask's edges and over onto the ribs. You are now ready to rub the fretboard true with the medium grit, 'free-cut' abrasive paper on the flat cork block; check the surface for straightness and use the winding sticks again to be quite certain. When the fretboard face is a silky-smooth consistent colour you are ready to fit the nut, frets and dot position markers (to the edge of the fretboard), but first clean out the dust from the fret slots with that broken piece of junior hacksaw blade.

11 NUT, FRETS AND POSITION DOTS

The nut – that on these instruments acts as a string spacer to the zero-fret – can be made from ivory, bone, brass, aluminium, coral, marble or whatever else is to hand as a hard material that does not fracture or split and can be cut, filed and polished to a fine finish. Bone is excellent, but does yellow with age; ivory is excellent and tends to stay white; the alloys will be harder to fashion to shape. Ebony is not recommended as a nut material because it is very brittle and can chip. Lignum vitae, the dense hardwood, can be used: it is self-lubricating to aid the strings to run smoothly through the slots! There are synthetic materials available from luthiers' suppliers such as Corian, that are dense, easy to work, stay white and do not distort. Beware of softer plastic materials: the strings will bite into them, they will distort and this means they lose the glue bond. Also, they do not glue well.

Use a small 'hobby' type vice screwed securely to one end of a 300mm length of 45 × 45mm planed square-section pine, utile or meranti (*see* Fig 148) which can be clamped in the bench vice; fix strips of cowhide to the metal jaws with Araldite adhesive to make them 'soft'. This type of vice is not expensive and is very versatile: an optional extra to allow you two free hands when fashioning the nut, tailpiece, bridge and bridge saddle.

Fashion the nut from the details in Fig 149. You will be cutting this from a larger 'blank' of the material. Cut the 'blank' to oversize with a hacksaw or band saw, then file it to shape, finish it with the medium grit, 'free-cut' abrasive paper on the flat cork block and then polish it with toothpaste, but leave it over-long, as you will scribe it to the exact width of the fretboard. Use the base width of the finished nut to scribe the peg-head veneer: cut *just* inside this line with the razor saw and chisel out any excess glue that has found its way onto the square-cut peg-head end of the fretboard. Push in the nut sideways into the slot; it should be a good sliding fit. If it is a reluctant fit, then use a fine flat file to take a little off the edge of the

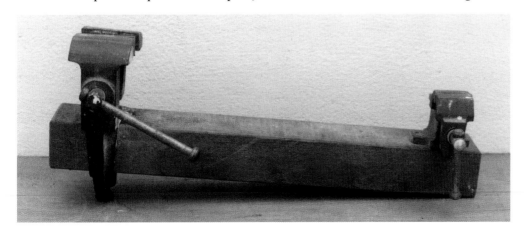

Fig 148 Small 'hobby' vices mounted on to wooden arm.

Fig 149 Details for the nut.

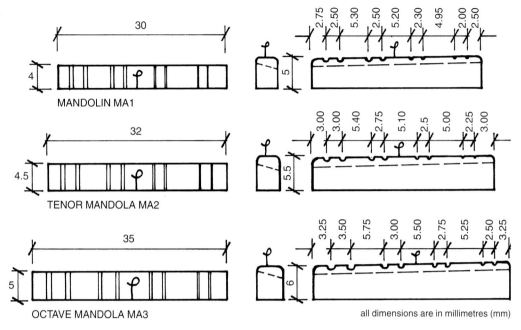

MANDOLIN MA1

TENOR MANDOLA MA2

OCTAVE MANDOLA MA3

all dimensions are in millimetres (mm)

peghead veneer. Offer the nut into the slot and scribe the ends to finished fretboard width, then rub smooth and polish these ends with toothpaste as well. Glue in the nut using a very thin film of C3 PVA and leave for about two hours to set hard. Do not mark and cut the slots for the strings yet: this is done after the frets are fitted.

FITTING THE FRETS

Firstly, ensure the belly mask is attached and leave it on until the text instructs otherwise. Guitar fretwire is too large for these instruments. Banjo fretwire is fine for the octave mandola MA3 and tenor mandola

MA2, but mandolin fretwire – the smallest section available – must be used for the mandolin MA1. The recommended sizes are as follows:

1.1mm wide ¥ 0.7mm high for mandolin;
1.6mm wide ¥ 0.85mm high for the mandolas.

Avoid buying coils of fretwire if you can; some manufacturers produce fretwire in about 500mm lengths, which *is* straight and not so dangerous. The coiled type is a large unmanageable spring which can stab you when snipping off lengths. If you can only obtain the coiled variety, then wear protective goggles when you handle it.

Cut the fretwire into strips about 7mm wider than the fretboard and lay them on your bench top in order of fitting: shortest to the zero-fret and longest to the 20th (or 21st) fret. The side-cut wire cutters are the best way to cut the individual lengths. Lay the instrument on its back on the cowhide mat and it is essential that the neck be supported by the hardwood 'V' block – used as an anvil in this role – under the zero-fret

Fig 150 Fret hammer and flush-cut wire snips.

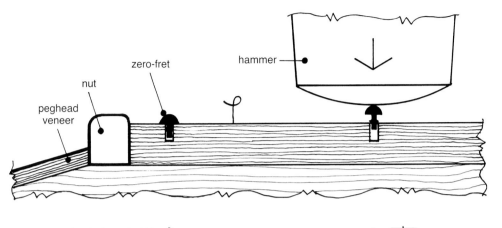

Fig 151 Tap frets into slots.

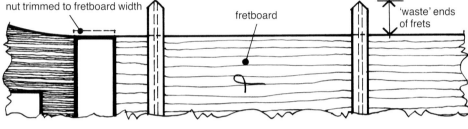

area. Because the nut has been fitted already (this is deliberate to prevent the fretboard end from shearing off when you tap in the zero-fret) you will need to use a piece of fretboard off-cut or any hard material about 6mm thick × 15mm wide and 75mm long to 'drift' in the zero-fret to prevent the hammer from bruising or chipping the nearby nut. A 'toffee' hammer is ideal for tapping in the frets and it already has a convex striking face (*see* Fig 150). Wipe on a very thin bead of C3 PVA adhesive to both sides of the tang of the fret and tap it into the fret slot from one side, working across the fretboard's width to the other, using light but sharp taps from the hammer. *Do not* tap in the middle of the fret first: the fret will distort and you will have difficulty getting it straight again. Ensure the zero-fret has seated squarely and tight to the fretboard face (*see* Fig 151). Now cut off the waste ends of the fret with the flush-ground side-cut wire cutters, shown on Fig 150, so they are almost flush with the sides of the fretboard. Then move the 'V' block to the 1st fret position and fit the 1st fret as before, but you will no longer require the 'drift':

take care not to hit the fretboard face as you do not want to have to remove dents. Do not hammer the frets so much that you start to flatten their convex profile.

Fit the other frets until you reach the heel of the neck; at this point you cannot use the 'V' block, so the button area of the neck

Fig 152 Dress the cut ends of the frets with the 'special' file.

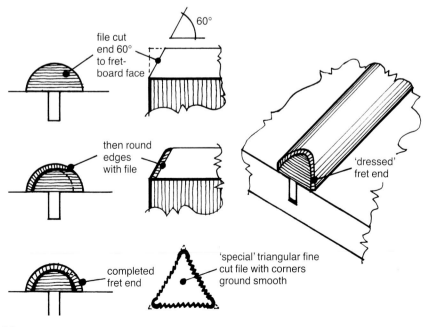

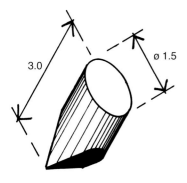

Fig 153 The fretboard edge dot markers.

needs to lie flat on the hide mat on a corner of the bench. You will need to tap in the frets from the 15th onwards with a little less force as there is only the shim, belly and bar B1 to support the fretboard here: use rapid, frequent and light taps to ensure the frets seat properly to the fretboard face. If you experience difficulty in this area, hold a 'dolly' to the underside of bar B1 as you tap in the 16th to 21st frets: the 'dolly' can be anything metal or heavy that will pass through the soundhole – a hammer head may suffice, but a roll of lead sheet about 35mm diameter and 60mm long is perfect.

The frets must now have their cut ends filed down flush to the fretboard edges and the domed edges dressed to an angle and rounded off with a small, fine triangular file specially prepared for this task: its toothed edges are ground down smooth – this detail ensures you only file down the fret ends and not the fretboard (*see* Fig 152). Use a fine cut flat file to grind the fret edges to the 60 degree angle, then the 'special' to dress the individual fret ends. There must be no sharp-edged facets to the fret ends: mandolinists do not play well with lacerated fingers! This job takes considerable patience – there are forty-two (or forty-four) fret ends to dress – but your reward will be the achievement of a neck and fretboard that feels and runs smoothly in the hand.

FITTING THE EDGE DOT MARKERS

Having filed and dressed the ends of all the frets, you can now drill the holes in the side of the fretboard for the edge marker dots. You can purchase these from luthiers' suppliers or make your own: 1.5mm diameter aluminium or silver wire is best. Copper or brass wire is all right but tarnishes and needs regular polishing. Clamp the soundbox (wrapped in the foam mat) gently in the bench vice so the edge of the fretboard lies horizontally. Ensure it is the face edge of the fretboard facing the player! Now mark on the dot positions with a bradawl point at the 3rd, 5th, 7th, 10th, 12th, 15th, 17th and 19th frets and drill out to a depth of about 3mm with the 1.5mm drill bit. Use the medium grit abrasive on a flat block to square-off the wire's end and then clip off a length about 3mm long so the wire cutter's jaws leave the cut end as a chisel point; it is this end that goes in the hole first (*see* Fig 153). Cut about ten such pieces (a couple are bound to disappear into the wood shavings), add a blob of C3 PVA adhesive to the hole, hold the dot with a slim pair of tweezers and tap in with a light hammer until the end is flush with the fretboard. Repeat until you have completed all the dots. Use a 'drift' of 100mm long × 6mm dowel to tap in the difficult dots at the 12th, 15th, 17th and 19th positions. Now polish the dot faces with the fine grade 1500 silicon carbide paper stuck onto an old credit card with double-sided sticky tape.

FILL THE FRET SLOT ENDS

Because the fret slots are cut over-depth to ensure that the shoulders of the frets are fitted tight to the fretboard face, the exposed slot ends at the fretboard edges need to be filled with a matching coloured wax obtainable from woodwork shops and good DIY stores. An alternative is cobblers' heelball, which works all right and can be found in shoe repairers and harness and saddlery shops. Colours are usually brown or black. This material is applied into the slot ends with a hot knife – on cooling it reverts to a hard substance. Once the slot ends are all filled, rub the fretboard edges lightly with the fine grade 1500 silicon carbide paper on an old credit card backing.

CLEAN UP FRETBOARD FACE

It may be that when hammering in the frets you have scuffed or dented the fretboard face with a slip or badly aimed hammer. Now the frets are fitted, the fretboard face needs a light scraping to clean it up and the tool for this is shown (*see* Fig 154). This scraper is made with an ordinary heavy-duty craft knife blade, sandwiched between two flat pieces of mahogany, size about 120 × 45 × 9mm, clamped together with three 18mm × 8 gauge brass CSK woodscrews. The sharp edge of the blade will need 'turning' over with a hard steel rod to make it into an effective scraper. If a light scrape between the frets does not remove the deeper dents or scuffs, then here is a tip: boil water in a kettle and use a small soft bristle paint-brush or 'cotton-bud' to apply a drop of boiling water to the dent; when cool, add another boiling drop. If you have a soldering iron then hold the hot bit in the puddle to keep it boiling. This may cure the dent by swelling the wood's cells and fibres to their (almost) uncrushed state. If this method does not prove effective, then scrape a little more off when the fretboard face has dried. Do not use any coloured filler to the fret-board to disguise a dent you can't remove; accept it as an honest mistake: perfection *is* elusive. A small dent may not look so bad when the frets are polished and the fret-board face oiled. If it is tiny it will doubtless go unnoticed when the strings are on.

POLISHING THE FRETS

You will need a mask to protect the fret-board surface when you polish the frets. Some luthiers mask with masking tape, leaving the frets exposed, but this is a tedious exercise and the natural oils in rosewood, for example, make the adhesive on the tape very sticky and you may have to clean up the fretboard with the scraper again. Simple masks can be made from an old credit card, the thinnest variety, with a slot cut in it lengthwise with the scalpel to the exact width of the fret (*see* Fig 155). You place this 'mask' over the fret, rub with the fine grade 1500 paper until the

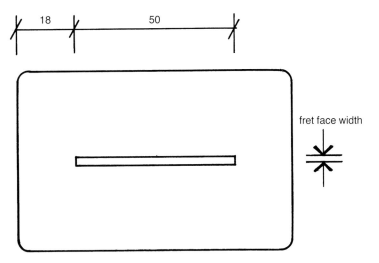

fret's surface is free of scuffs. Then get a piece of cowhide about 50 × 75mm, apply metal polish sparingly to the suede side and then polish the fret to a shine, back and forth along the fret.

Do not file or stone down the frets to level them; if the fretboard face was levelled straight and smooth before you fitted the frets, then dressing them should prove unnecessary. Only resort to re-dress a fret's profile if it is a problem when the strings are on, the truss rod adjusted for correct relief and the action is set to optimum: if it is higher than the other frets, then reduce it, re-dress and polish. Now get a dry, coarse rag (old denim jean's material is good) and rub the frets and fretboard vigorously. This done, you can now progress to mark on the string spacings for the nut slots.

TOP: Fig 154 A home-made fretboard scraper.
ABOVE: Fig 155 A fret polishing mask.

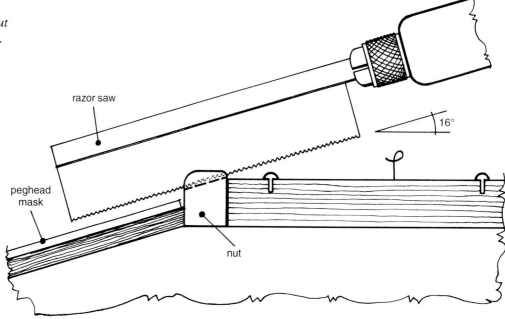

Fig 156 Slotting the fitted nut for strings to peghead 'break'.

SLOTTING THE NUT

From the details previously given on Fig 149 in this Chapter, mark the string spacings on the nut with a hard, sharp pencil. Pay due attention to the margins between the fretboard edges and the first and last string: too narrow means that these first and last strings can be muted by your hand or pushed off the fretboard edge when 'pitch-bending'. You will notice that the spacing between the unison pairs increases as the gauges increase; this is to allow for the greater amplitude of the heavier strings to prevent them from clashing into each other. On the long-scaled instruments with less string tension, the gap between the unison pairs must not be less than dimensioned. You may vary the larger spaces between the pairs of strings to suit your own needs, for example, if you require a wider fretboard than recommended.

To cut the slots, first mask the peghead face with an old credit card: stick it in place with masking tape; this precaution will prevent the end of the razor saw or needle files from gouging holes in the peghead veneer. Cut each string slot first with the razor saw

held at the same reclined 16 degree angle of the peghead: cut down *almost* to the fretboard's face (*see* Fig 156) but ensure you *do not* saw or file into the surface of the zero-fret. Now file out the width of the slots with the needle files according to the string gauges recommended in Chapter 14. Another tip: you can retain old wound strings cut into lengths about 150mm long and use them as flexible round 'files', tensioned in the jaws of the piercing saw to dress the string slots perfectly to the same gauge to be used. Generally, the razor saw or fretting saw (not fret saw) tend to cut enough of a slot for strings up to about 0.66mm (.026in), but above this gauge you must select which needle file is most appropriate. The slot must not be too tight for the string, otherwise tuning difficulties or broken strings can be the result. It is possible to enlarge a slot width by tilting the file from side to side, but do not overcut the slot's width because the string can squeak about on the zero-fret. The nut is now finished and you may remove the peghead's mask and clean off the filing dust of the nut's material with an ordinary household paint-brush.

12 FINISHING AND FINISHES

The instrument is complete now and a very final rub down *with the grain* to the bare wood of the peghead and neck should be done with the 800 grade 'wet-or-dry' silicon carbide abrasive paper. Where rubbing down or polishing is mentioned, this means 'by hand': power sanders, however cunningly designed, are not suitable, neither are rotary sanders, polishing wheels or any high-speed device. When rubbing down and finishing, always lay the instrument on the foam mat to your bench top. Now remove the belly mask.

Always use the 'wet-or-dry' paper *dry* to bare woods. Round off the sharp edges to the peghead and remove all file and scratch marks to peghead end grain, hook, back of neck and heel; the surfaces should be finished quite smooth. *Do not* rub down the sides of the fretboard anymore – this component is already to 'finished' width. The sides of the neck heel and ribs where they meet the internal angle of the shoulders are difficult areas to rub smooth; a piece of the 800 grade 'wet-or-dry' abrasive paper wrapped and taped around the edge of an old (but stiff) credit card is the best tool to work into these tight corners cleanly. You may find the home-made scraper, used to clean up the fretboard, very useful to remove rough spots from the shoulder areas, but it may leave the odd scratch, so follow up with the 800 grade paper. When you have the neck surfaces clean and smooth, mask the heel area with tape and then rub down the ribs to finish; this way you will not scuff or scratch a finished adjacent surface.

If the bindings' edges seem sharp, then rub these down to achieve a small rounded edge: sharp edges to the soundbox's back will dig uncomfortably into the player's thigh (*see* Fig 157). Now turn your attention to finishing the soundhole edges; achieve a full rounded edge section (*see*

Fig 158) using the 800 grade abrasive paper, but be careful when you reach the tighter radii of the end of the ellipse as a line of soft earlywood will cut down more quickly than the latewood and the radius can turn ugly. A piece of 800 grade abrasive paper wrapped around a short piece of broomstick or 25mm diameter dowel

Fig 157 Rub the sharp edges off the bindings.

Fig 158 Detail for the soundhole edge profile.

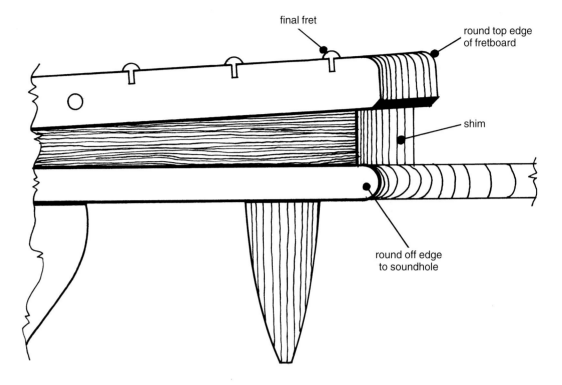

final fret

round top edge
of fretboard

shim

round off edge
to soundhole

will prevent you from locally over-cutting the smaller radii. Having used the 800 grade paper to the neck and soundhole edges, move on to the finer 1200 grade, and rub down with the grain – using a cork or rubber backing pad to the flat areas – until every surface is better than silky smooth. The finest bare wood surface achieved now will mean less work 'flattening' each successive coat of finishing oil. You do not want to waste time, or expensive oils, laying on finishes to remove them by trying to smooth the roughness of a surface. Now you are ready to apply the first (or sealer) coat of oil.

FINISHES

Luthiers' suppliers or specialist woodworking stores will present you with a good choice of fine abrasives, flatting papers, polishing pads, tack cloths, disposable gloves and the range of finishing oils recommended. It is worth your while to obtain a

price list and catalogue from the specialists as some of these fine-quality materials are just not available at your local DIY store; the specialists, I have found, are quick to respond by mail order and are actually less expensive. Australia and the USA seem to be well-served by excellent ironmongers, tool stockists and DIY stores that carry an amazing range of good quality materials. The abrasive papers and finishes mentioned in the text are generally available wherever you live, but do check out the other options from the trade suppliers. Suppliers to the automotive finishing trades are a good source of fine abrasives, flatting papers and polishing/buffing pads, but resist the temptation to try their lacquers, cutting-down compounds and silicone polishes: what is compatible on steel and car paintwork may not be compatible on rosewood, spruce, mahogany, sycamore, tung oil- or linseed oil-based penetrating oils.

You may use tung oil, Danish oil, teak oil or Tru-oil to the instrument, but use a lemon oil application to the fretboard. The choice of which oil to use for the peghead, neck, back, ribs and belly will be determined by preference. Tung oil and Danish oil dries quite quickly and is compatible with the natural oils in rosewood. Teak oil dries a little slower, is the least expensive but is not quite so compatible with the rosewoods; teak oil gives a more glossy lustre. Tru-oil provides a fine, high lustre built-up finish, but is expensive in comparison: it was originally produced for rifle and shotgun stocks, but is now commonly

oil will need to be applied: this builds up the finish and seals the pores of the grain. Firstly, wear cotton painter's gloves and wipe the instrument with white spirit on a clean cotton cloth: this will remove greasy areas and the oils left on the surface by your hands. Now allow the white spirit to evaporate and, when the wood is dry, wipe every surface with a tack cloth, then apply the oil with a clean cotton rag, rubbing well in across the grain and then along it; then wipe off the excess across the grain, working in the sequence of belly, ribs,

Fig 159 The low-lustre, silky finish of Danish oil.

used by luthiers, who, like myself, are glad to make use of superior and user-friendly alternatives to the traditional varnishes and modern lacquers. Oil finishes are not so high-gloss, but do feel and look silky (*see* Fig 159).

If you devise a hook or bar that will pass through a tuning machine hole in the peghead so that the instrument can be hung from the ceiling, this will allow you to give the whole instrument one coat of oil in one go. As stated in Chapter 3, several coats of

back, peghead and neck. Now hang the instrument up somewhere warm, dry and as dust-free as possible. Allow the sealer coat to dry for one whole day – perhaps longer in cooler, damper climates – then *very lightly* 'cut back' with the 1200 grade paper: you are flattening the oil film at this stage not 'rubbing down' wood anymore. Wipe off the dust with a tack cloth and then apply another coat of oil; when dry, lightly flatten all the surfaces with grade 1500 paper but now used wet to help lubricate and prevent the very fine grit paper from clogging. Repeat this process exactly for seven full coats to the belly and neck and *at least* five elsewhere. The final coat should be permitted to harden over a period of at least one week, before lightly flatting with the wet 1500 grade paper and then polishing the finish *by hand*, with just a burnishing pad and power to your elbow: it's as simple as that! 'Finishing', using these oils is, at least, a two-week timetable.

You may be wondering where the colour staining of the tonewoods comes into the finishing process, as it is a little late once the oil finish has been applied. Using stain is not recommended for any of the tonewoods; I am not being purist (for once) – stain can ruin a finish if it dries patchy. You may not know this until it is applied, when it will be too late to change course. If you have selected attractive tonewoods, then the oiled finish will enhance and deepen their natural colour, figure and lustre far more. You will find your finished instrument quite beautiful enough without stain; spruce, sycamore and mahogany will darken over time with exposure to daylight, and rosewood is already beautiful enough. The natural oil finishes do 'yellow' with age as well.

If you do desire to stain the neck, belly or soundbox then I recommend a fine-quality water-based stain: this product is least likely to leave you with patches and smears, although it does 'raise the grain'. All I can advise you to do is to follow the manufacturer's instructions, and apply the stain, let it dry thoroughly, then apply the oiled finish as described before.

One advantage of the natural oiled finish is that should the instrument get scratched or scuffed – it will if it gets played – it is then easy to redress the damage and build up the oil finish, something that is very difficult to do with traditional varnish or thick synthetic lacquers. If a spirit stain is used mixed with the oil finish (sometimes recommended!), then matching its density of colour and depth to redress a scuff mark will be more difficult. The oiled finishes can be cleaned simply with a soft cotton cloth dampened with warm water and soft soap; wipe off with clean water and a soft dry cotton cloth. No sealers, proprietary polishes and waxes are required, nor desired. Make the effort to burnish the neck of the instrument with a dry rubbing pad, this must feel – and look – like the sheen of French polish. Avoid using polishing compounds and proprietary 'guitar' polishes to shine up your instrument during future preening: these are products designed specifically for 'hard' finishes such as catalyst lacquers and are quite unsuitable for natural oil finishes. Natural beeswax polishes are not recommended as the warmth of your hand will make the instrument's surface tacky and clog up the pores. Now you can fit the 'hardware'.

13 TUNING MACHINES, TAILPIECE AND TRUSS ROD COVER

Place the instrument on the foam mat on your bench and support the neck with the 'V' block. You may need to ream out the string post holes with the round file to clean out any finishing oil that will have built up inside, but do not open up the holes any more than the original drill diameters specified. Depending on which type of tuning machine you have chosen, the four-on-a-plate or the individual 'minis', these must be fitted the correct way round. The four-on-a-plate variety should be posterior mounted to the peghead with the worm drive of the button shaft *above* the string post cogs (*see* Fig 160): this ensures that as wear occurs, the string tension will always force the cog into the worm drive, so the gears do not develop any slack and cause problems with keeping the strings tuned. If you are fitting the four-on-a-plate type, then you must push in the face collars to the string post holes in the peghead with a hardwood 'drift' and light hammer (*see* Fig 161) then mount the tuning machines and screw fix from the rear in the same manner as described for the 'minis'. The four-on-a-plate type have no friction adjustment to the button shafts. Do not apply Vaseline or grease to lubricate the worm gears: this will accumulate dust and grit and cause rapid wear. The types of tuning machines recommended are:

◆ Gotoh SG38-05 mini in chrome, four left, four right
◆ Schaller M6 A mini in chrome, four left, four right, or
◆ Schaller four-on-a-plate chrome with pearloid buttons.

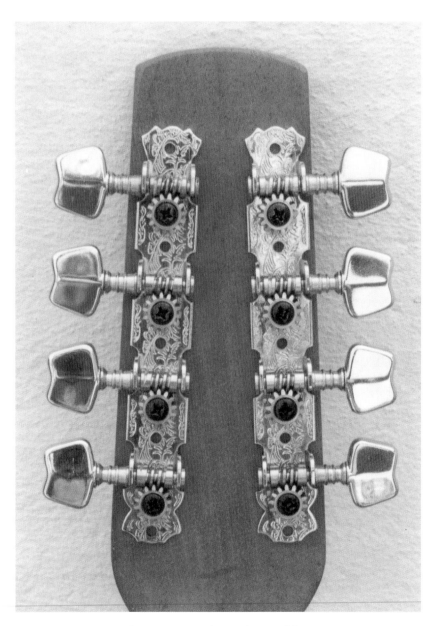

Fig 160 Four-on-a-plate rear-mounting tuning machines.

BELOW: Fig 161 Four-on-a-plate collars/bushing to peghead face.

ABOVE: Fig 162 Peghead rear mounting of the 'minis'.
BELOW: Fig 163 Peghead face fixing of the 'minis'.

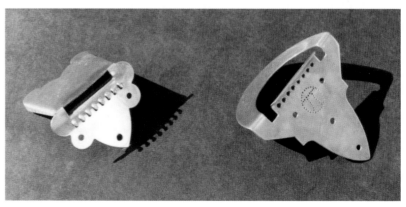

RIGHT: Fig 164 Tailpieces for loop-end or ball-end strings.

All the above types are available in gold-plated finishes, but these are expensive and the gold wears off quite quickly on the edges; chrome or nickel plating is more robust. Most music shops will order you a set of six tuning machines, which is not enough: you must therefore specify: 'four left and four right'. Luthiers' suppliers will sell them singly and usually at less cost.

The individual 'minis' recommended should be posterior mounted as shown (*see* Fig 162). These superior-quality tuning machines are also secured in place with a collar and lock nut from the face of the peghead (*see* Fig 163), that clamps the body of the machine head to the thickness of the peghead. When you have fitted the 'minis' and turned the lock nuts to finger-tight to hold them steady in the holes, use a small rule or try-square to align them so they all have the button shafts parallel to each other. Both types of tuning machine are screw-fixed to the underside of the peghead using small dome-headed screws, usually cross-headed: you will need to drill pilot holes 4mm deep and perpendicular to the peghead with the 1.5mm diameter drill bit. Insert the screws tight, turn the peghead over and use a 10mm spanner to tighten the hexagonal nuts firmly on the peghead face. The 'mini' tuning machines are now fitted, but you may need to tighten up the friction adjusting screws at the end of the buttons if they feel slack: these machines are smooth turning, but there should be no 'play'.

THE TAILPIECE

Mandolin and mandola strings are normally manufactured with loop ends, sold in a complete set and do not give much choice in gauges, windings, lengths, and far more commonly are hard to obtain except from specialists. For these reasons, a tail-piece that will accept ball-end strings gives you greater choice and availability: you can pick up single steel guitar strings anywhere, in any gauge and in any winding. The Gibson style tailpiece accepts loop-end strings; the 'D' buckle style will accept ball-end strings (*see* Fig 164). For reasons I have yet to fathom, the 'D' buckle tailpiece made from brass improves sustain – this may be because it cannot flex and dissipate energy or perhaps brass is acoustically special and reflects some energy back down the string. There are tailpieces on the market made from thin, pressed steel sheet, with pathetic hooks that bend or shear off (or break the loop-end) and these are not worth using. You could opt for no tailpiece, but insert a fillet of rosewood or ebony on the very tail-end of the belly and fix four brass panel pins into pre-drilled pilot holes in the tail-block as 'hitch-pins': all very traditional, but you will still be restricted to the availability of loop-end strings.

It is important that the tailpiece does not hold the end of the strings much above the belly's surface, but just clear of it. This detail will ensure that the strings' break angle will remain as designed. The Gibson tailpiece floats above the belly because the Gibson mandolin has a high, carved arch-top, therefore the break angle is much greater.

To make a brass 'D' buckle tailpiece you will need brass sheet about 1mm thick; cut it out using drilled holes and the piercing saw according to the pattern and dimensions shown (*see* Fig 165). Mark with a centre-punch and drill out the string and screw-fixing holes to the diameters specified and then bend it 'cold' to the dotted lines clamped up tightly in the vice jaws with two MDF cauls, using a heavy hammer and a flat-ended hardwood drift, to the shape required (*see* Fig 166). File off the sharp edges with a fine flat file and rub it down with the 1200 grade silicon carbide paper and 'Brasso' metal polish, or, just rub it down and get it nickel plated. Fit it to the tail of the instrument using 10mm × 4 gauge dome-headed brass screws, but drill pilot holes for the screws first with a 3mm diameter drill bit to a depth of 6mm (*see* Fig 167).

Fig 165 Detail for the 'D' buckle tailpiece.

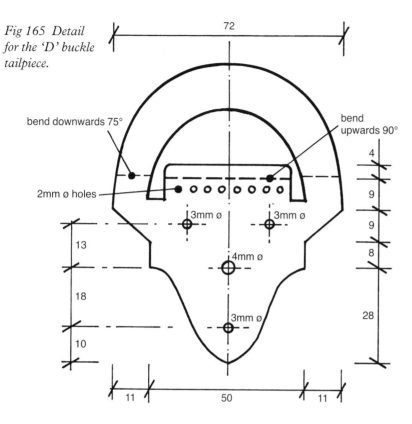

THE TRUSS ROD COVER

The recess in the peghead for access to adjust the truss rod needs a cover plate to hide the necessary but not very attractive internal nuts and bolts. Off-cuts from the ribs' or back's material need never be wasted as it is quite suitable to fashion this into a cover plate. You could use stainless steel, aluminium, brass or plastic sheet for the cover plate, but I recommend you make good use of the tonewoods' 'waste'. Flamed sycamore and the rosewoods make excellent cover plates; but mahogany, for some reason, fails to adapt to this role. Ebony is difficult to work down to the thinness required and will fracture easily.

The thickness will need to be reduced to about 1mm for rosewood and about 1.5mm for sycamore: clamp the workpiece to the bench on the hide mat in the same way as you did when planing the peghead veneer. The block plane will shave cleanly, and finish with the steel cabinet scraper to achieve fair faces both sides. Mark out the cover plate's shape from the details given (*see* Fig 168) or design your own, but keep it approximately within the sizes suggested and the hole centres for the screw fixings as dimensioned, and avoid drilling pilot holes for the screws within the area between the truss rod anchor plate and the nut. The

BELOW: Fig 166 The 'D' buckle tailpiece bent to shape.
BELOW RIGHT: Fig 167 The tailpiece fitted to the centreline of the tail.

You may wish to fix a strap button to the tailpiece – if you do, then always pre-drill pilot holes first to the screw's shank diameter and to a depth of about 5mm less than the length of the screw: this will prevent the ribs from splitting or – even worse – the internal tailblock being cleft into two halves.

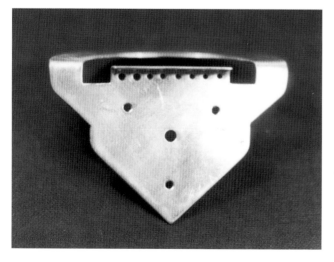

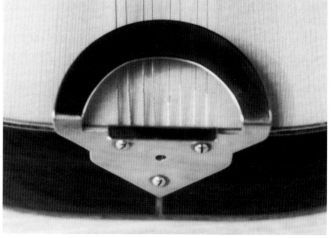

smallest possible screws should be used: cheese-headed S.S. machine screws are perfect and have a very fine thread that bites well into the dense peghead veneer (*see* Fig 169). Avoid drilling the screws' pilot holes into the peghead material: the holes only need to be veneer deep.

Cut out the plate's outline with the fret saw, dress the edges smooth with the flat file, scribe the end to the nut's face and round off the edges of the face side. To finish, rub down with the 1200 grade silicon carbide paper, apply a coat of whichever finishing oil you are using, wipe off the excess and rub vigorously with a suede leather off-cut to polish it on the face side. You need not fit it to the peghead yet, as adjustment to the truss rod will need to be undertaken once the instrument has been strung up to concert pitch and the action established, so put it somewhere safe until you will fix it in place in the following Chapter.

If you do experience difficulty in obtaining small screws to fit the truss rod cover plate, then try a clockmaker's or repairer's shop: they keep an amazing selection of S.S. and brass machine screws. Model makers' suppliers may also prove fruitful.

ONE LAST DETAIL

In Chapter 8 mention was made of the fact that the 18mm flat bit's centre point – used to drill out the peghead truss rod recess – may have cut through the thickness of the peg-head to leave an unwelcome hole in the underside face forward of the hook. So, now is the time to lay the instrument on its belly on the foam mat and support the neck on the 'V' block while you drill out this hole to 4 (or 5)mm diameter and add a blob of C3 PVA or Titebond adhesive and push in a mother-of-pearl or abalone fret-board marker dot of 4 (or 5)mm until it is flush with the peghead's surface. Wipe away surplus glue with a damp, soft rag. The instrument is now finished, complete and in need of a bridge and a set of strings.

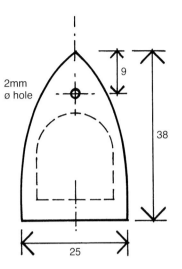

Fig 168 Detail for truss rod cover plate.

Fig 169 A truss rod cover plate screw-fixed in place.

14 BRIDGE, STRINGS AND ACTION

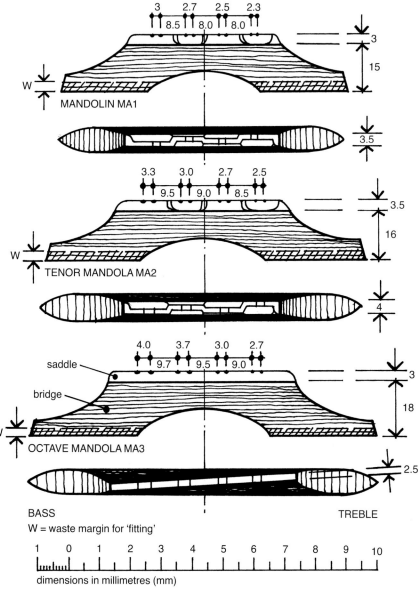

3   2.7   2.5   2.3
8.5   8.0   8.0

3

15

W

MANDOLIN MA1

3.5

3.3   3.0   2.7   2.5
9.5   9.0   8.5

3.5

16

W

TENOR MANDOLA MA2

4

4.0   3.7   3.0   2.7
9.7   9.5   9.0

saddle

bridge

3

18

W

OCTAVE MANDOLA MA3

2.5

BASS   TREBLE

W = waste margin for 'fitting'

1 0 1 2 3 4 5 6 7 8 9 10

dimensions in millimetres (mm)

ABOVE: Fig 170 Details for the bridge.
RIGHT: Fig 171 Compensated indented bridge saddles for MA1 and MA2.

The bridge can be made from an off-cut of the fretboard material: rosewood and rock maple are excellent. You may use ebony, but it is more difficult to work. Use the 'hobby' vice as previously shown in Fig 148, Chapter 11, to allow you two free hands while the small workpiece is held tight in the cowhide-faced jaws. You will need an off-cut of suitable size, planed square: 150 × 18 × 7mm; the grain must be quarter-sawn with the radial grain aligned with the sides. Fashion the bridge to the details shown (*see* Fig 170), cutting out the arch and insteps with the coping saw or scroll saw, dress these smooth with the half-round file and plane the top edge flat to the widths specified. You will note that instruments mandolin MA1 and tenor mandola MA2 have their saddles indented for string compensation (*see* Fig 171) whilst the octave mandola MA3 has a single-slanted saddle (*see* Fig 172). Allow the feet of the bridge enough 'waste' to be 'fitted' later on. The bridge requires tapering from foot to

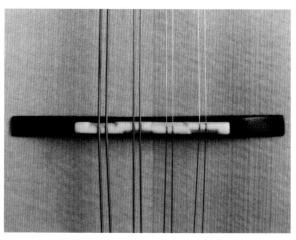

saddle and the block plane or 25mm chisel are the preferred tools for this task. Clamp the bridge material in the 'hobby' vice whichever angle suits you: the cowhide-faced jaws enable you to hold it steady without distorting or stressing the workpiece.

The bridge saddle material can be bone, ivory, mother-of-pearl, brass, aluminium or you may use the synthetic materials such as Corian or Micarta. Brass and aluminium work extremely well on the lower-pitched mandolas. Bone, ivory or mother-of-pearl is recommended for mandolins. Fashion the blank into the rectangular section specified on Fig 170, but leave it over-long, rub it down with the medium grit, 'free-cut' abrasive on a hardwood block and bond the saddle on to the bridge's top edge using Araldite standard epoxy resin adhesive. If the bridge is rosewood, then de-oil it with cigarette lighter fuel before gluing on the saddle. Tape the saddle on to the bridge with masking tape and leave it somewhere warm for sixteen hours.

The next task requires accurate measuring out and fine workmanship. Mark on the string spacing with a small nick from the razor saw; templates are useful (*see* Fig 173) and use the fine, flat needle file to fashion the indents for string compensation. This done, then trim the waste ends off the saddle with the razor saw (or piercing saw), file on a rounded end and smooth the ends to the bridge's shoulders. Mask the bridge and polish the saddle with toothpaste (or metal polish if you have used brass or aluminium). Now mask the saddle and give the bridge a coat of finishing oil, wipe off the excess and rub to a sheen with an off-cut of suede leather. Allow the oil one whole day to dry properly.

Use the needle files to open up the grooves for the strings to the gauges specified in the following section. The grooves must not be too deep, just about half the diameter of the string: use old wound strings in the correct gauges as flexible 'files' to achieve the right groove width and angle

it downwards – towards the tailpiece – to follow the 'break' of the strings (*see* Fig 174). Simple 'v' cuts made with a fine triangular file may seem an easier option, but these will cause sharp edges and broken strings.

If you use a brass saddle, then the tone will be rich, warm and with excellent sustain, but brass is hard-edged and broken

Fig 172 Compensated slanted bridge saddle for MA3.

Fig 173 String spacing templates for nut and saddle.

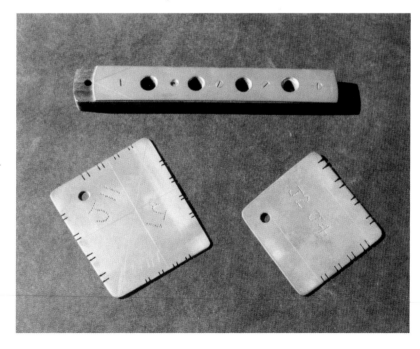

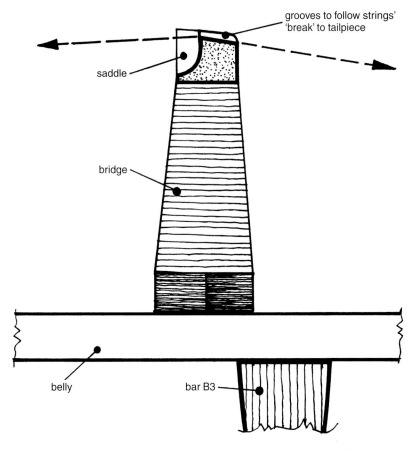

Fig 174 Cutting string grooves to saddle.

to hold on a strip of medium grit, 'free-cut' abrasive paper across the belly's width at the bridge position. Hold the bridge perpendicular to the belly and rub it backwards and forwards until the feet sit perfectly to the belly's doming. Do not yet reduce the bridge height to that specified, allow a margin for removal later on: this is the 'first fit'.

STRINGS

Roundwound phosphor bronze steel-cored strings are recommended for the wound strings, and plain steel, plated with nickel or silver, for the plain strings. Ball-ended strings are required for the 'D' buckle tailpiece. The gauges that are preferred for the scale-lengths of these instruments are shown in the table below.

To fit the strings correctly is vital to maintain tuning and prevent breakages. Once the ball or loop ends have been attached through or over the hooks or pins, the free end of the string is then passed through the hole in the tuning machine post and the string wound around in the directions shown (*see* Fig 176). The manner in which the free end of string is wrapped around the post prior to winding up to pitch is just as important as whether the strings spiral clockwise or counter-clockwise: if the string slips from its initial tie to the post then breakage will occur. The method recommended is illustrated in the sequence of the four photos shown (*see* Fig 177). The 'string post' in this case was a mock up, enlarged for clarity. The initial wrap around is *over* the free end, *under* the first full-turn and then *under*. Usually 2 to 3

strings too common. To avoid this occurrence file the grooves with *slightly* rounded edges, but not too much, otherwise the strings will not be 'stopped' correctly: they can buzz and rattle and mislead you to a futile search for the source of the troubles. The zero-fret rarely gives trouble: check saddle or tailpiece.

The feet of the bridge require fitting to the doming of the belly, so use masking tape

	4th pair	3rd pair	2nd pair	1st pair
Mandolin MA1	G: 0.91w	D: 0.61w	A: 0.28	E: 0.23
Tenor Mandola MA2	C: 1.11w	G: 0.71w	D: 0.40	A: 0.30
Octave Mandola MA3	G: 1.22w	D: 0.91w	A: 0.61w	E: 0.33

NOTE: 'w' refers to wound string and *see* Fig 175 for metric to imperial conversions.

wraps around is sufficient for the 4th and 3rd strings, 4 to 5 wraps around for the 2nd and 1st strings. *Do not* allow the string to wrap around the post by overriding the previous wrap. Fit the strings on in the following order, but without the bridge in place: 4th and 1st pairs, then 3rd and 2nd. Do not tighten the strings up too much, just enough to hold them in place on the string posts of the tuning machines.

Cut out two triangular-shaped pieces of insulating tape, about 15mm long × 5mm wide tapering to a point, and using the steel rule measure the theoretical scale-length from the zero-fret to the belly plus 4mm and stick your 'pointer' markers at this exact spot on the belly: this is the approximate position for the pointed ends of the bridge, before correct compensation and intonation are established later in this Chapter. Slide a piece of thick paper between the strings and belly, then insert the bridge lying flat on its side under the slack strings at this point and raise it perpendicular to the belly, ensuring you do not scratch or dent the soft spruce. Pull out the sheet of paper and align the bridge ends with the 'pointers'. Now tension up all the strings to the correct tunings at concert pitch: A = 440Hz, using corresponding piano keys, or a quartz tuner. A chromatic quartz tuner is a most useful device and they are no longer expensive.

The instrument should be left strung up to concert pitch for at least a week to allow the belly, body and neck to stabilize to these sudden stresses and compressions and to acclimatize to the relative humidity of your home. After a week the belly will have pushed itself back up a little and measurements can then be taken to correct and 'first fit' the initial bridge height, action and check the intonation. It *can* take up to six months for the belly to settle down, so never under-cut the bridge's height: you will need to 'second fit' the bridge at a later date, preferably when the instrument has been played regularly over a period of at least three months.

Metric to Imperial Conversions for String Gauges

mm	in	mm	in
0.20	0.008	0.23	0.009
0.25	0.010	0.28	0.011
0.30	0.012	0.33	0.013
0.36	0.014	0.38	0.015
0.40	0.016	0.43	0.017
0.46	0.018	0.48	0.019
0.51	0.020	0.53	0.021
0.56	0.022	0.58	0.023
0.61	0.024	0.64	0.025
0.66	0.026	0.68	0.027
0.71	0.028	0.73	0.029
0.76	0.030	0.79	0.031
0.81	0.032	0.83	0.033
0.86	0.034	0.89	0.035
0.91	0.036	0.94	0.037
0.97	0.038	0.99	0.039
1.01	0.040	1.04	0.041
1.07	0.042	1.09	0.043
1.11	0.044	1.14	0.045
1.17	0.046	1.19	0.047
1.22	0.048	1.24	0.049
1.27	0.050	1.32	0.052

ABOVE: Fig 175 String gauges conversion chart: mm to inches.
LEFT: Fig 176 Strings must wind correctly around posts.

Fig 177 String tied correctly in sequences shown.

ACTION

The 'first fit' of the bridge will be too high, but with string tension having been applied at concert pitch, you can check the relief of the neck by sighting your eye down the length of the fretboard edge – looking from the peghead end. Is the fretboard bowing up too much? Is it dead straight? There needs to be a slight bow of approximately 1mm for the mandolin MA1, 1.5, for the tenor mandola MA2 and 2, for the octave mandola MA3, which can be measured with the steel straight-edge lying on the frets along the centreline of the fretboard; then measure the perpendicular distance with a steel rule between the straight-edge and the 12th fret (*see* Fig 178). If necessary,

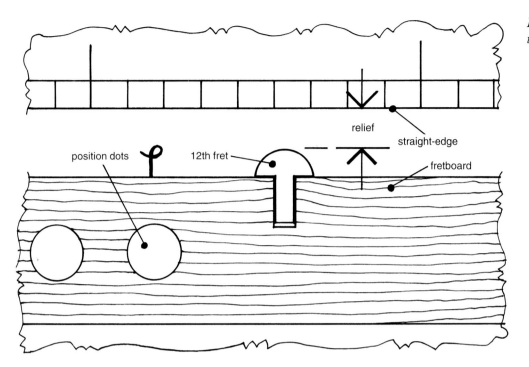

Fig 178 Measure 'relief' of tensioned neck at 12th fret.

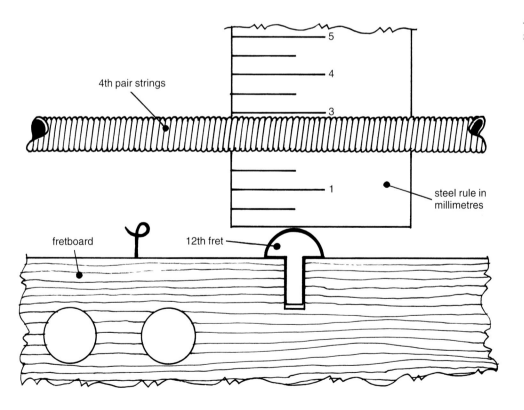

Fig 179 Strings' action measured at 12th fret.

Fig 180 Bev Lawton's string-lifter (modified by author).

the truss rod tension to give the fretboard slightly more relief. It is always worthwhile to make two bridges (one with a brass saddle?) and leave one 'unfitted' for future use.

A device that makes establishing and setting the action much easier is the 'string-lifter' as shown (*see* Fig 180). The base is lined with a thin strip of suede leather to prevent bruising or scratching the belly. It is adjustable in height and takes on the role of a temporary bridge to permit the instrument to be strung up at concert pitch with the belly in compression and all the stresses and strains in place. After a week or two, you can adjust the 12th fret to 4th pair of strings' clearance to the dimensions previously recommended and measure the height between the belly's surface and the strings, then scribe your bridge to 'fit' this height: the 'first fit' is now complete.

adjust the tension on the truss rod at the peghead recess and lock the brass hexagonal nuts against each other using the tiny spanners. The height of the strings above the 12th fret will, at this stage, be too much (*see* Fig 179) but if you aim for a 4th string clearance of 2mm for the mandolin MA1, 2.25mm for the tenor mandola MA2 and 2.75mm for the octave mandola MA3, this will allow a waste margin for reduction when the 'second fit' of the bridge takes place to achieve optimum action. Remove the insulating tape 'pointers'.

Setting the action for optimum playability will depend on the player's technique, and the figures given above for 12th fret to 4th string clearances can probably be reduced by 0.25mm for the final set-up, but this cannot be done too soon after the instrument has been completed: the instrument needs 'playing in' before fine adjustments can be made. If you do under-cut the bridge causing too low an action, you may slacken off

INTONATION

You will need to check the intonation at the 12th fret with the quartz tuner before adjusting the bridge position for string compensation, and then fit the tear-drop markers to the belly to ensure the bridge is always in the right place; it is a common problem when changing strings: the bridge may get moved off its alignment and intonation will suffer. Because every instrument will differ slightly, there is no universal law for the actual distance from zero-fret to 4th strings' length. Generally, 4mm more than the theoretical scale-length for the 4th pair is about right, and about 2mm more for the 1st pair (*see* Fig 181). When the 'second fit' to the bridge height is done, this initial compensation may need reducing slightly: only the quartz tuner can tell you. The 'tear-drop' markers can be made from thin-gauge black or brown hard plastic plectra, cut to shape with nail scissors, the edges rubbed smooth with the 1200 grade abrasive paper and then stuck in position on the belly with double-sided adhesive tape.

Fig 181 Bridge position beyond theoretical scale-length.

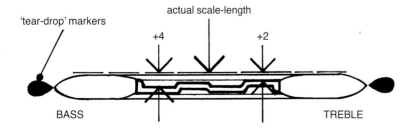

15 ORIGINS, TYPES AND TUNINGS

This final Chapter has been included as a prelude to further reading of the publications listed in the following Bibliography, that document the evolution and history of the *mandora* (Italy and Germany), *mandore* (France), *mandola* and *mandolino* (Italy), and in anglicized form *mandolin*, in greater detail. All are well-researched and comprise photographs, line drawings and detailed descriptions of examples from private collections and museums. What follows from my own pen is a summary of the origins, kindred instruments and known tunings, just to whet your appetite.

THE MANDORE

Small, lute-like, gut-strung, shallow bowl-backed, high-pitched instruments date from the late Medieval period and were known as *gitterns* (England), *guiterne* (France) and *quinterns* (Germany). They came to be known in the mid-sixteenth century as *mandora* or *mandola*, but *mandore* in France. The earlier types had three, or, more commonly, four courses of single strings running from a reclined peghead to a fixed (tie) bridge. The neck and soundbox were sometimes integral: carved from one solid piece of wood. The bellies were flat and the fingerboard was flush with the belly. Fretting was tied gut, with seven to nine frets as usual, but some had inset ivory frets beyond the fingerboard; some were fretless. Single circular soundholes were carved 'roses' (*see* Fig 182).

They were popular melodic instruments, especially in France, and were claimed to be played with relative ease (compared to the lute?). Some later mandores were partially double strung, but retained the four courses. Mandores were probably tuned in fourth and fifth open tunings: an example

Fig 182 Seventeenth-century mandore.

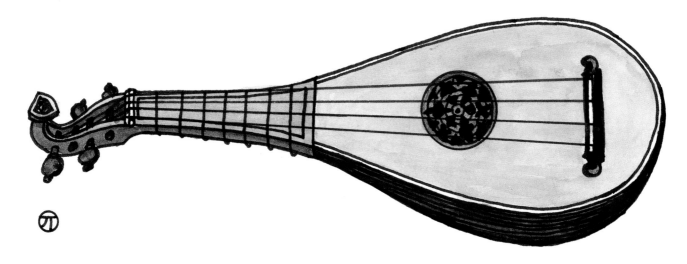

(Michael Praetorius, 1619) gives one tuning, and quoting the 1st string first – as musicologists prefer – d", g', d' and g for a four-course mandore – almost the same compass as a Neapolitan mandolin: e", a', d' and g. These instruments were played with the plectrum, quill or finger(s). Praetorius also mentions that the scale-length was 'exactly half that of the lute'.

The French four-course mandore and Italian *pandora* (or *pandura*) eventually gave way (about 1650) to five- and six-course Italian mandolas and mandolini, and by about the end of the seventeenth century had slipped into obscurity.

THE MANDOLINO

This 'soprano lute' developed from the mandore about 1670, the name suggesting a diminutive *mandola*, high-pitched from b" down to g', strung with gut to a fixed bridge. Antonio Stradivari made some of these and had templates for several varieties. A five-course, ten-stringed instrument of his survives from 1680: the body is bowl-backed, shallow, very almond-shaped with a flat belly displaying a carved soundhole rose. The neck has ten tied-gut frets. Other *mandolini* from the mid-seventeenth century onwards employed five or six double courses of gut strings and were,

it seems, tuned g", d", a', e', b and g. This little 'soprano lute' was to become known as the *Milanese* (Baroque) mandolin: the instrument and tuning required for Vivaldi's famous mandolin concerti (*see* Fig 183). The Presbler family of Milan made fine examples of this instrument – hence its name. It was produced in other cities, as well.

This improved variation on the obsolete four-course mandore held its own for 200 years before giving way to the resurgence of the Neapolitan mandolin at the end of the nineteenth century. Happily, this long-lost *Baroque* mandolin has been resurrected in the last decade and is being played for music from the Baroque period.

THE NEAPOLITAN MANDOLIN

This instrument does not seem to have developed much before 1760. Early types would have had a combination of wire and gut stringing, reverting to the mandore's four courses, but double-strung and tuned as the violin in e", a', d' and g. The advent of the Neapolitan mandolin would indicate the desire for a melodic plucked instrument that would fit in effortlessly within the violin's compass and supremacy

Fig 183 Eighteenth-century Baroque (Milanese) mandolin.

Fig 184 Eighteenth-century Neapolitan mandolin.

in the Baroque era. It would have made a natural 'second instrument' for violinists.

The finest examples of mid-eighteenth-century Neapolitan mandolins were made by the Vinaccia (or Vinaccio) family of luthiers in Naples. These very ornate mandolins were deep bowl-backed, fingerboard flush with the belly, an open round sound-hole and the almond-shaped belly being raked towards the tail at a point just behind a 'floating' pressure bridge; it is this particular detail – along with ten silver or ivory frets – that identifies the early Neapolitan mandolin as being partially wire-strung, with an anchor point for the strings on the tail of the instrument, similar to the larger scale-length cittern. Later improvements brought the fingerboard over onto the belly and 'T' or 'mushroom' section brass or nickel frets to instruments around 1850, and a little later geared metal tuning machines were adopted. The nineteenth-century Neapolitan mandolins developed the fashion for open oval soundholes. Tortoiseshell lozenge, escutcheon or butterfly-shaped scratchplates were standard on all bellies as the plectrum was used rather than finger(s). The scale-lengths were about 300 to 335mm (*see* Fig 184).

The Neopolitan mandolin's playability and brightness and the ease with which it could be tuned led to it supplanting the ear-lier Baroque (Milanese) mandolin. To most ears the Neapolitan's timbre is preferred. To my ears its tonal range is more balanced; the true Baroque mandolin is powerful on the trebles, but weak on the bass, but this is unavoidable on a short-scaled, gut-strung instrument that relies on heavy gauge (but relaxed) wound strings. This is the very good reason why the theorbo-lute has very long, but brightly vibrant bass stringing. Now, if the Baroque mandolin had a wider body … a strategically located treble bar … a slightly longer scale-length … there *is* an interesting development overdue.

THE PORTUGUESE MANDOLIN

Flat-backed, flat-top Neapolitan mandolins were also made, some based on the pear-shaped cittern body. The Spanish *bandurria* could claim responsibility for this variation; it was in existence since the mid-sixteenth century and Philip J. Bone called it the 'Spanish mandolin', having a scale-length of about 300mm, gut-strung with a fixed bridge on the earlier models, but wire-strung with a 'floating' bridge on the later in five or six double courses. Another likely candidate for this inspiration is perhaps the Portuguese guitar, *guitarra*, from the early-eighteenth century. This instrument has a

ABOVE: *Fig 185 Twentieth-century 'Portuguese' mandolin, 'Troughton's No.1'.*
BELOW: *Fig 186 Nineteenth-century Portuguese guitar,* guitarra.

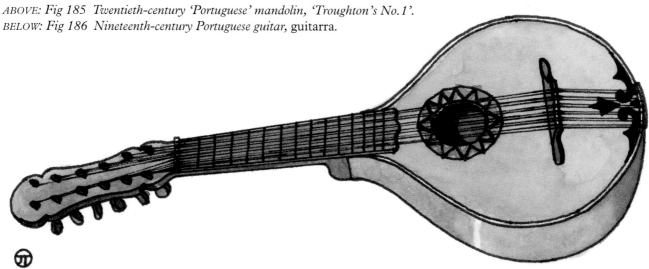

scale-length similar to today's tenor mandola (420 to 430mm), wire-strung in five or six double courses and with metal frets, open round soundholes on later models, but more importantly, it has a 'floating' pressure bridge. The lower three courses are, however, tuned in octave pairs. It would seem natural that the flat-backed Neapolitan varieties adopted the 'Portuguese' title as a description of body shape rather than geographic or ethnic origins (*see* Fig 185). I have never heard the flat-back mandolin spoken of as a 'Spanish'. A Portuguese *guitarra*, made by H.R. Ferro of Lisbon in the nineteenth century is shown (*see* Fig 186). It does look rather like an old friend!

146

MANDOLIN PLAN MA1

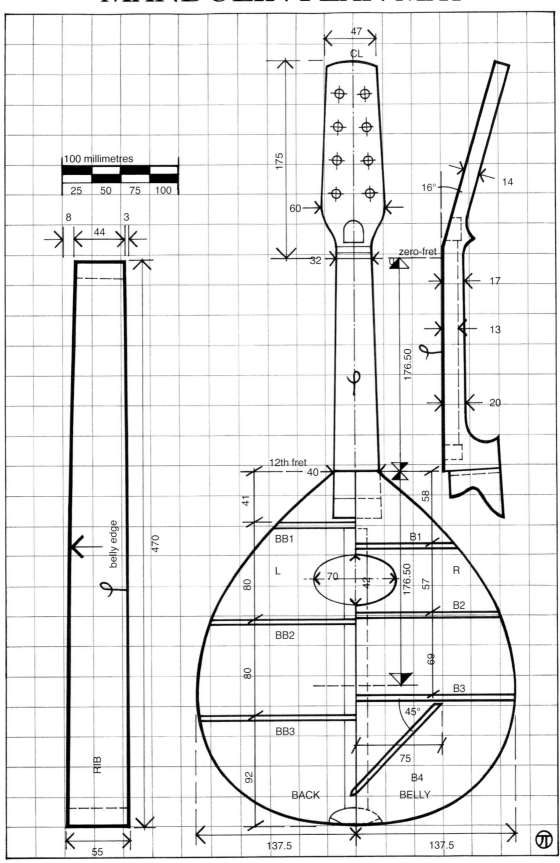

TENOR MANDOLA PLAN MA2

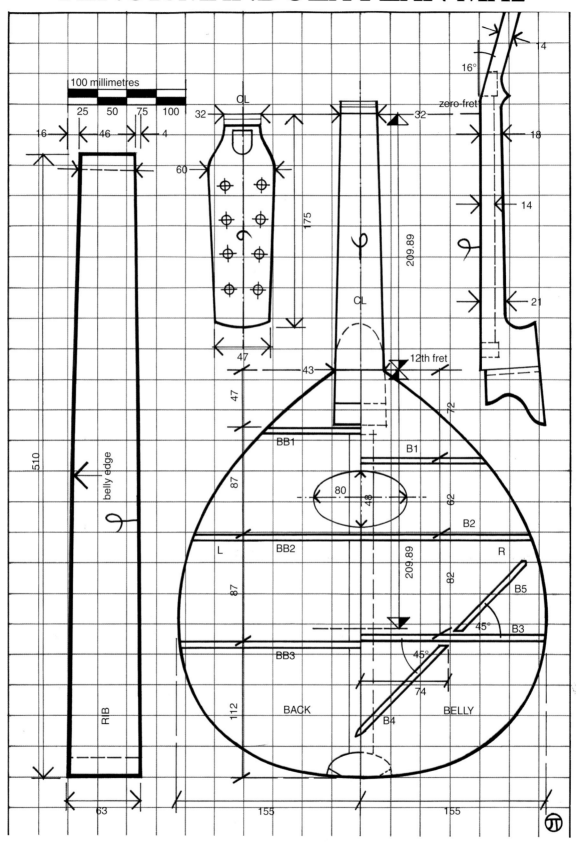

OCTAVE MANDOLA PLAN MA3

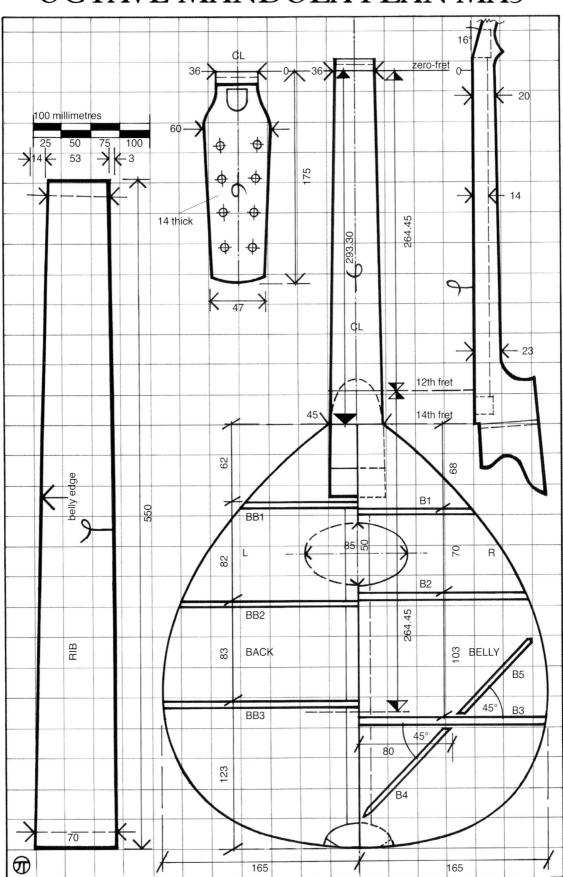

GLOSSARY

Action
The height of the strings above the fretboard or fingerboard. Optimum action will permit ease of playing and correct intonation at all fret positions.

Air Drying
The traditional seasoning of felled and sawn timber stacked under cover whilst gradual evaporation of moisture in the cells and fibres of the wood takes place.

Amplitude
The extent to which a vibrating string will move away from 'at rest'; this distance depending on the energy given it by being plucked, hammered or bowed.

Back
The thin pieces of hardwood, usually 'book-matched' and joined at the centre-line to make up the back of the instrument: a component of the soundbox.

Bars
The light, structural internal wooden components that support the belly and back and maintain the dome. The bars to the belly are not simply supports: they must flex and enhance the acoustic properties of the belly.

Belly
The thin, light pieces of softwood that are 'book-matched' and joined at the centre-line to make up the two halves of the soundboard (or top) of the instrument to amplify the strings' vibrations and dynamics. The belly has the soundhole cut into it.

Bindings
The thin hardwood strips that are let into rebates cut on the edges of the belly/ribs' and back /ribs' joins to cover the end grain and provide a robust edging.

Book-Matched
The arrangement of joining the two pieces of quarter-sawn wood, cut from the same part of the log with one piece turned over to give a mirror image of the grain pattern of the other.

Break
This refers to the angle the strings make when passing over the nut to the reclined peghead or over the bridge to the tailpiece. A high break angle promotes greater string tension and therefore increased pressure on the nut (or zero-fret) and bridge. The angle is measured at the degree of divergence from the straight string.

Bridge
The hardwood component that acts as a stopping point for the scale-length of the strings and supports them at the correct height (for optimum action), transmitting the strings' vibrations to the belly.

Bridge Saddle
The hard material bonded to the top edge of the bridge on which the strings 'stop' and run on to the tailpiece or hitch pins. This material is commonly bone, ivory, brass or synthetic dense compound and is compensated for correct intonation with a slant or series of indents.

Button
The area of the back that extends on to the heel of the neck.

Camber
The slight convex face of the transverse bars and the gentle curvature of the ribs' profile. These features promote the 'dome' to prevent the belly and back going 'hollow' (or dishing).

Cambium Layer
This is the material on the tree trunk between the bark and the sapwood. Cell growth on its inner surface produces the next annual growth ring of sapwood, while the outer surface of the cambium produces the growth of bark.

Cauls
These are pieces – sometimes fashioned – of smooth-faced boards or off-cuts of timber that act as pads or pressure plates to aid clamping and gluing of workpieces to prevent bruising or local distortion that would be caused by the clamp jaws.

Cello Clamps
Adjustable wooden spindle clamps with a long-bolt and wing-nut. Used for clamping the belly when being glued onto the ribs.

Checks
The short radial splitting in sawn timber due to sudden and variable drying out and shrinkage; most obvious as 'surface checking'.

Clear
Sawn timber that is best quality, free from all defects, knots, shakes, pith and bark. The stuff from which musical instruments are made.

Conversion
The manner in which the trunk of a tree or log is sawn lengthwise into planks or scantlings to determine the direction of end grain to obtain the desired face grain, figuring or strength. For instruments the conversion required is quarter-sawn.

Coping Saw
A small bow saw with a narrow-backed, coarse-toothed blade about 160mm long for cutting curved profiles.

Dimension
The exact measurement for the finished or fashioned length, width or thickness of a component or workpiece.

Dome
The slight convex swelling of the belly (top) and back, maintained by the transverse bars and ribs' profile. A very necessary feature with an acoustic advantage.

Earlywood
The softer, paler and wider area of the annual growth ring in timber created in spring; most obvious in softwoods, but can be difficult to see in the 'diffuse-porous' tropical hardwoods.

Emergent Grain
Where the cell cavities are exposed on a cut or planed surface either because the grain is divergent or the cut is at an angle, such as at the peghead or the scalloped bar ends. It is like end grain but at a less obtuse angle.

End Grain
The annual growth rings and cell cavities as seen from a transverse cut across a plank or scantling.

Extractives
These are organic and inorganic compounds found in the structure of wood giving a particular species its characteristic coloration, odour and durability. The heartwood contains the most extractives in its outer layers. These compounds can be 'extracted' from the wood by solvent or distilling, for example, terpenes and resins.

Figure

The pattern or shapes made by the grain on the face of a plank, panel or scantling. This is generally the aspect of the grain seen on the radial and tangential faces of a board or panel.

Fretboard

The flat section of hardwood (usually rosewood, ebony or rock maple) bonded to the face of the neck and continuing across the belly to the soundhole to provide the surface on which the strings are stopped on the frets.

Finished (F)

The section, component or workpiece as it is dimensioned when planed or sanded smooth.

Frets

The 'T'-section pieces of nickel-silver wire that are fitted into fine slots cut on the face of the fretboard at precise diminishing intervals to give the stopping points for the strings. The fret spacings are calculated to give twelve tones of equal temperament to one perfect octave.

Fret Saw

A small, long-armed bow saw with a fine, narrow-backed blade about 125mm long for cutting tight curves in panels and planks.

Fretting Saw

A small, hard-backed, fine-toothed saw for cutting the fret slots in the fretboard. This saw is not to be confused with the 'fret saw'.

Gauge

The overall diameter (thickness) of the cross-section of a string, including any wrap-around covering; represented as thousandths of an inch (USA) or in millimetres (Europe). For example: 0.017in or 0.43mm. Gauges extend from 0.009in up to 0.052in for the instruments featured in this book.

Grain

The direction of the long cellular vessels in wood that conduct the sap and nutrients up the living tree. Commonly 'grain' is defined as the lengthwise direction of the radial or tangential face of the pattern of annual growth rings.

Green

The state of timber as it is felled and converted into planks, with a saturated cell and cell wall condition having a high moisture content (MC) of up to 120 per cent.

Hardwood

The timber from broadleaved trees, that tends to be more dense and more durable than softwoods. This term refers principally to the botanical group rather than hardness of the wood.

Head Veneer

The thin slice of attractive hardwood that is glued to the peghead face to cover the emergent grain of the neck and provide a robust facing. Typical head veneers are made from exotic tropical hardwoods, 'flamed' sycamore or walnut.

Heartwood

The structural core of the tree trunk comprising the mature and usually darker wood that no longer conducts sap and nutrients for growth.

Hook

The swelling carved at the point where the back of the neck changes to the angle of the reclined peghead. This strengthens the area where the truss rod plate acts.

Inlays

The decorative material or wood veneer that is set and glued into shallow recesses cut into the workpiece and scraped or rubbed down flush with the surface; similar in principle to marquetry.

Interlocked Grain

The feature of grain found in tropical hardwoods that are diffuse-porous and have an alternating spiral growth: one year clockwise, next year anti-clockwise. This gives 'ribbon' figure to the radial face of the wood and causes havoc with planing because of the changing polarity of the cells. In other words, it is difficult to plane 'with the grain'.

Intonation

The exactness of the pitch (frequency) of a note sounded, that is not 'out of tune' by the slightest degree. Good intonation is dependent on accurate fret spacings, optimum action and bridge saddle position (not necessarily theoretical scale-length).

Kiln Drying

The seasoning of timber carried out in large kilns, using hot air and steam regulated to speed up the time of reducing moisture content of timber to be used or fixed internally. Kiln-dried material must be stored internally.

Latewood

The denser, darker and narrower part of the annual growth ring that is created during the end of the summer growing season. Obvious on pitch pine.

Linings

The small rectangular section lengths of quarter-sawn selected woods that are bent and glued to the internal faces of the ribs to form a substantial join for the belly and back connections to the ribs.

Long-Grained

The run of the grain lengthwise along a plank, scantling or workpiece.

Medullary Ray

Small groups of cells that radiate from the centre of the tree trunk like spokes of a wheel and display the flecks or 'silver figure' as seen, for example, on the quarter-sawn radial faces of hardwoods.

Moisture Content (MC)

This is the amount of water vapour present in the fibrous tissue of seasoned timber, expressed as a percentage of the dry weight; for example 9 per cent MC.

Movement

The extent of shrinkage or swelling of a piece of seasoned wood due to loss or absorption of water vapour corresponding to the relative humidity of air.

Neck

The arm that springs from the soundbox and is fashioned from a quarter-sawn block. It provides the means of stopping the strings by hand to raise or lower the pitch.

Neck Angle (or Tiller)

The degree of backward tilt in the neck from the plane of the belly to ensure the optimum height of the bridge and string angle 'break' for good action, dynamic response and projection.

Nut

The hard material stopping point for the open strings at the top end of the fretboard, which is notched to space the string centres correctly and direct them to the tuning machine posts. The instruments detailed in this book employ a 'zero-fret' which acts as the nut (the 'nut' in this case acts as a spacer, not a stopping point).

Open Grain

The large open cells displayed on porous, coarse-grained hardwoods such as rosewood, mahogany, oak and ash.

Plain

A steel, nylon or gut string without any wound covering, used for the treble strings.

Peghead (or Pegbox)

The flat head area carved from the neck block that reclines backwards from the plane of the fretboard at the nut and serves to mount the pegs or tuning machines.

Pitch (1)

The number of cycles per second (frequency or Hertz) of a sound. High notes have higher pitches (shorter wavelengths); low notes have longer wavelengths. The audible range for the (healthy) human ear can extend from pitches of about 20Hz to 20,000Hz.

Pitch (2)

The distance between the strings as set out at the bridge saddle or nut; in other words, the space between their centres. (This is a confusing alternative term used by luthiers, so all future reference will state 'string centres' rather than 'string pitch' in this quest for clarity.)

Pith

The very core of the tree trunk or log, being the weaker, softer initial growth cells, prone to fungal attack.

Plain-Sawn

The conversion of timber from the trunk or log that produces boards and scantlings with the end grain running at acute angles to the radial faces. Quite simply: of no use to the instrument-maker.

Projection

The ability and efficiency of any instrument to convey its sound to an audience.

Purfling

Small-section strips of laminated hardwood or fibre for inlaying to the edge of the belly or back, traditionally used on members of the violin family. A 'purfling cutter' is the tool for cutting the outlines of the inlay channel, the 'toothpick' chisel then excavates waste material from the channel.

Quarter-Sawn

The conversion of the trunk or log into boards and scantlings that have the end grain running at or close to right angles to the face-side. An expensive way to convert a log, but the only one that will provide suitable 'tonewoods'.

Radial

The aspect of the annual growth ring (end grain) as seen from a cut along the log on its axis.

Rake

The transverse bending of the belly at a point behind the bridge that was and is still employed on 'traditional' Neapolitan mandolins. This feature braces the belly against longitudinal and transverse distortion (caused by string tension and bridge pressure) and gives a better 'break' to the string angle from bridge to tail.

Relief

The slight bending (set) in the neck and fretboard caused by string tension (and maintained by the truss rod adjustment) to take account of the amplitude of the vibrating strings. A lack of any relief will cause the vibrating strings to rattle or buzz on the frets forward of the open or stopped strings.

Resonance

The sound as enhanced and sustained by the sympathetic reflection of the soundbox and air volume contained therein. The belly is 'tuned' to have a resonant pitch of between four to five semitones above the lowest note on the open bottom string. (The air resonance is usually a bit less: between three to four semitones above.)

Ribs

The thin, bent hardwood sides of a stringed instrument, especially of the violin family and segmental bowl-backed lute, Neapolitan mandolin, Greek bouzouki and

Arab oud. For flat-back instruments, the sides are referred to as the 'ribs' as well.

Sapwood

The younger wood in a tree trunk that surrounds the heartwood and conveys the sap and nutrients through its living cells to nourish the tree.

Scale-Length

The preferred distance of the stopping points for the open strings, from which the fret intervals are calculated to make the instrument convenient to play over its whole tonal range.

Scantlings

Sawn timber lengths that are not boards or planks but more square in section; usually less than 125 × 125mm.

Scribe

To mark and cut a workpiece to a line or profile accurately, where it has to marry or fit to a particular finished or specifically shaped component.

Set

The distortion of the neck caused by prolonged stress from the tension of the strings, that will partially remain even when the strings are slackened or removed.

Shakes

The longitudinal cracks that are due to growth defects and stresses caused by shrinkage. 'Ring' shakes will follow a line of annual growth ring.

Shim

A piece of specially cut and fashioned material to act as a raising piece.

Sides

See 'Ribs'.

Softwood

The timber from coniferous trees, which tends to be paler, lighter in weight, less dense and less robust than hardwoods. This term refers principally to the botanical group rather than softness.

Straight Grain

The grain running true with the length of the log or workpiece.

String Post

The cylindrical metal peg of a tuning machine that is provided with a notch or hole to thread through the plain end of a steel string. Good string posts would have a 'waist' like a ship's capstan.

Sustain

The endurance of a note once plucked or hammered, to its gradual decay.

Tailblock

The piece of fashioned quarter-sawn wooden block that holds the glued tail-join of the ribs and provides the substantial fixing for the strings' tailpiece.

Tailpiece

The fashioned brass or hardwood component that is screwed or hooked to the tailblock and anchors the loop-end or ball-end of the strings to the tail of the instrument.

Tangential

The aspect of the annual growth rings as seen when cut lengthwise down the log at a tangent to a growth ring: at right-angles to the radial plane.

Template

A thin sheet of material, such as plywood, plastic or brass, cut to a pattern of a specific component, that is used to replicate the shape or outline on to the workpiece by tracing around its profile.

Timbre
The distinguishing characteristic of a sound, but not pitch, of a particular instrument.

Tone
This describes a note of definite pitch, but is commonly used to convey a preference for a pleasing (if subjective) quality of sound; for example: 'That fiddle has a very fine tone.'

Tonewoods
Any timber material that is quarter-sawn, clear and selected for its tonal properties in the construction of a musical instrument.

Transverse
The aspect of the annual growth ring as seen on a cut made across the log at a right-angle to the long axis, showing the end grain.

Treble Bar(s)
The carefully fashioned and strategically fitted piece(s) of spruce glued to the underside of the belly to stiffen the treble side of the soundboard so it has better projection and response to the higher notes, as a 'sound post' does in a violin.

Truss Rod
The adjustable, high tensile, stainless steel rod that is inserted into the neck to counteract the bending caused by string tension.

Tuning Machines
The geared metal pegs that are mounted to the peghead and wind up the strings to the pitches desired by rotating the button on the shaft end.

Warp
The distortion of a workpiece caused by poor seasoning and uneven shrinkage.

Waste
The area or portion of the workpiece that will be trimmed off at a later stage; this allows for a certain flexibility if a 'finished' size needs to be a bit bigger to fit.

Wild Grain
Divergent and wandering cell structures that will give difficulty in 'working with the grain' when planing in any given direction.

Winding (1)
The gradual rotary twist along the length of an otherwise straight board or scantling caused by spiral stresses induced by poor stacking and seasoning.

Winding (2)
The spiral wound wrapping on a (plain) string to increase its gauge, brilliance and overtones; used for the middle to bass strings.

Wolf Note
The pitch of an unwelcome sympathetic resonance (commonly the fifth harmonic) in a soundbox that grossly enhances that pitch's loudness over the fundamental. More common in cellos.

Workpiece
The component you are marking, cutting or fashioning to a determined size and shape.

Zero-Fret
The alternative open string stopping point at the top end of the fretboard, instead of the nut; used for definitive fret spacing, correct intonation, consistent dynamics and low action. This is preferable to a nut on steel-strung instruments.

BIBLIOGRAPHY

Baines, Anthony, *European and American Musical Instruments* (Batsford, 1966).

Baines, Anthony, *Catalogue of Musical Instruments in the Victoria and Albert Museum* Vol. 2. (HMSO, 1968).

Buchanan, George, *The Making of Stringed Instruments: A Workshop Guide* (Batsford, 1989).

Boyden, David, *The Hill Collection of Musical Instruments* (Oxford University Press, 1969).

Buchner, Alexander, *Musical Instruments through the Ages* (Spring Books, 1959).

Coates, Kevin, *The Mandoline: an unsung serenader* (Early Music, Vol. 5, No.1, January 1977), pp. 75–87.

Jeanes, Sir James, *Science and Music* (Cambridge University Press, 1937).

Morey, Stephen, *Mandolins of the 18th Century* (Cremona, Editrice Turris, 1993).

Paganelli, Sergio, *Musical Instruments from the Renaissance to the 19th Century* (Cassell, 1988).

Prince, William, *et al.*, *Build your own Spanish Guitar, Balalaika and Violin* (Model and Allied Publications, 1970).

Taylor, Zachary, *Make and Play a Lute* (Argus, 1983).

Taylor, Zachary, *Decorative Wood Inlay* (The Crowood Press, 1997).

Tyler, James, 'The Mandore in the 16th and 17th Centuries' (*Early Music*, Vol. 9, No. 1, January 1981), pp. 22–31.

Tyler, James, 'The Italian Mandolin and Mandola' (*Early Music*, Vol. 9, No. 4, October 1981), pp. 438–446.

INDEX